LITERARY CRITICISM AND CULTURAL THEORY

OUTSTANDING DISSERTATIONS

edited by

William E. Cain

Wellesley College

A ROUTLEDGE SERIES

OTHER BOOKS IN THIS SERIES:

WRITING THE CITY
Urban Visions & Literary Modernism

Desmond Harding

ROUTLEDGE
NEW YORK & LONDON

Published in 2003 by
Routledge
711 Third Avenue
New York, NY 10017

Published in Great Britain by
Routledge
2 Park Square, Milton Park
Abingdon, Oxfordshire OX14 4RN

Library of Congress Cataloging-in-Publication Data

Harding, Desmond, 1967-
   Writing the city : urban visions and literary modernism / by Desmond
Harding.
      p. cm. -- (Literary criticism and cultural theory)
Includes bibliographical references (p.) and index.
   ISBN 0-415-94276-4 (hardback)
   1. Joyce, James, 1882-1941--Views on city and town life. 2. Joyce,
James, 1882-1941--Knowledge--Dublin (Ireland) 3. Dos Passos, John,
1896-1970--Criticism and interpretation. 4. Literature,
Comparative--Irish and American. 5. Literature, Comparative--American
and Irish. 6. Modernism (Literature)--United States. 7. Modernism
(Literature)--Ireland. 8. Dublin (Ireland)--In literature. 9. City and
town life in literature. 10. Cities and towns in literature. I. Title.
II. Series.
   PR6019.O9 Z5745 2003
   823'.912--dc21

                                        2002010035

   ISBN13: 978-0-415-94276-8 (hbk)
   ISBN13: 978-0-415-51282-4 (pbk)

Contents

Acknowledgments

This book is a result of the work I completed for my Ph.D. dissertation at the University of Southern California. I wish to thank Ronald Gottesman, the advisor to this project, who allowed me to move at my own pace and to roam wherever the idea of the city took me. I am indebted to his generosity of mind and heart, and am grateful for his abiding friendship. I was also fortunate to have the company of distinguished faculty members such as Thomas B. Gustafson, Anthony Kemp, Marshall Cohen, James Kincaid, and Joseph Dane, who supported me in the preparation and writing of this book. I am particularly grateful to Thomas Gustafson, who read and reread with the attention, criticism, and sympathy that comes with long fellowship.

During the years I worked on this project I was an Assistant Lecturer in the Writing Program at the University of Southern California. I wish to thank Betty Bamberg, John Holland, Jack Blum, and Stephen M. Byars for supporting me not only during my tenure as a graduate student, but also for continuing to provide me with the opportunity to enrich and deepen my current teaching practices as a Senior Lecturer. I owe thanks also to Ken Taylor and the Division of Student Affairs for enabling me to complete my graduate studies by working within the residential college system as a Residence Coordinator. I am also indebted to my colleagues in the Writing Program for providing me with both friendship and critical support: Joy Ross, William S. Feuer, Ryan J. Stark, Desmond Dewsnap, Phyllis J. Franzek, Nora Ashe, and Kathi Inman Berens.

I would like to thank the following for their friendship and support down the years: Ian D. MacKillop, Maurice Couve de Murville, David Saint, Kevin Starr, Peter Manning, James Forde, Annabelle Forde, Simon Bristowe, Matthew Bristowe, Eamon Kelly, Peter Bennett, William St. Clair, David E. Davis, and Edward Silva.

A special note of thanks goes to Damian Treffs and Paul Foster Johnson, editors at Routledge, and Danielle Savin, production editor at Routledge, who were instrumental in the publication of this book.

And now for those forever closest to me. To Johanna M. Josefsson I extend my deep love and thanks for helping me bring this project to its conclusion. And to my mother, Elizabeth, my brother, Norman, and my father James, I owe a debt of gratitude above all others. Although separated by an ocean and a continent, my family has supported me loyally and with a full heart throughout my years of labor on this work. To them this book is dedicated.

Preface

The silhouette of the great city, its roofs and chimneys, the towers and domes on the horizon! What a language is imparted to us through one look at Nuremberg or Florence, Damascus or Moscow, Peking or Buenos Aires. What do we know of the Classical cities, seeing that we do not know the lines that they presented under the Southern noon, under clouds in the morning, in the starry night? The courses of the streets, straight or crooked, broad or narrow; the houses low or tall, bright or dark, that in all Western cities turn their facades, their faces, and in all Eastern cities their backs, blank wall and railing, towards the street; the spirit of squares and corners, impasses and prospects, fountains and monuments, churches or temples or mosques, amphitheaters and railway stations, bazaars and town halls! The suburbs, too, of neat garden-villas or of jumbled blocks of flats, rubbish heaps and allotments; the fashionable quarter and the slum area, the suburb of Classical Rome and the Faubourg Saint-Germain of Paris, ancient Baiae and modern Nice, the little town-picture like Bruges and Gothenburg and the sea of houses like Babylon, Tenochtitlan, Rome, and London! All this has history and *is* history.

~ Oswald Spengler, "The Soul of the City"

From Plato's conception of the human soul as analogous to the ideal city to Sigmund Freud's evocation of Rome as a metaphor for the eternal laws of the mind, the empirical city and its subjectively perceived image in Western culture has always existed as a complex and discontinuous site of convergent interests rather than a logically or conceptually clarified idea. Arguably, the greatest work of art created by the city is the city itself, for in its totality urban civilization represents the apex of human achievement. Moreover, as an art form in search of its own perfectability, the city also stands for the central foundation upon which the broad range of human experience draws its energy and charts its course. Indeed, culture-capitals such as Athens, Jerusalem, Alexandria, Rome, Vienna, Paris, London, New York, and Los Angeles have long been looked to as symbols through which writers legitimate their struggles for cultural authority.

In the context of American history in particular, European literary models and cultural discourses have provided a wealth of conceptual and symbolic frameworks for the chronicling of American urban topoi in relation to their Atlantic counterparts. In our own time, the city has once again been opened up in multifarious ways by American and continental writers, urban historians, and literary theoreticians in their interdisciplinary pursuit of a new poststructuralist vocabulary of urban experience. The metropolis we are now confronted with is a "de-centered" postmodernist city, the culmination of a progressive devaluation of the Enlightenment idea of the city as the form and symbol of an integrated social relationship. Yet the pervading sense of ambivalence that commonly informs transatlantic responses to the postindustrial megalopolis is not essentially "new"; if anything, such hermeneutic quests are symptomatic of a shared sense of crisis recuperated down the years, which finds its most radical expression with the advent of the modernist city. In tracing the contours of European and American urban modernism, we not only enter fully into the enduring significance of the city as a charged symbol of human consciousness, but also experience the city anew as it speaks to us in the form of unfolding discourses marked by debate, disagreement, and intervention.

Writing the City: Urban Visions & Literary Modernism makes visible the coalescence of culture, history, and language raised in the act of reading the representative fictions of James Joyce and John Dos Passos as textual codings of a poetics of transatlantic urban modernism. In particular, I attempt to redefine critical emphases and theoretical conceptions of urban modernism as the function of a London-Paris-New York axis—an assumption that all too often elides the vital historical importance of Dublin as central to the formation of an Atlantic system of metropolitan identities and discourses. These Atlantic identities should not be viewed as discrete categories of "center" and "margin"; rather, I prefer to illustrate the interplay and hybridization of identity across seemingly disparate cultural formations, so as to contribute further to our ever-increasing understanding of modernism. The modernist epoch involved a global shift across a range of cultural, social, political, and economic contexts each marked in their own way by struggle and contradiction, ambiguity and anguish, renewal and faith. In order to understand both the localism and universality of international modernism, therefore, we need to develop comparative approaches that make it possible to synthesize cultural discourses that have no direct ties to one another yet exhibit correlative patterns of thought.

By expanding the concept of writing and representation and their relation to the city-as-text to include the claims made in Joyce's *Dubliners* (1914), *A Portrait of the Artist as a Young Man* (1916), *Ulysses* (1922), and Dos Passos' *Manhattan Transfer* (1925), I argue that Joyce's internationalist vision of the Irish capital, which takes form at the violent nexus of Ireland's national emergence, generates powerful epistemic and cultural tropes that reconceive the idea of the modernist city as a moral phenomenon in transcultural and transhistorical terms. Joyce's importance for cultural relations of the Atlantic rim is underscored by his own struggle for Irish cultural authority. Positioning himself as the privileged voice of modern Ireland, Joyce subverts the coherent, authoritative pronouncements of nineteenth-century British imperialist discourses, while simultaneously challenging the false consciousness of provincial Catholic Nationalist ideology. In keeping with the book's interpretive transatlantic paradigm, a large portion of *Writing the City* is given over to Dos Passos' role in the re-construction of a new form of American urban poetics, one marked by linguistic transformations and dislocations of style and form to represent the mix of sounds, styles and cultures that is modern America: Manhattan. Americans have always looked to New York as the gateway between Europe and the United States as well as the center of the nation's literary consciousness; indeed, from Washington Irving's mock-heroic descriptions of the city to Walt Whitman's increasingly guarded sense of New York as a symbol of democratic optimism, the city has offered thematic and formal challenges for generations of American writers. Central to Dos Passos' conception of New York, and by extension American modernism, is the legacy of Jefferson's failed vision of the republic, an idealized sense of community inexorably eroded by the rise of Hamiltonian federalism and the industrial state. Assuming the role of modernist historian and cultural saboteur, Dos Passos reconceptualizes the image of the metropolis by transforming the idea of the European city in history into an American urban Colussus.

Chapter one begins by tracing the aesthetic philosophies and critical ideologies of urban modernism as a means for providing a context for the transatlantic paradigm underpinning *Writing the City*. Using interpretative strategies taken from literary criticism, social history, urban studies, sociology, and cultural studies, I investigate the fundamental connection between European and American modernism as a shared historical moment, and locate the significance of this association in the wider interdisciplinary context of evolving conceptions of the city in transatlantic intellectual thought from the Enlightenment through postmodernism.

In more local terms, chapter two examines Joyce's topographical conception of Dublin in *Dubliners* as a structurally grounded discourse that straddles naturalist and modernist literary formations. Writing at the close of a European epoch of capital and culture, Joyce betrays the diachronic realities of Dublin as a form of hereditary pathology even as he poeticizes the entropy of modern existence, creating a new urban landscape—and the language used to speak its reality—out of the fragments of Irish history.

By extension, chapter three on "The Dead," which forms the heart of the book, demonstrates the ways in which Joyce transplants the philosophical contours of Wordsworth's epitaphic mode to the locus of the metropolis. Opening up an ontological space similar to the Romantic poet's conception of language-as-incarnation, "The Dead" serves to mediate competing conceptions of urban modernity and historical consciousness by forging a link between Joyce's aesthetic vision—and passion—for Ireland at the expense of unmasking nationalist mythologies of the peasant periphery as the cultural locus of the nation.

Chapter four analyzes the workings of Joyce's sociological imagination in *Portrait* alongside the contemporary theoretical investigations of pioneering sociologist Georg Simmel, in order to illuminate in thematic and nonlinear terms the ways in which these writers blur the epistemological and disciplinary boundaries separating the metropolitan novel, social theory, and sociology.

While a substantial portion of *Writing the City* investigates Joyce's reconfiguration of cultural modernity, chapter five focuses on the broad impact of Joyce's urban fiction on the aesthetic principles and critical ideologies of American modernism, of which Dos Passos is a paradigmatic example. In the context of American letters, the proletarian theory and practice of representative city-former Dos Passos is commonly regarded as grounded in a tradition of pragmatism, social criticism, and political partisanship dating from Emerson and Thoreau. While this association is certainly resonant, I instead establish Dos Passos' entropic urban fiction as rooted firmly in a transatlantic pattern of thought, one that deconstructs the boundaries between history and fiction, creating a new kind of cultural history and a new kind of fiction.

CHAPTER ONE

"Saxa Loquuntur"[1]
The Modernist City

To make a novel out of a city, to represent the streets and the various districts as *dramatis personae*, each one with a character in conflict with
every other; to give life to human figures and situations as if they were
spontaneous growths from the cobblestones of the streets [. . .] to work in
such a way that at every changing moment the true protagonist was the
living city, its biological continuity, the monster that was Paris—this is
what Balzac felt impelled to do when he began to write *Ferragus*.

~ Italo Calvino, "The City as Protagonist in Balzac"

ROME: THE ETERNAL CITY

On 2 September 1901, Sigmund Freud fulfilled a long-frustrated dream of
visiting Rome, a city whose cultural and religious significance had weighed
on the clinical psychologist's mind for many years.[2] The impact of the *Urbs
Aeterna* was as instantaneous as it was enervating: within an hour of arriv-
ing on the overnight train from Castello, Freud had bathed and written
home that he felt a "proper Roman."[3] For the next twelve days he devoted
himself to St. Peter's, the Vatican Museum, and the Museo Nazionale,
where he encountered Michelangelo's statue of Moses for the first time.
Freud marveled at the Pantheon, exclaiming "so this is what I have been
afraid of for so many years!"[4] And he roamed the rolling Alban hills before
reveling, finally, in the Palatine, his favorite corner of the city. On 14 September, Freud departed Rome with a heavy heart for his home in Vienna.
The consummation of the desire to go to Rome had been of the highest
emotional significance; indeed, as he later recalled, it was the "high point
of my life [. . .] I could have worshipped the abased and mutilated rem-
nant of the Temple of Minerva near the forum of Nerva."[5]

Despite the euphoria Freud experienced while in Rome, the symbolic importance of the city continued to oscillate in his mind between two icon-oclastic poles. On the one hand, he revered the imagination and erudition of ancient Rome as the *archae* of European civilization.[6] At the same time, the metropolis represented the "lie of salvation"[7] embodied in Christian Rome, a latent manifestation that had in time overturned and superseded its classical antecedent. The first of these commingled cities, the topos of ancient Rome and renaissance Rome, was a cause for rejoicing; the other, Christian Rome, was a source of fear and distrust. At a deeply personal level, however, Freud's correspondence to friends, family, and colleagues celebrated Rome as a life-affirming antidote to the anti-Semitic climate of his own "hated Vienna"[8]: "it [feels] quite natural to be in Rome; I have no sense of being a foreigner here."[9]

All the same, for Freud the troubling dichotomy of Rome remained. Critics and biographers alike have argued that Freud's "tormented, long-cherished and long-frustrated wish to visit Rome"[10] was almost obses-sional, neurotic even.[11] Taking Freud's methodological presuppositions to heart, some have even looked to Freud's relationship with Rome as a sort of skeleton key with which to unlock "some secret of his inner life."[12] Some commentators maintain, for example, that the city represents "a charged and ambivalent symbol [that] stood for Freud's most potent con-cealed erotic, and only slightly less concealed aggressive wishes, and glanced at their secret history."[13] Viewed alongside the persistent search for meaning in the Freud-Rome dialectic, Freud's attachment to the phan-tasmal city remains as enigmatic as it is elusive. This point is all the more palpable given the psychical importance attached to the city in Freud's case studies, theoretical writings, correspondence, and reflections.[14]

Perhaps the most compelling instance of the centrality of Rome occurs in *Civilization and Its Discontents* (1930), Freud's provocative meditation on the irreparable conflict between the individual and his or her institu-tional surroundings, in which he argues that the study of human institu-tions must begin with the study of human nature. In the opening chapter, Freud invites the reader to consider as an analogy for the human mind the city of Rome, which he presents in transhistorical and cinemascopic terms. In order to clarify the principle "that in mental life nothing which has once been formed can perish—that everything is somehow preserved and that in suitable circumstances [. . .] it can be brought to light,"[15] Freud summons up a stratified vision of Rome thus:

> Let us, by a flight of the imagination, suppose that Rome is not a human habitation but a psychical entity with a similarly long and copious past—an entity, that is to say, in which nothing that has come into existence will have passed away and all the earlier phases of development exist along-side the later ones. This would mean that in Rome the palaces of the Cae-sars and the Septizonium of Septimus Severus would still be rising to their

old height on the Palatine and that the castle of S. Angelo would still be carrying on its battlements the beautiful statues which graced it until the siege by the Goths, and so on. But more than this. In the place occupied by the Palazzo Cafarelli would once more stand—without the Palazzo having to be removed—the Temple of Jupiter Capitolinus; and this not only in its latest shape, as the Romans of the Empire saw it, but also in its earliest, when it still showed Etruscan forms and was ornamented with terra cotta antefixes. Where the Coliseum now stands we could at the same time admire Nero's vanished Golden House. On the Piazza of the Pantheon we should find not only the Pantheon of to-day, as it was bequeathed to us by Hadrian, but, on the same site, the original edifice erected by Agrippa; indeed, the same piece of ground would be supporting the church of Santa Maria sopra Minerva and the ancient temple over which it was built. And the observer would perhaps only have to change the direction of his glance or his position in order to call up the one view or the other.[16]

In this instance Freud masterfully excavates the historicity of Rome in keeping with Mikhail M. Bakhtin's notion of the chronotope.[17] According to Bakhtin, narratives must always represent space in the dimension of time: "Time, as it were, takes on flesh, becomes artistically visible; likewise, space becomes charged and responsive to the movements of time, plot and history."[18] In Freud's own time-space vision of an historically discontinuous Rome, the remains of the republican "Roma Quadrata" and the phase of the "Septimontium" are dovetailed so as to produce a fragmentary succession of virtual cities. Historical difference is eroded, and the archaeological traces of earlier settlements become enmeshed with the post-Renaissance jumble of the modern metropolis, so as to produce a simultaneous city flush with the weight of time and history. Freud's attempt to develop a structural theory of the mind by evoking the palimpsest of Rome is remarkable in several ways. In the first instance the conceit is coterminus with Freud's dramatic theory that "the unconscious knows no time, contains all times, annihilates the distinction (in time) between desire and fulfillment, is eternal."[19] By extension, the metaphor is symbolic of Freud's personal triumph in coming to terms with his own life-long obsession with Rome.

Though certainly not the first to conceive of the mind-city metaphor as a way of shaping our understanding of the workings of human consciousness, Freud's metaphor isolates "the concept of an invisible dimension [. . .] in which the textual city incorporates space and time: the present, the past, and the implied future"[20] beyond the constricting formal boundaries of received notions of 'reality.'[21] In addition, Freud's provocative strategy invites comparison with modern innovations within the novel (especially rapid multiple perspectives) in which *a priori* nonlinear conceptions of the city replaced the broken discourse of classic realism. Within this "mythic or 'fourth' dimension, the city's fragmentation is complete," in that "the many experiences of the characters are complemented by the contents of their consciousness, which enter the text as independent agents."[22] More-over, and as one commentator astutely notes, Freud's speculations "draw attention to the redemptive project that leaves its mark on the archaeological metaphor, in spite of the dangers involved, for what cannot be lost also has the chance to be saved."[23]

This last point is of particular importance for the larger critical impulse of *Writing the City*, in that Freud's evocative metaphor is suggestively close to the ways in which European and American modernist writers, particularly those experimenting with the form of the urban novel in the opening decades of the twentieth century, broke with outmoded nineteenth-century narrative modes of representation based primarily on sequential-causal principles.[24] Indeed, as the distended Victorian epoch drew to a close, already subjective perceptions and their attendant inner responses—predicated on a growing sense of restlessness and desire—were being developed by artists as a paradigm for more authentic accounts of everyday life than the rationalizing tendencies of positivist thought.

The heightened sense of subjective experience at work within the modernist novel challenged such cornerstones as mimesis, Aristotelian logic, Euclidean geometry, and Newtonian physics, which progressively appeared inadequate for coming to terms with the world of experience, especially the world of art.[25] Moreover, the debate was further agitated by Einstein's Theory of Relativity, which categorically denied the possibility of a privileged point of view from which "reality" could be adequately and unequivocally observed or delineated. In an essay entitled "Rodin" (1911), German sociologist and cultural philosopher Georg Simmel praised the sculptor's work on the basis that it aesthetically heightened the tensions of modern life while simultaneously releasing the individual from the anxieties of contemporary existence. More particularly, for Simmel the experience of modernity was grounded in the individual's attempt to negotiate—and incorporate—external reality in relation to the psychic interiority of the self:

> The essence of modernity as such is psychologism, the experiencing and interpretation of the world in terms of the reactions of our inner life, and indeed as an inner world, the dissolution of fixed contents in the fluid element of the soul, from which all that is substantive is filtered and whose forms are merely forms of motion.[26]

According to Simmel, by first energizing and then unifying in aesthetic terms the form and function of art in his sculpture (and ultimately in the viewer), Rodin embodies and thus captures the essence of modernity. The external world is part of our inner world; accordingly, the substantive elements of reality are reduced to a ceaseless flux, and their fleeting, fragmentary, and contradictory moments are all incorporated into human subjectivity.

THE CITY IN HISTORY

"If the City is a text," Joyce Carol Oates asks, "how shall we read it?"[27] Cities are as old as the term *civilization*; indeed, more than any other phenomenon the city has provided the critical mass which produces civilization.[28] Even the basic etymology of the word reveals its ancient past, for behind the English word *city* lie the Latin words *civis* (citizen) and *civitas* (citizenry, citizenship). Of course humans have been reading cities in all sorts of ways since the generally agreed upon beginnings of civilization in Mesopotamia, circa 3500 BCE. When we read cities we invariably raise questions about how cities come into being, how they take shape and grow, and what purposes they play in social, political and cultural change.[29] According to Lewis Mumford,

> The city is characteristic of most civilizations and is often considered their fullest expression. Its origins can be traced back beyond the 'urban revolutions' which took place [. . .] in Mesopotamia in the third millennium BC to the archaeological remains of Jericho and Catal Hoyuc (Anatolia). After all these centuries, the quality of urban life is still man's central concern.[30]

Mumford, perhaps the most prolific urban historian of the twentieth century, articulated his own urban ideal in *The Culture of Cities* (1938) when he declared: "The city is the form and symbol of an integrated social relationship: it is the seat of the temple, the market, the hall of justice, the academy of learning. Here is where human experience is transformed into viable signs, symbols, patterns of conduct, systems of order."[31] In many ways, Mumford's notion of the city as a uniquely human phenomenon where unity, cohesion, and coherence are the primary goals is in keeping with Aristotle's classical sense of the laws governing private man, as delineated in *Politics*. Echoing Mumford's idealistic hopes for the city, Jane Jacobs' examination of the city praises the idea of order (often dictated from below) in the form of diversity, vitality, plurality, and responsiveness to human need in her discussion of city sidewalks, parks, neighborhoods, and districts.[32] As both a container and transmitter of culture, the idea of the city for Mumford constituted possibility, with civilization passing on from one generation to the next the fruits of human achievement. And yet it was on these same grounds that Mumford, who, toward the end of a life immersed in the history and culture of cities and city planning, faulted his native New York, an urban sprawl he felt had abandoned the idea of the city in history.

Mumford's lament is in fact representative of an ancient tradition of urban *angst*. Indeed, from Juvenal's *Satires* to Augustine's "City of God" to Virgil's *Eclogues*, an antagonistic sense of duality is central to the image of the city in classical and Judeo-Christian culture. In the Old Testament, the expulsion of Adam and Eve from the pastoral idyll of Eden gave rise to the first settlement. Cain, the architect and builder of humankind's first planned community, constructed the first mythical city even as his hands were fresh from killing his brother, Abel. Babel itself was later cast out of the sky, while the venal twin-cities of Sodom and Gomorrah fell into corruption. Outside biblical narrative, in *The Bacchae*, Pentheus surrounds his city with walls, but secretly yearns for the libidinal vitality and freedom of the countryside that is lacking in his own realm, and which he consequently attempts to fortify his urban civilization against. In our own time, the diverse influences and common roots of Western civilization have given rise to a global pantheon of mythologized cities that not only exist as symbolic expressions of humanity in the form of distinct economic or political systems, but also have become part of the collective psyche of world history. At its furthest geographical and historical extreme, Richard Lehan argues that contemporary Los Angeles is metaphorically representative of the culmination of the "Idea of the West," which had its origin in late seventeenth- and early eighteenth-century Europe in such texts as Daniel Defoe's *Robinson Crusoe* (1719). Carried west across the Atlantic and the North American continent to the Pacific, Lehan contends that this idea was embraced under such names as the Frontier Movement, Manifest Destiny, and the California Dream.[33]

From a European urban-historical perspective, intellectual historian Carl Schorske has isolated three major conceptions of the city in history since the eighteenth century: the Enlightenment city of Virtue, which for Voltaire, Adam Smith, and Gottlieb Fichte variously embodied the dynamic of civilization; the anti-rational industrial Victorian city of Vice denounced by Blake and Wordsworth, Engels and Marx; and, finally, Spengler's terminal modern city, an entity "beyond good and evil."[34] Speaking in the broadest cultural terms, Schorske's three recursive stages embody the mythologized metaphoric associations often associated with the city in history, from the classical period to the present. Intrinsic to Schorske's discontinuous concept of the city are the New Jerusalem of the Book of Revelation; St. Augustine's City of God (intimating the perfectability of man and woman); the soul-punishing urban crucible of sin dedicated to Mammon in the form of Babylon or Sodom; and the deracinated, decentered city of Babel, which feeds on the communitarian disconnection of the spirit of the polis, a city of "permanent transience."[35]

Schorske's schematic analysis is symptomatic of an enduring insistence in the West to answer a central, perhaps even impossible, question asked of the city since the city began: What *is* the city? In literary terms, Blanche H. Gelfant has divided the American city novel into three main types: the "portrait," in which the city is revealed through the experiences of a single character, often a youth from the country; the "ecological," which focuses on one element of the city, for example a neighborhood, a street, or even a house; and the "synpotic," in which the city itself becomes the major protagonist.[36] While Gelfant's schema allows for a useful discussion of American fiction during the period between 1890 and 1940, Schorske is nonetheless quick to point out that all such attempts to provide an answer to the question "What is the city?" are highly questionable. Schorske's skepticism is well founded, for any attempt to provide a definitive answer is surely suspect. Not only is the idea of the city a sub-topic in literature, painting, history, psychology, and sociology, but it has also become a focused concern in the multidisciplinary field of urban studies.[37] In Schorske's final stage of progression for the city (the coda of urban history), humanity is figured like Poe's "Man of the Crowd": neo-nomadic, and dependent upon the spectacle of the ever-changing urban scene to fill the "void of a desocialized consciousness."[38] This last classification is particularly relevant for urban studies, in that in keeping with an overarching theme of historical discontinuity, Schorske's pronouncement defines for the nineteenth-century city a new and radical break with its past. Up until this point, notions of self-perception and identity had not yet completely fused with the increasingly intrusive presence of the city as the essential ground of modern existence.

Raymond Williams notes that attempts to codify the genealogy of the modern city that involve the mapping of historical discontinuities are themselves culturally symptomatic of periods of "ideological transition."[39] In other words, like artistic responses, social scientific commentaries more often than not surface when debates concerning the city are at their most intense. As Schorske's reflective argument reiterates, historically there exists an identifiable series of what Williams terms "rhetorical contrasts"[40] between the town (more often than not identified as an overdetermined sense of greed and corruption) and country life (symbolic of an idealized golden past)[41] that together are consistent with the mythology of the city. Schorske's own particular brand of urban rhetoric is prescient in that it foreshadows perhaps our own (latent) ideological transition to a new period of cultural pessimism regarding the city. Indeed, we now find ourselves at the end of a period in which, as many contemporary urban theorists and writers would have us believe, there has been a progressive devaluation (symptomatic of a cultural and intellectual crisis) of "the city as a concept"[42] in western culture since the Enlightenment.[43]

The work of William Sharpe and Leonard Wallock is a notable contribution to this debate. Their prescriptive trilateral analysis of the evolutionary phases of the city allows room for a degree of sympathy with Schorske on the grounds that his analysis highlights not so much a progressive devaluation of the city as the progressive betrayal of the city as affirmation.[44] Elaborating on the perceived sense of crisis affecting urban society and culture, Sharpe and Wallock contend that we are now at a point of structural transition, a Viconian *ricorso*, if you will, to a new kind of city and are thus experiencing a "crisis of terminology"[45] similar to that felt by observers of early industrial Manchester and later by the modernist investigators of Paris, London and New York. In our post-modernist stage of the

city's evolution, we now speak of a de-centered city that no longer con-
forms to the definitions of even our own recent past.[46] Calling for "a new
vocabulary of urban experience,"[47] Sharpe and Wallock urge the reader to
be attentive to the fact that "perceptions of the urban landscape are inseparable from the words we use to describe them and from the activities of
reading, naming, and metaphorizing that make all our formulations possible."[48] Moreover, uneasy with constricting empirical designations, for example, the city as a "non place urban realm"[49] in its third phase of
deracinated development, Sharpe and Wallock are also loathe to trade in
dehistoricizing terms that erase the genealogical spatial and temporal significance of the city as a function of civilization.[50]

In contrast to this sense of defeated expectation, pioneering urban theorist Kevin Lynch early on isolated and analyzed the principles of identity
and structure as key factors that inform the idea of the city as a complex
yet negotiable phenomenon. For Lynch, the "legibility" or "visibility"[51] of
the cityscape is not only crucial for the "imageability of city form,"[52] but
also necessary for the consciousness that perceives it. In linguistic terms,
Lynch has argued that "just as this printed page, if it is legible, can be visu-
ally grasped as a related pattern of recognizable symbols, so a legible city
would be one whose districts or pathways are easily identifiable and are
easily grouped together into an over-all pattern."[53] The attempt to define
"the series of psychological transformations by which an individual ac-
quires, codes, stores, recalls, and decodes information about the relative locations and attributes of phenomena in his or her everyday
environment,"[54] also known as "cognitive mapping," is just one example
of urban theorists staking their claim on an area of study that all too often
has often been the preserve of the literary artist or historian.

In terms of the semantics of urban legibility, the city has also been
opened up by poststructuralist theoreticians as a system of signification dependent on certain fixed relations and shared values for its comprehensibil-
ity or interpretation.[55] In the case of language, Jacques Derrida has
similarly challenged the way we read and write the world. For example, in
the seminal essay "Structure, Sign, and Play in the Discourse of the Human
Sciences," he pronounced:

> If totalization no longer has any meaning it is not because the infinity of a
> field cannot be covered by a finite glance or a finite discourse, but because
> the nature of the field—that is, language and a finite language—excludes
> totalization [. . .] instead of being too large, there is something missing
> from [the field]: a center which arrests and founds the freeplay of substitu-
> tions.[56]

In linguistic terms, it can be argued that the city defies any attempt to
designate a "meaning," "signified," or "center," eliding its own signification at every turn. In Derridean terms, if the traditional functions of the
city are now displaced to other parts of a more homogeneously urbanized

environment (as has become the case, say with American "edge cities"), then the effect will resemble the loss of semantic apprehensibility. Consonant with recent approaches to the city as a de-centered artifact, the city-as-text in turn provides a feeding ground for post-structural exigencies of meaning. Urban fiction thus represents a hospitable field of play, a paradigm of *différance*, of linguistic freeplay, defying unity, wholeness, and the authority invested in a unified subject. Indeed, this multifarious genre of writing lends itself as much to poststructuralist notions of the decentralized city as it does to poststructuralist literary theory.

The city has always embodied such diametrically opposed and/or ambivalent attitudes such as those outlined above. Moreover, as Western civilization has evolved the progressive disconnection between the physical presence of the city and its subjectively perceived image has become increasingly emphasized in terms of a perceived cultural and social crisis. While the roots of this epistemological sea change are as deep as they are complex, it was toward the end of the nineteenth century in particular that this sense of fragmentation in European and American urban culture became more pronounced, as artists and investigators, working across a range of mediums, attempted to redefine notions of perception and environment.

Prior to the nineteenth century the city was taken by most social theorists to be the image of society as opposed to some special, unique form of social life (this identification also plays itself out in the writings of Aristotle, Plato, and Augustine). During the re-emergence of city life during the late Middle Ages a similar sense of the city resurfaced in the work of Machiavelli. In the eighteenth century, the idea of the city as a mirror reflecting the larger realities of society was once more restated in the more authoritative social theory of Jean Jacques Rousseau, despite the work of such social thinkers as Jean Bodin, who attempted to isolate the city as a unique societal phenomenon. If anything, the city modernist artists rebelled against is very much an Enlightenment construct. Constituting a revolutionary turn away from an agrarian settlement to an urban mercantilist metropolis, the Enlightenment city, founded upon the idea of Reason's triumph over Nature, laid the groundwork for much of life as we know it today, absorbing and controlling the mythic nature of the city in the process. It has been argued that this "urban drama played itself out against a Europe transformed by Enlightenment values, by an America that offered a New Jerusalem, and by a Wilderness and a frontier against which the city assumed its meaning."[57]

The idea of the city as an absolute image of society was jettisoned with the coming of the Industrial Revolution, an epoch that elevated the city to an unprecedented height unknown since the time of Rome. Even before the invention of printing, some Renaissance codices of Ptolemy's *Geography* had included, in addition to the ancient maps of the whole world and its various regions, a series of more-or-less symbolic city plans featuring

Venice, Milan, Florence, Rome, Constantinople, Damascus, Jerusalem, and Alexandria. The cities of the Renaissance were often depicted in harmonious iconographic terms in all their civic historical roots. By contrast, the modern city was set adrift from its cultural past, an amorphous entity that often eluded representation. Siennese painters such as Duccio, working in the fourteenth century, envisioned Italian cities as objects one might hold in one's hand. For example, *Christ Entering Jerusalem* (1285–1295) is a example of this microcosmic view of an urban world comprising towers, domes, and palaces enclosed by a wall, and entered by a gate. Sienna, at that time an independent and wealthy city-state set on a hill, was a world, economy, and system of belief unto itself, so it is perhaps not surprising that Duccio chose to envision the city situated on a lofty vantage-point. One of the earliest surviving images of an Irish town or city is that of *Waterford* (c. 1370), as traced by G. V. du Noyer, with the natural world once again beyond the city wall (rabbits frolicking in meadows, and fish jumping in the River Suir).

The *Liber Chronicarum*, published in Latin and German by Hartmann Schedel in 1493 at Nuremberg (and often referred to as the *Nuremberg Chronicle*), illustrated a series of monuments, buildings, and cities both ancient and modern. Printed from woodcuts, the *Chronicarum* marked the beginning of a new interest in the physical aspect of the city, highlighting "spatial dimensions over historical narrative preoccupied with the flow of time."[58] Renaissance London would have to wait until the late sixteenth century before such a belief as Duccio's in the centrality of Italian urban culture would reveal the city to itself, and to the world. The "Braun-Hogenberg Map View" of London, otherwise known as *Civitates Orbis Terrarum* (1572), presented a panoramic bird's-eye-view of municipal order from the southern side of the Thames. Following the Great Fire of London in 1666 and the reconstruction of the city, however, the central tenets of Enlightenment reason and order generated a whole new tradition of city planning and cartography (and the place of the individual within that order), with London as its primary subject. By the nineteenth century the spatial, temporal, and kinetic relations of the city had been radically altered: the city became *in toto* the seat of international political and economic power, influencing mass human migration, new means of labor, and revolutionary modes of production. While Karl Marx declared that the city was the primary location of alienation, his studies also concluded that this new labor was more than a function of the factory system or capitalism (phenomena that had been in existence in one form or another in towns and cities well before the Renaissance). The modern city had become a world unto itself.

More often than not fictional representations of nineteenth-century European metropoli formed empirically strange environments beyond human scale for their fictive heroes; for example, the Haussmanization of Paris in Zola's *L'Assomoir* (1877), the dark and unknown urban interior of Mayhew's *London Labor and the London Poor* (1851), or the mysterious land-scape of Dickens' *Bleak House* (1853). Yet despite the sense of alienation engendered by such urban visions, the city had not yet attained that centripetal force we now associate so readily with the urban fictions of literary modernism. If nineteenth-century urban novels explored the isolation of the individual from the idea of historical community in negative terms, the twentieth-century city went one step further by sundering the very notion of historical continuity in favor of unhistorical miscellany.

Modernism's obsession with history in turn mutated into a new form of urban neurosis in which the city rather than its inhabitants became the protagonist. Consequently, modernist writers embodied a self-conscious awareness of historical and social relativity that played on the archetypal and historical features of the city in order to challenge the idea of the metropolis as an essentially static, fixed, and, ultimately, knowable object. In certain instances, this new method of representation was preempted by similar feelings of alienation and/or disconnection; for example James Thomson's *The City of Dreadful Night* (1874), which takes form at the edge of the modernist period. The modern cities of developing western nations were now figured as dynamic and kaleidoscopic environments, radically new and shifting signs of discontinuity that evoked dissociation in the midst of community: Eliot's fragmented London; Biely's mysterious Petersburg; Sue's surrealistic Paris; Dos Passos' protean Manhattan; and Joyce's transhistorical Dublin.

THE ROOTS OF MODERNITY: BAUDELAIRE AND THE CITY

> One thing distinguishes modernity from all that is past and gives it its particular character: knowledge of the eternal becoming and disappearance of all things in ceaseless flight and insight into the connectedness of all things, into the dependency of each thing upon every other in the unending chain of what exists.
>
> ~ David Frisby quoting Hermann Bahr

In *One Way Street* (1928) Walter Benjamin isolated Paris as the locus-point for his prehistory of modernity, and chose as its interpreter poet and flâneur Charles Baudelaire. Benjamin's native informant symbolizes one of the first sustained and brilliant instances of the relationship between the urban self and the urban environment that functions on both material and spiritual planes.[59] In his review of the 1846 salon, Baudelaire proclaimed that "the epic quality of modern life" was an exclusively urban experience, and urged his fellow artists to make the life of cities the subject of their work: "scenes of high life and of the thousands of uprooted lives that haunt the underworld of a great city [. . .] are there to show us that we have only to open our eyes to see and know the heroism of our day."[60] In the same way that Thomas De Quincey's drug-induced fantasies departed radically from Wordsworth's natural landscape, Baudelaire, in choosing Paris as the subject and site of his unique voyage into the heart of modernity, usurped Romanticism's elevation of the country as the cultural and spiritual locale of a more cultivated sensibility. Yet while in *Confessions of an English Opium Eater* (1822) De Quincey journeys into "a heretical space in which he celebrates disorientation from the normal sensate, social and divine worlds," the English writer, unlike Baudelaire, "never really articulated a formal literary doctrine based on extraordinary sense perception"[61] in which the city functioned as the principal site of modernity.

Baudelaire defined his concept of modernity most forcefully in the essay "The Painter of Modern Life" (1859–60) when he declared: "La modernité, c'est le transitoire, le fugitif, le contingent, la moitié, de l'art, dont l'autre moitié est l'éternel et l'immutable."[62] For Baudelaire, the modern artist was, in paradoxical terms, "the painter of the passing moment and of all suggestions of eternity that it contains."[63] (Baudelaire's painter also reminds us of Poe's "Man of the Crowd," for whom "curiosity has become a fatal, irresistible passion."[64]) In turn, Baudelaire's painter, the modern artist, gazes upon the landscapes of the city—"landscapes of stone, caressed by the mist or buffeted by the sun"[65]—surveying the eternal beauty of creation as a monument to freedom in the "outward show of life, such as is to be seen in the capitals of the civilised world."[66]

Yet Baudelaire's modern artist is more than just a flâneur, in that he systematically searches for the beauty of modernity, releasing it from the most trivial externalities. Entry into the crowd, the *tableau* of life, is as through entering "a magical society of dreams"; consequently, the artist is like "a mirror as vast as the crowd itself" that reproduces "the multiplicity of life and the flickering grace of all the elements of life [. . .] at every instant rendering and explaining it in pictures more living than life itself, which is always unstable and fugitive."[67] While Baudelaire's painter may well give little to the darker side of modernity, the dangers of urban existence are taken up more fully in *Les Fleurs du Mal* (1861). At the same time, Baudelaire's aesthetics of modernity does not seek to replace the aesthetic of a timeless past with that of a timeless present.[68] Rather, the image of the modern world is often presented in terms of its opposite, one that reveals "the harsh refuse of modernity," indeed "the savagery that lurks in the midst of civilisation" and its "living monstrosities."[69]

READING MODERNITY

> Surely no literary term has raised more controversy and misunderstanding than the modest little word *modernism*.[70]
>
> ~ Marjorie Perloff, "Modernist Studies"

As readers and critics we have become attuned to the institutionalized assessment of modernism as an art disintegration.[71] Almost by its very nature modernism is commonly defined "an art of despair and pain; a dissonant, fragmented art that confronts meaninglessness; an art bred by the city where the scale of life dwarfs the individual and where each isolated person lives in bewilderment, shifting patterns of relationship with others, or in no discernible patterns at all."[72] Or so we are told.[73] Yet while modernist art is certainly grounded in conflict, the forms and foci of urban modernism remain nonetheless standardized, critically speaking, in distinct cultural, historical and geographical terms. Raymond Williams has argued forcefully that narrow applications of the concept of modernism to avant-garde responses to the city alone in the first decades of the century often preclude an attendant and invasive "hidden history."[74] In other words, in the case of modernist texts, criticism that ignores the work of Wordsworth, Dickens, Thomson, and Engels (to name but a few) necessarily delimits a shared sense of urban history. Moreover, the dominant conception of modernism as an art of disintegration further simplifies the heterogeneity of the positions and manifestoes generated in response to the conditions of modern urban life by artists working within and across a wide range of mediums. By reducing modernism to an art of entropy, we not only lose touch with the complexity of the multi-form phenomenon itself, but also simplify the richness of modernism's primary subject: the city as historical-cultural palimpsest. While the city is certainly home to many forms of disintegration, we should consider the possibilities it also provides as a site of liberation from the very forces that would seem to crush the individual.

International debates on the material conditions of the city in the early decades of the twentieth century were often marked by a renewed sense of urgency. From the tenements of New York to the streets of Dublin to the salons of Weimar Berlin and beyond to revolutionary gatherings in St. Petersburg, we read a variety of challenges to, and rejections of, urban experience. Certainly, from among these varied responses a consensus emerged, which is more often than not epitomized by the sense of the city as a menacing force beyond the capacity of human experience to control or even sometimes comprehend. From a literary perspective this type of judgment is most forcefully pronounced in T. S. Eliot's excoriation of the cultural and spiritual topos of London in *The Waste Land* (1922)—*the* "unreal city" of modernity. At the same time, while Eliot's imprimatur abides, we might do well to consider more of what *The Waste Land* fails to tell us about the idea of the city in modern consciousness than what it exposes. For example, from the urban historian's perspective at the heart of such antagonistic responses such as Eliot's lies a central "historical paradox" germane to the concept of modernism, that is "the great cities of Edwardian Europe represent[ed] one of the highest levels of metropolitan civilization."[75]

Continental artists, however, both pre-empted the terrain of Eliot's cultural critique in their own representations of the city as well as prefigured in programmatic and dynamic terms the very tensions central to modernist art. In joyous terms, for example, F. T. Marinetti's *First Futurist Manifesto* (1909) declared: "we will sing of the multicolored polyphonic tides of revolution in the modern capitals [. . .] of the vibrant nightly fervour of arsenals and shipyards blazing with violent electric moons."[76] As Judy Davies notes, "the Futurists sought energetically to close the rift between the artist and his world. Not for them the provinces, but the city: and an abiding scorn for the economic and intellectual tyranny of institutions—the gallery or the academy—that mediated between the work of art and its destinatees."[77] Concurrently, by 1912 both Paris and the Eiffel Tower were still popularly regarded as "archetypal symbols of the modern world."[78] Indeed, between 1910 and 1912 French painter Robert Delaunay painted a series of cubist studies of the tower with varying emphases. But "underlying the triumphant image of modern technology," however, "is the archetype of the Tower of Babel."[79] In contrast to Delaunay's somewhat ambiguous response to Eiffel's tower, or the more celebratory *City of Paris* (1910), German artist George Grosz's Futurist painting *The Big City* (1916–1917) presents a vision of urban pandemonium and colliding energies exploding within the metropolis that reflect Grosz's fascination and loathing for Berlin. There is no such ambiguity at work in the work of Grosz's contemporary, Otto Dix. In *Big City Triptych* (1927), for example, Dix explicitly presents a monstrous caricature of Weimar culture in the juxtaposition of cabaret dancers, overdressed revelers, prostitutes, crippled war veterans and demonic figures that for him embody post-World War I Berlin.

Whereas European artisans working in the visual arts were slow to absorb and express the Baudelaire's call for a new urban art with new forms of expression, French writers responded immediately, especially Flaubert, Vigny, Rimbaud, and Laforgue. For the French and German painters who did respond to Baudelaire's injunction, their work is typically framed by the exuberance of Impressionist Claude Monet and by the apocalyptic visions of Expressionists such as Ludwig Meidner. Moreover, in contrast to their literary counterparts Impressionists such as Monet, Degas, Seurat, and Renoir celebrated the everyday pleasures and travails of city life. As a consequence, the dehumanizing effects of the metropolis (as expressed by Zola's naturalist studies) are surprisingly absent in French painting. Monet in particular responded enthusiastically to the shimmering, linear energy of Hausmann's new Paris in his Boulevard des Capucines (1873), whereas Cézanne, Van Gogh, and Gaugin in time fled the pressures of the metropolis, retreating into nature. During the period immediately following Baudelaire's investigations, it was left to painters such as Belgian James Ensor in *The Entry of Christ into Brussels* (1888), or Norwegian Edvard Munch's urban neurosis and urban poverty in *Spring Evening on Karl Johan* (1891), to engage with the darker tide of modern life, as they moved beyond the fashionable quarters of the city.

The later work of Expressionist painters such as Meidner illustrates the move to render images of the city in harsher terms compared with Futurists or Impressionists. Although Meidner's aesthetic rejection of Impressionism was foreshadowed in many ways by Ernst Ludwig Kirchner's *The Street* (1913), it was the 1912 Futurist exhibition held at *Der Sturm*, the leading avant-garde gallery in Berlin, that set the stage for Meidner's break. One painting in particular entitled *The Street Enters the House* (1912) by Umberto Boccioni, which illustrates the aural sensation of the metropolis in the form of a building site entering a woman's house using distorted and exaggerated colors, highlights the overpowering imminence of the city as a protean force. Meidner, immersing himself in the shock of the new, responded critically in particular to Monet and Pissarro, following the 1914 first Impressionist exhibition in Paris. In his own urban visions such as *I and the City* (1913), Meidner proposed a new formal language to capture the sense and presence of the city as *Weltstadt*, or World-as-City thus: "Let us paint what is close to us, our city world! the wild streets, the elegance of iron suspension bridges, gas tanks which hang in white-cloud mountains, the roaring colours of buses and express locomotives [. . .] and then night [. . .] big city night."[80]

The city as a new and exciting phenomenon is especially prevalent in German cinema of the Weimar Republic.[81] For example, Fritz Lang's commercially successful and entertaining *Metropolis* (1926)[82] presents not so much a vision of the modernist city but a city of the future, and in doing so universalizes the city, invoking biblical archetypes in the form of the massive control tower, which is called "The New Tower of Babel." Meanwhile, Walther Ruttmann's *Berlin, die Symphonie der Grosstadt* (1927)[83] is an avant-garde day-in-the-life documentary of Berlin, which is especially memorable in that along with focusing on the city the film consciously draws attention to "itself showing Berlin."[84] In addition, Sergei Eisenstein's *October* (1928)[85] takes its cue from the very real historical events surrounding the Russian revolution which occurred on 25 October 1917, and locates the battle for the establishment of the socialist revolution and the triumph of the proletariat squarely in the city of St. Petersburg as the site of a revolutionary struggle for power.

As the mass of twentieth-century urban art reveals, the experience of modernity in Europe and America is often described in terms of a violent discontinuity between past and present, and often grounded in a series of intense transformations. Not surprisingly, evidence for the compelling centrality of the metropolis to the literature of Western industrializing nations alone is now a moot point.[86] To all intents and purposes it has become impossible to ignore the presence of the city when we speak about avant-garde movements in the early decades of the twentieth century. In a volume of widely disseminated essays that surveys some of modernism's dominant urban centers at points of high cultural intensity, one critic contends:

When we think of Modernism, we cannot avoid thinking of these urban climates, and the ideas that ran through them: through Berlin, Vienna, Moscow and St. Petersburg around the turn of the century and into the early years of the war; through London in the years immediately before the wars; through Zurich, New York and Chicago during it; and through Paris at all times.[87]

It is certainly a truism, as Bradbury and McFarlane note, that the body of movements and manifestoes that made for the debates and directions of modernism are associated with such materially dominant culture-capitals as Paris, Rome, Vienna, Munich, Berlin, Zurich, New York, London and Chicago. In keeping with this institutionalized assessment, much of the English language discussion concerning the so-called internationality of modernism has "steadfastly held to the London-Paris-New York axis"[88] at the expense of reading and interpreting the multiform movements of modernism as a transnational phenomenon. While such responses to the cultural productions of this Atlantic axis constitute valid expressions of the idea of the city as a transcultural and transhistorical phenomenon, they can also be read as the product of an exclusive sense of literary and critical inertia. Moreover, these discourses continue to be dictated by the privileged intellectual and cultural climates of the highly selective metropoli they serve.

If cities such as London, Paris, and Rome, New York, Chicago and Los Angeles constitute evocative mythic cities of modern European and American culture, fate and history have conspired to elide the presence of a city like Dublin—in spite of so-called "pluralistic if not relativistic"[89] attempts to identify such a center as being of "significance" in the writing of *Ulysses*, modernism's quintessential literary city of the imagination. Until Joyce the representation of a city like Dublin served to mark that point furthest from any singularly vivid potential for mythification and/or attempt at cultural self-definition. Ireland, quite simply, lay outside history. Ironically, in our own time, New York, arguably the quintessential material city of modernism, has also been singled out in certain corners but for quite different reasons. If Dublin is a site of cultural "lack," then New York now embodies its own historical lack in the continual recycling and reinvention of history as the foundation for an ever-new urban scene. For example, surveying the urban island from the vantage point of a walker in the metropolis, Michel de Certeau argues that New York has been

transformed into a texturology in which extremes coincide—extremes of ambition and degradation, brutal oppositions of races and styles, contrasts between yesterday's buildings, already turned into trash cans, and today's urban irruptions that block out its space. Unlike Rome, New York has never learned the art of growing old by playing on all its pasts. Its presents itself, from hour to hour, in the act of throwing away its previous accomplishments and challenging the future. [. . .] On this stage of concrete, steel and glass, cut out between two oceans (the Atlantic and the American) by a frigid body of water, the tallest letters in the world compose a gigantic rhetoric of excess in both expenditure and production.[90]

A TALE OF TWO CITIZENS

James Augustine Aloysius Joyce was one of twelve children, only eight of whom survived childhood. He was born into middle-class wealth and domestic security in Rathgar, a suburb of Dublin, on 2 February 1882. Due to a combination of drink, sloth and feckless imprudence, his father, John Stanislaus Joyce, managed to steer the family fortunes from prosperity to near penury. James' mother, May Joyce, died a premature death at the age of 44. Educated by Jesuits at Clongowes Wood College and later at Belvedere College, Joyce entered University College Dublin in 1898. After graduating in 1902, he went to Paris to study medicine, but soon abandoned his studies. In April 1903 Joyce returned home to visit his dying mother, but after her death on 13 August 1903 he remained in Ireland, living in a tower at Sandymount with Oliver St. John Gogarty (the model for Malachi Mulligan in *Ulysses*). On 16 June 1904, the date Joyceans celebrate Bloomsday (also the date upon which *Ulysses* takes place), Joyce met his future wife, Nora Barnacle. In 1904 Joyce published early versions of stories in *Dubliners*; the collection was later completed with the writing of "The Dead" in 1907.

In 1904 James and Nora left Ireland, and spent the rest of their lives on the Continent. Joyce did, however, return to his native country, once 1909, and for the last time in 1912. In 1914 he began work on *Ulysses*, the same year in which *Dubliners* was published. In 1915 Joyce published a play entitled *Exiles*, followed by *A Portrait of the Artist as a Young Man*, in 1916. Having spent the first part of his self-exile living in the cities of Pola, Trieste, and Zurich (where they moved at the outbreak of World War I), Joyce, together with Nora, their son, Georgio, and daughter, Lucia, moved to Paris in 1919, where they lived until the fall of France during World War II. *Ulysses* was published in Paris in 1922. In 1923 Joyce began to write "Work in Progress," the book that became *Finnegans Wake*, which was published in complete form in 1939. On 4 July 1931, Joyce and Nora married in London. Joyce spent the last year of his life in Zurich, where he died in 1941 following abdominal surgery for a perforated ulcer. He lies buried in Fluntern Cemetery, adjacent to the zoo where, as Nora once remarked, he liked to sit and listen to the lions roar.

An ocean and half a continent away, John Dos Passos (born John Roderigo Madison) was born some fourteen years after Joyce's birth in a Chicago hotel room on 14 January 1896. It was not until 1910, however, upon the death of his father's legal wife, that he was able to extricate himself from the unfortunate consequences of an illegitimate birth to assume the surname Dos Passos. He spent part of a peripatetic childhood in Europe before returning to the United States to attend the Choate School.

Graduating in 1911, he traveled extensively throughout Europe and the Mediterranean (he would spend a great deal of his subsequent life traveling the globe in search of material for his books) before entering Harvard in 1912 as John R. Dos Passos, Jr. One year after his graduation in 1917, Dos Passos, Sr., a self-made corporate lawyer (and son of a Portuguese immigrant), died.

When the United States entered World War I, Dos Passos joined the Norton-Harjes ambulance unit, serving in Italy and France. His wartime experiences animate the war novels, *One Man's Initiation—1917* (1920) and *Three Soldiers* (1921). In 1925 Dos Passos published *Manhattan Transfer*, an experimental and controversial novel that launched his career as a radical modernist author. Building on his political involvement while at Harvard, Dos Passos committed himself during the 1920s and 1930s to fighting a capitalist system he saw as the breeder of war, depression, societal unrest, and fascism. No incident more thoroughly symbolizes his disaffection with American society than the trial and execution of the Italian anarchists Nicola Sacco and Bartolomeo Vanzetti on 22 August 1927, on whose behalf Dos Passos had campaigned. In response to their deaths, Dos Passos essentially "seceded" from the Union. Between 1927 and 1936 he composed and published the trilogy *The 42nd Parallel*, *Nineteen Nineteen*, and *The Big Money*. Yet the 1930s also marked a volta in Dos Passos' political allegiances, and by the end of the decade he was openly denouncing Communism. He briefly returned to his old ideological stomping grounds with Roosevelt's New Deal, but, disillusioned once more, gradually drifted in time toward the ideologies of Robert Taft and Richard Nixon. In his later years and with his best writing now behind him, he feared governmental bureaucrats and labor union bosses with the same vehemence he had once attacked war-mongering Wall Street capitalists. In the course of his lifetime, Dos Passos completed a series of thirteen chronicles—beginning with *One Man's Initiation—1917* and ending with his final work, *Century's Ebb* (published posthumously in 1975)—which together examine the life of the twentieth century from a variety of perspectives. Dos Passos' twentieth century ended when he died of congestive heart failure in Baltimore at about 9:00 A.M. on 28 September 1970.

WRITING THE MODERNIST CITY

Generally speaking, if twentieth-century American history began with the armed conflict of World War I, which then gave way to a cultural revolution in the form of modernism, then twentieth-century Irish history emerged, it can be argued, with the cultural revolution of the Irish Literary Revival followed by the military revolution of Easter 1916. While this is still not the commonly held view concerning modern Irish history, it is precisely within this space—the violent cultural-historical moment of Ireland's national emergence—that Joyce's fiction takes form. Such a revaluation

Ireland's revolutionary character from 1890 onwards is outlined by Irish historian Connor Cruise O'Brien:

> In the summary historical retrospect which we all acquire at school [. . .] this period 1891 to 1916 forms, I think, a sort of crease in time, a feature-less valley between the commanding chain of the Rising and the solitary enigmatic peak of Parnell. It was a time in which nothing happened; nothing except [. . .] a revolution in land ownership, the beginning of a quest for a lost language and culture, and the preparation of [. . .] two successful rebellions. Yet despite these momentous events it is not only to us with our memories of school history that the period seems empty: it seemed so to many contemporaries.[91]

While O'Brien's comments provide a corrective jab to typically formalist criticism of the period, Joyce himself was not only acutely aware in his own work of the social and cultural foment of the times, but also highly at-tuned to the dangers inherent in the rhetoric of so-called revolution. As we know, Joyce spent his life opposing the snares of nationalism, religion, and language as blocking agents to Ireland's union with Europe's intellectual community. In *Ulysses*, for example, Stephen Dedalus mocks the notion of literary Celtic Ireland: "Five lines of text and ten pages of notes about the folk and the fishgods of Dundrum. Printed by the weird [Yeats] sisters in the year of the big wind (*U* 11).[92] In Joyce's mind, such a view of Ireland was an isolationist cultural construct built on the narcissistic foundation of ancient myths and heroes, which was then being forged by the cultural work of Yeats, Lady Gregory and their Abbey Theater supporters.

Speaking to the broad historical reaches of his brother's work, Stanis-laus writes in *My Brother's Keeper: James Joyce's Early Years*:

> My brother's work came at the close of an epoch of Irish, perhaps one may say, of European history, to give a comprehensive picture of it in the daily life of a large city. He always held that he was lucky to have been born in a city that is old and historic enough to be considered a represen-tative European capital, and small enough to be viewed as a whole; and he believed that circumstances of birth, talent, and character had made him its interpreter.[93]

Later in his life, Joyce himself outlined in genealogical terms to Adolf Hoffmeister a larger sense of the importance of Dublin, especially the cen-tripetal-centrifugal significance of the city in relation to the development of his fiction:

> Each of my books is a book about Dublin. Dublin is a city of scarcely three hundred thousand population, but it has become the universal city of my work. *Dubliners* was my last look at that city. Then I looked at the people around me. *Portrait* was the picture of my spiritual self. *Ulysses* transformed individual impressions and emotions to give them general significance. 'Work in Progress' has a significance completely above real-

ity; transcending humans, things, sense, and entering the realm of complete abstraction.[94]

Taken together, Stanislaus' description of his brother as the privileged voice of modern Ireland in relation to Europe and Joyce's own comment present a grand mytho-historical conception of Dublin radiating out from the artist-as-creator. By the same token there is also an elemental charge of truth in Stanislaus' words, especially with regard to Joyce's use of language as a vehicle for chronicling the moral history of *fin de siècle* Dublin.

As Hayden White argues, the mythologized antithesis between history and literature that dates back to Aristotle's famous dictum is no longer as obvious or, indeed, as natural as we have long thought. According to White, all historical texts are fundamentally literary artifacts: if there is an element of the historical in all poetry, there is an element of poetry in every historical account of the world. This is because in our historical account of the world we are dependent on, in ways that we are not, say, in the natural sciences, the techniques of figurative language for our narrative representations. Moreover, precisely because history has no subject matter uniquely its own, "it is always written as part of a contest between contending poetic configurations of what the past might consist."[95] While Joyce's comment to Frank Budgeon that, in *Ulysses*, he wanted "to give a picture of Dublin so complete that if the city one day disappeared from the earth it could be reconstructed out of my book"[96] may appear boastful, the city as the primary site of Joyce's sense of modernity invades the world of the text in both historical and literary terms.

The Dublin Joyce was born into, of all Victorian cities, had declined in economic size, power and prestige throughout the nineteenth century.[97] In 1800 Dublin was the second largest city in the British Isles next to imperial London, but by 1860 it had slipped to fifth place.[98] F. S. L. Lyons describes the debilitating conditions of the city's poor, then on a par with the worst of Europe, at the end of the nineteenth century:

> About thirty per cent (87, 000) of the people in Dublin lived in the slums which were for the most part the worn-out shells of Georgian mansions. Over 2000 families lived in single room tenements [. . .] without heat or light or water (save for a tap in a passage or backyard) or adequate sanitation. Inevitably, the death-rate was the highest in the country, while infant mortality was the worst, not just in Ireland, but in the British Isles. Disease of every kind, especially tuberculosis, was rife and malnutrition was endemic.[99]

Much of this decline has been traced to Britain's success on the high seas as a naval power as well as Ireland's inability to establish itself as an international trading partner.[100] For the Anglo-Irish, the history of the Ireland of Burke and Grattan and Swift and Emmet was the record of Anglo-Irish dominance. But for Joyce Irish history was the nightmare from which he was trying to awake: "History for him meant Catholicism, meant sub-

servience to the Ascendancy, meant subordination to Britain, meant isolation from Europe, meant a small island turned in upon itself, meant the fall
of Parnell and every kind of national ignominy."[101] Given that collusion
and oppression together continued to play their part in oppressing Ireland,
Joyce presented an incisive version of history—a "nicely polished looking-
glass"[102]—the Irish had to see for themselves.

As the nineteenth century drew to a close, a metamorphosis of a different sort was changing the face of American history. In 1890 America was
transformed with the Census Bureau's announcement that the frontier no
longer existed (in 1893 Frederick Jackson Turner re-presented this closure
in cultural terms). Yet if one part of America's youth matured on the plains
in the West, by the 1920s the United States, a country reared on a Jeffersonian rural paradigm, had transitioned through Jacksonian democracy to
a new nation dominated by Hamiltonian economics. The new center of life
at the end of the nineteenth century was the modern metropolis in the East.
In 1910, 54.2 percent of the country lived in villages of fewer than 2, 500
inhabitants; by 1920, only 48.6 percent could call themselves rural inhabitants. For the first time in American history, less than half the people dwelt
in villages and on farms, and from 1910–1920 some six million people
abandoned the countryside for the city. In 1920, 51.4 percent of the nation
lived in cities; by 1930, the United States was only 44 percent rural.[103]
Nowhere were these profound changes felt more than in New York, the
historical gateway linking the Old World and the New World, and long
America's most important city as well as the center of the nation's literary
consciousness.

Between 1880 and 1919 more than 23 million people immigrated to the
United States, and of these, seventeen million entered through New York
City. By 1910, immigrants in New York made up 41 per cent of the total
population.[104] This explosion in size was made all the more dramatic with
the consolidation on 1 January 1898 of New York within its present
boundaries so as to include, in addition to the island of Manhattan, the
Bronx, Brooklyn, Queens, and Staten Island. Overnight, New York became the most extensive and populous city in the United States (its population increased from two million to 3.4 million).[105]

As the index of reality shifted from the countryside to the city, a dramatic visual aesthetic was born in the form of the skyscraper. While the
technology of cast-iron joists and columns as the skeleton of a multi-story
building had come from Europe, it was in New York that the innovation
was seized upon in the conscious construction of public space. Following
the long preeminent image of John Roebling's Brooklyn Bridge (completed
in 1883) as symbolic of America's industrial potential, it was architect
Daniel H. Burnham's Flatiron Building, built in 1902 (and arguably the
world's first skyscraper), that trumpeted the arrival of the twentieth century in New York. Rising for twenty-three floors, the Flatiron mesmerized
Alfred Stieglitz, who attempted to capture its image in photograph after

photograph. The building symbolized in material and architectural terms a consummation of America's growing sense of economic, industrial, and cultural hegemony. During the 1920s the Grand Central section of Manhattan was transformed as the race to rebuild the City turned into a race for the skies. On 1 May 1931 the race ended when the Empire State Building soared past the Bank of Manhattan's 71 stories and the Chrysler Building's 77 stories. Constructed over a period of twelve months, the 102-story Empire State was the tallest building in the world.

For those like Stieglitz, skyscrapers such as the Flatiron were the architectural embodiment of a new form of American civilization comparable in cultural significance to the Acropolis for the Greeks or the Pantheon for the Romans. But as Gertrude Stein noted, the genesis of modernity had taken place in America well before the twentieth century:

> America [is] the oldest country in the world because, by the civil war and the commercial conceptions that followed it, America created the twentieth century, and, since all the other countries are now either living or commencing to be living a twentieth century life, America, having begun the creation of the twentieth century in the sixties of the nineteenth century, is now the oldest [modern] country in the world. [punctuation added][106]

In other words, "due to specific historical conditions [the accelerated economic growth of post-Civil War America] that made the fast development of innovative, aggressive capitalism the only logical mode of economic development, nineteenth-century America initiated not nineteenth-century culture as it was conceived and on view in Europe and Britain, but twentieth-century culture, a culture as yet only in Europe's future."[107] In the twentieth century New York became an empire city, the capital of modern world history and the product of American industrial capitalism. However, while modern New York embraced a revolutionary future in keeping with its own protean past and present, its writers were meanwhile being "borne back ceaselessly into the past"[108] in their search for alternate visions of the city.

The first description of New York was written by Italian explorer Giovanni da Verrazano in 1524.[109] In addition to describing the topography and waterways of the region, de Verrazano detailed a meeting with Algonquin natives he claims to have discovered, who approached the explorers joyfully and greeted them with wonder. Four hundred years later, it was still possible, in the words of F. Scott Fitzgerald, to imagine how "the old island here that flowered once for Dutch sailors' eyes" constituted "a fresh, green breast of the new world," a place that gave itself "to the last and greatest of all human dreams."[110] From the very beginning, Americans looked to themselves as progenitors of a new concept of progress. In John Winthrop's *A Model of Christian Charity* (1630), one manifestation of this discourse was the trope of Puritan civilization (New England) as a "city upon a hill."[111] As America evolved from a colony (Christian) to a republic

(Enlightenment) that same sense of manifest destiny remained, as evinced by the Constitution and the Bill of Rights. With the exception of perhaps Philadelphia, New York more than any other American city symbolized the nation's historical commitment to the Western philosophical concept of democracy. As a result, since its beginnings as a Dutch trading post in the seventeenth century, New York has offered thematic and formal challenges for the imaginations of American and European writers who have attempted to articulate their own competing best and worst conceptions of the nation as a democratic polity. By 1837 Ralph Waldo Emerson could declare American literary independence in a Harvard lecture on the grounds that the United States had "listened too long to the courtly muses of England."[112] From a historical perspective, however, the influence—and fear—of European urban culture in all its forms, which runs deep in American society, spurred American writers to challenge their colonial past in order to create a new urban reality. Yet in many ways that reality was flawed from the beginning.

Thomas Jefferson himself saw the necessity for an industrialized America along European lines, but insisted that such industry be balanced by an equally powerful agricultural base. The Jeffersonian vision of America dominated intellectual debate for nearly two hundred years, but was progressively eroded by the advent of Alexander Hamilton's federalism and the rise of the industrial state. In *The Scarlet Letter* (1850) Nathaniel Hawthorne reconfigures the terrain of the American version of the nature-culture debate by transforming pre-Jeffersonian America into a series of discrete spaces: the wilderness of space signified by the cottage (site of Hester Prynne's exclusion and extension of the menacing prison-house); the transitory liberating space of the forest; and the repressive space of the settlement itself, complete with the symbolic matrix of the patriarchially controlled marketplace, prison-house, scaffold, and cemetery. For Hawthorne, official society (Bellingham et al.) and the individualism of his characters may well contribute to a prison-like isolation, but it is the "community, in its fully totalitarian and repressive aspect, which Hawthorne shows to be the profound enemy of the 'sweet society' possible between individuals."[113]

In the essay "Nature" (1836), Ralph Waldo Emerson formulated his doctrine of correspondences as the function of the relationship between matter and spirit, each material aspect of nature reflecting its spiritual counterpart. Similarly, in 1844 Karl Marx argued, in the midst of European industrial expansion, for the intrinsic relationship between man and nature, or what he termed "species being,"[114] in the following terms:

> The universality of man appears in practice precisely in the universality which makes all nature his *inorganic* body—both inasmuch as nature is (1) his direct means of life, and (2) the material, the object, and the instrument of his life activity. Nature is man's *inorganic body*—nature, that is, in so far as it is not itself the human body. Man *lives* on nature—means that nature is his body, with which he must remain in continuous inter-

change if he is not to die. That man's physical and spiritual life is linked to
nature means simply that nature is linked to itself, for man is a part of nature.[115]

According to Marx, it was the special relationship between man and nature that nineteenth-century political economy fractured, estranging man
from both nature and the process of his own active functions. For Emerson, the woods of New England variously represented perpetual youth in
opposition to the life of streets or villages, and it was this dialectical opposition that Henry David Thoreau translated from theory into practice in
Walden (1854). While Emerson contended that nature provided an advantage for the mind over the artificial and curtailed life of cities, it was left to
Thoreau, who appropriated this position in his own moral protest against
the oversocialized vanity of the New England town of Concord, to rail
against the factory system he believed had depressed not only man but
also nature. The threat of civilization for Thoreau in *Walden* was that
rather than civilizing the individual, society succeeded in barbarizing the
human spirit, reducing humankind, in Marx's formulation, to the level of
an "animal."

While in longitudinal terms there has always been a sense of ambivalence, distrust even, concerning the city in American history, debates have
continually focused their attention on New York as the embodiment of national decline, decay, and degeneration. One critic has declared:

> Through the years, New York has been accused of being too European,
> too suspiciously cosmopolitan, too aggressive and materialistic, too hur-
> ried and hectic, a city where family life and home life do not flourish but
> where—it is asserted or suspected—iniquity does. New York seems to sum
> up all the negative balances in the rural animus against cities, in the sec-
> tional argument against centralization and cosmopolitanism, and in the
> frontier bias against cities which do not share the mystic pioneer experi-
> ence. No other American city is the target of such great or complete an-
> tagonism.[116]

In the nineteenth century, for example, the contrast between Washington
Irving's mock-heroic *A History of New York, from the Beginning of the
World to the End of the Dutch Dynasty by Diedrich Knickerbocker* (1809)
and, say, James Fennimore Cooper's more anguished analysis of an increasingly materialistic America in *The American Democrat* (1838) is reflective
of the way in which New York becomes progressively identified with a literature of disillusionment. Later in *Pierre: or, The Ambiguities* (1852) and
"Bartleby, the Scrivener: A Story of Wall Street" (1853) Herman Melville
mercilessly satirized the soul-crushing emptiness at the heart of New York
and its attendant capitalist culture. However, whereas Melville's visions of
New York variously ended with images of suicide and despair, Walt Whitman, that "Dweller in Mannahatta my city,"[117] extolled—and fretted

over—the American city, especially New York City. In the joyous "Crossing Brooklyn Ferry"(1856) Whitman created a mythic vision that united the city's masses—past, present and future—into a redemptive whole. But while in *Leaves of Grass* (1855) Whitman's poetry celebrated the urban masses, songs of himself, and the possibilities of democracy for an ethnically diverse nation, by the time he published *Democratic Vistas* (1871) "he had begun to develop reservations about democracy in America, doubts that undermined his passion for New York City."[118] Despite such reservations, however, Whitman's poetry continued to celebrate New York—and America—as a testament to the American people and the nation even as the ravages of the Civil War gave way to the venalities of the Gilded Age.

Linda Patterson Miller argues that Edgar Allan Poe, like many of his contemporaries, does not attempt to revile the city, but rather, in his tales and essays, to interpret and evaluate a broader sense of anxiety that mirrors the "ambivalences many Americans had toward the burgeoning urban complex."[119] Unlike Wordsworth's disgust with the aural and visual pollution produced by the London populace, Poe indulged his morbid fascination for the debilitating and dangerous effects of nineteenth-century urban expansion. For example, the narrator of "The Sphinx" (1846) flees to the country in order to save his life from the cholera epidemic of the thickly populated city of New York. Accepting the invitation of a relative to spend a "fortnight with him in the retirement of his *cottage orne* on the banks of the Hudson, they pass the time "rambling in the woods, sketching, boating, fishing, bathing, music and books." However, they cannot escape "the gloom and desolation of the neighboring city," where, as the narrator relates, "they learned to expect daily the loss of some friend [. . .] The very air from the South seemed to us redolent with death."[120]

By the time of writing the tales of ratiocination, "Murders in the Rue Morgue" (1841) and "The Purloined Letter" (1845), Poe's obsession with the city had mutated into a fascination with urban crime. These tales may well take as their locale the city of Paris, but "it was actually an American phenomenon drawn from the Philadelphia and New York of the time."[121] As Dupin (Poe's ur-Dr. Watson) tells us in the "Rue Morgue" case, it is typically in the darkness and "amid the wild lights and shadows of the populous city"[122] that the sleuths of deduction sally forth into the metropolis to conduct their investigations. And in the course of their work, Poe's characters present an evocative and menacing topography of the city's working class population in close proximity to dangerous excitements and the menace of crime. In "The Purloined Letter," meanwhile, the narrator tells us that Dupin hires a man as a decoy to fire a musket into an afternoon Parisian crowd. However, the neurasthenic crowd is used to the arbitrary violence of city life, and the man is subsequently allowed to go his way as a lunatic or a drunkard.

By the 1880s, as the rapid rise of industry, urbanization, and population expansion during the post-Civil War era transformed the nation, "*the city* became a shorthand for everything threatening in American society."[123] In the national bestseller *Our Country: Its Possible Future and Its Present Crisis* (1885), a text that recycles tired fragments of denunciation common to criticisms of the city on both sides of the Atlantic, Josiah Strong tailored a culturally conservative attack so as to single out immigrant communities as the source of urban degeneration. Jeremiad-like, Strong argued that while the city was the "nerve center of our civilization," it was also the "storm center" of civilization, where all manner of lawlessness and lewdness and *ennui* and surfeit existed amid "foreigners and wage workers."[124] By contrast, just as the investigations of Chicago School sociologists W. I. Thomas, Robert Park, Ernest Burgess, and Robert Redfield would later inform the literary imaginations of writers like James T. Farrell, Nelson Algren, and Richard Wright, so Jacob Riis' more sympathetic *How the Other Half Lives* (1890) exposed the shocking living conditions endured by immigrants in the very slums Strong identified. Riis' investigative eye exposed such examples of human misery as New York's infamous Five Points, a loathsome ghetto so bleak that even Charles Dickens was shocked when he viewed it shortly after its construction in 1842.[125] In 1888, a leading magazine described a typical dumbbell-shaped tenement (prohibited after 1901) situated in the predominantly Jewish Lower East Side as follows:

> They are great prison-like structures of brick, with narrow doors and windows, cramped passages and steep rickety stairs. They are built through from one street to the other with a somewhat narrower building connecting them. [. . .] The narrow court-yard [. . .] in the middle is a damp foul-smelling place, supposed to do duty as an airshaft; had the foul fiend designed these great barracks they could not have been more villainously arranged to avoid any chance of ventilation. [. . .] In case of fire it would be impossible for the occupants of the crowded rooms to escape by the narrow stairways.[126]

Whereas Henry James had written about New York's upper-class during the 1830s and 1840s in *Washington Square* (1881), William Dean Howells' *A Hazard of New Fortunes* (1890), Stephen Crane's *Maggie: A Girl of the Streets* (1893), and Theodore Dreiser's *Sister Carrie* (1900) further illuminated the misery, luxury, and restless confusion that now characterized the American city. In *Maggie*, Crane in particular captured the material life of the tenement experience in Zolaesque style, exposing the miserable physical and human conditions of a sector of the city that for the more privileged remained a dark and threatening mystery."[127] Yet is was with Dreiser's *Sister Carrie*, with its treatment of alienation, materialism, mechanization, the breakdown of tradition, sexuality, and the inevitable conflict between the individual and society, and all set in the vortex of the city, that the modern New York City novel was born.

In 1899, Thorstein Veblen had satirized the rise of a new class in the cities indulging in "conspicuous consumerism" and a lower class obsessed with "pecuniary emulation," consciously separating themselves from the world of labor relations.[128] Perhaps Dreiser's importance lies in the fact that more than any other writer, his realism prefigures American modernist fiction's own critique of consumer culture. As Walter Benn Michaels notes, "where Howells identifies character with autonomy, Dreiser [. . .] identifies it with desire, an involvement with the world so central to one's self that the distinctions between what one is and what one wants tends to disappear."[129] Even as the nineteenth century drew to a close, therefore, there was already a sense of aesthetic dissent from the materialism and puritanism of American life we more easily associate with fiction of the 1920s. However, as American writers continued their conversation with the American city as an urban phenomenon into the new century, the tenor and focus of their debates were being radically altered by the formation of a new European urban culture.

In *The Autobiography of an Ex-Colored Man* (1912), James Weldon Johnson personified New York as a Janus-faced witch guarding the hypocritical confines of a white New World society within, while enticing the immigrant hordes of the Old World without, to enter in: "New York City is the most fatally fascinating thing in America. She sits like a great witch at the gate of the country, showing her alluring white face and hiding her crooked hands and feet under the folds of her wide garments—constantly enticing thousands."[130] As the title of the novel suggests, *The Autobiography* plays with the concept of racial identification; in particular, Johnson "exposes the white world's worst crime, its encirclement of the black man's self and its denial of his right to voice and freedom"[131] by not allowing the nameless narrator to accept either a black or white identity in the binary that white society has set for him. Not only is Johnson's narrator denied an identity based on color, but he is also frustrated in his attempts to fulfill his artistic intentions, of finding, in other words, his own cultural voice. Indeed, Europe for Johnson's ex-colored man provides little more than stereotypical observations of Paris and London. Throughout the book "the narrator defines himself as an artist and his views as those of an artist, and yet while he continues to play the piano, primarily for the amusement of a rich white patron who takes him to Europe, he creates nothing."[132]

By 1922 Harold Stearn's anthology of protest essays titled *Civilization in the United States* had declared American civilization culturally bankrupt, and that the best thing for the cultural intelligentsia was to get out and head for Paris, a city whose enduring magnestism would attract generations of American artists.[133] Yet despite such polemical outbursts, 1920s New York, the nation's publishing capital since the 1840s, had become a literary world unto itself. In effect, the city became a cultural landscape punctuated by literary magazines such as *The Little Review*, *The Dial*, and *Opportunity*, stylish magazines like the *Smart Set*, *Vanity Fair*, and the

New Yorker, and of course newspapers such as *The New York Times* and
New York World. Despite the carnage of the calamitous war in Europe
(1914–1918), many Americans like Stearns continued to have faith in the
notion of Europe as a culturally and historically enriching alternative to
the crass commercialism and puritanical values of President Wilson's postwar America.

At the same time, young writers like Dos Passos, who had grown up
when Europe was the center of world power, were shocked with what they
believed was the precipitate decline in European civilization. In the early
essay "A Humble Protest" (1916), Dos Passos had already objected to a
capitalistic pyramidal structure for society, which he believed was the underlying cause for the diseased state of Europe and America.[134] As the discursive essay "Young Spain" ([1917] anthologized in *Rosinante to the
Road Again* [1922]) reveals, Dos Passos saw western civilization historically, with the individual connected to the heritage of a shared cultural
past, a theme that remained a life-long obsession. Reflecting on the enigma
of Almorox, a small Andalusian village near Madrid, Dos Passos writes:

> It was all so mellow, so strangely aloof from the modern world of feverish
> change, this life of the peasants of Almorox. Everywhere roots striking
> into the infinite past. [. . .] [There] always remained the love for the place,
> the strong anarchistic reliance on the individual man, way beaten by gen-
> erations of men who had tilled and loved and lain in the cherishing sun
> with no feeling of a reality outside of themselves, outside of the bare en-
> compassing hills of their commune, except the God which was the synthe-
> sis of their souls and of their lives.[135]

After he returned to America following World War I, Dos Passos carried
the seeds of this culturally conservative (agrarian/mythical) vision of history with him to New York, where competing transatlantic versions of history were already being played out in dynamic terms. The most significant
and far-reaching consequence of Dos Passos' experience of New York from
1920 onwards was his deep interest in the various experimental artistic
and literary movements that were then informing the city's artistic culture.
Looking back on the decade in 1931, Dos Passos described in particular
what was at the time coming to be known as modernism:

> The poetry of Blaise Cendrars was part of the creative tidal wave that
> spread over the world from the Paris of before the last European war.
> Under various tags: futurism, cubism, vorticism, modernism, most of the
> best work in the arts of our time has been the direct product of this explo-
> sion, that had an influence in its sphere comparable with the October rev-
> olution in social organization and politics and the Einstein formula in
> physics. Cendrars and Apollinaire, poets, were on the first cubist barri-
> cades with the group that included Picasso, Modigliani, Marinetti, Cha-
> gall; that profoundly influenced Maiakovsky, Meyerhold, Eisenstein;
> whose ideas carom through Joyce, Gertrude Stein, T. S. Eliot (first pub-
> lished in Wyndham Lewis's 'Blast'). The music of Stravinski and Prokovi-

eff and Diageleff's Ballet hail from this same Paris already in the disintegration of victory, as do the windows of Saks Fifth Avenue, skyscraper
furniture, the Lenin Memorial in Moscow, the paintings of Diego Rivera
in Mexico City and the newritz styles of advertising in American magazines.[136]

Like an antiquarian cataloguing the prized contents of a cabinet full of exotic specimens, Dos Passos-as-curator arranges and itemizes in formal
terms a collection of artists whose work we now embrace without reservation as canonical avant-garde works. Sandwiched between cubist artists of
one shade or another and the progenitors of modern music and dance lies
Joyce—appropriately heading a list comprising Stein and Eliot. Like their
European counterparts, the vast majority of American critics writing in the
1920s and 1930s associated formal experimentation with revolutionary or
anti-bourgeois tendencies. Yet in American cultural debates, it was Joyce's
art in particular as the cause (or symptom) of contemporary social ills that
became the focus of heated discussions rather than the nature his unarticu-
lated political views.[137] By contrast it was Dos Passos American critics
looked to (with as much praise as dismay) as a model of socially active art.
In a diary entry dated 21 July 1918, Dos Passos noted the following:

> Finished reading for the second time James Joyce's 'Portrait of the
> Artist'—pray God I shant start imitating it off the face of the earth, Cuth-
> bert-like [reference to Cuthbert Wright, a Harvard acquaintance]—I ad-
> mire it hugely—It is so wonderfully succinct and follows such curious
> by-ways of expression—old abandoned roads that are overgrown but
> where the air is cleaner than in the modern dusty thoroughfares—con-
> stantly churned by other people's footsteps.[138]

Like many of his generation, Joyce's fiction marked a literary precedent for
the young Dos Passos. However, beyond the gushing praise for a literary
master's technical achievements, Dos Passos' choice of metaphor intimates
a central difference between the two concerning their responses to the
modern city. For Dos Passos and Joyce the city was the expression of the
human experience it embodied, and this included all personal history.
However, whereas Joyce mapped the collective and individual histories of
the urban aggregate in terms of social, cultural, and political paralysis, the
vision of his European metropolis does not detract from a progressive amelioration over time of that vision, indeed of Joyce's conditional reconciliation with the city of Dublin. Dos Passos, on the other hand, never fully
reconciled himself to the soul-destroying nuclear texture of New York as
the embodiment of American history betrayed. Dos Passos' American
modernism, rooted in a tradition of pragmatism, social criticism, and political partisanship, was in many ways in keeping with the long-standing influence in American letters of Emerson and Thoreau. In Dos Passos'
organic conception of civilization, however, the tragedy of modern history
was symbolized by a "restless industrial world of joyless enforced labor

and incessant goading war," a world in which America was "a malignant Colossus trampling out the hope of the Western world."[139] The New York of the synoptic novel *Manhattan Transfer* is a synecdoche for this phase of history, representing a "sanitary civilization of a scientized New World Order," a world that had enslaved itself to a debilitating "industrial system" offering little succor, except in the hectic pleasures of suffocating life in cities."[140]

Like Dos Passos, Joyce predicated his own history of modernity in *Dubliners* on an organic conception of urban society when he claimed, "I call the series *Dubliners* to betray the soul of that hemiplegia or paralysis which many consider a city."[141] Moreover, Joyce was also obsessed with the epistemology of the self caught in the flux of international and universal history; but, like Stephen Dedalus, "he chronicled with patience what he saw, detaching himself from it and tasting its mortifying flavor in secret."[142] Joyce the artist, in other words, learned to disengage himself from political activity, creating in his art an autonomous, self-reflexive world. By contrast, "the history of Dos Passos' political opinions has tended to overshadow his fiction"[143] so as to subsume his literary achievements and his place as a great American modernist author. Borrowing heavily from Giambattista Vico's cyclical theory of history, Joyce always wrote about Dublin, because by getting to the heart of this city, he felt he could get to the heart of all the cities of the great urban civilizations in history. But the *corso-ricorso* of the Joyce-Dublin dialectic is not, as many critics seem to think, a progressive detachment from the nets of family, home, and religion. Rather, Joyce's conception of himself as a self-exiled Irishman became more complex the more distance, time, and space he put between himself and his native city.

Written across the face of Europe in cities as diverse as Dublin, Pola, Trieste, Rome, Paris, and Zurich during a period of historical transformation, Joyce's lean, myopic eye progressively forged an internationalist vision of Dublin in two interlocking and recursive ways: first, in terms of a naturalistic, quantified, and knowable object in which the moral, cultural and social destitution of turn-of-the-century metropolitan Ireland is offered up as an oppositional reading against nationalistic and romantic conceptions provided by the Celtic Twilight. At the same time, Joyce's inherently sympathetic relationship with and articulation of the modern city and its inhabitants as a locus for modern consciousness transforms the sordid particulars of "Dear, Dirty Dublin" into an imaginative urban vision of the city in universal terms. Read together, the politics of Joyce's and Dos Passos' fictions may be seen as a massive attempt to deconstruct two versions of historical process: the mythology of modern Ireland, and superpower U.S.A.

CHAPTER TWO

Dubliners
The City Betrayed

By infallible presentiment he saw, that not always doth life's beginning gloom conclude in gladness; that wedding-bells peal not ever in the last scene of life's fifth act; that while the countless tribes of common novels laboriously spin veils of mystery, only to complacently clear them up at last; and while the countless tribe of common dramas do but repeat the same; yet the profounder emanations of the human mind, intended to illustrate all that can be humanly known of human life, these never unravel their own intricacies, and have no proper endings; but in imperfect, unanticipated, and disappointing sequels (as mutilated stumps), hurry to abrupt intermergings with the eternal tides of time and fate.

~ Herman Melville, *Pierre: or, The Ambiguities* (1852)

I am afraid I am more interested, Mr. Connolly, in the Dublin street names than in the riddle of the universe.

~ James Joyce, in an interview with Cyril Connolly

THE SPACE OF *DUBLINERS*

In "Semiology and Urbanism," Roland Barthes attempts a semiotics of the city in response to the abiding significance of human and physical space.[1] In the first instance, Barthes notes the relative failure, on the part of many urban theoreticians and their functional studies, to explicate fully the infinity of meaning the modern city affords. At the same time, he assures the reader in more encouraging terms that urban studies also shows a growing awareness of the function and importance of symbols in the study of urban space, or what Barthes terms "significant space."[2] Before proceeding to consider central Paris in semiotic terms, Barthes notes that, in historical terms, the study of geographical space in general has always been characterized by relativism in terms of its denotation and study. For example, from the identification of human habitations in Greek antiquity in the maps of Anaximander and Hecataeus to the "mental cartography" of paradigmatic maps of the known world by Herodotus to Claude Levi-Strauss's semiological study of an African Boro Village, the notion of human space (geographical space) in western cultural history has always constituted a structurally grounded and contested discourse.[3]

Toward the end of the essay, however, Barthes regretfully announces that, despite his best efforts, he has nonetheless failed to "really [come] to grips with any methodological issues"[4] pertinent to a semiology of the city. He too, it seems, has failed to reveal the infinity of meaning germane to the city. Barthes is of course being ironic; in fact, this semantic turn is really a sleight of hand for the main thrust of a quite different argument. What Barthes is advocating for, it appears, is the need, based on certain precedents taken from the broad reaches of history, for a "naive attitude, like that of a reader" on the part of literary commentators, who have read the city in terms of its signification. These alone, he notes, "are the only ones who so far have dealt with urban semantics."[5] With the exception of urban theoreticians such as Kevin Lynch, Barthes contends, finally, that "it is far less important to multiply functional studies of the city than to multiply these city readings, of which, so far, unfortunately, writers alone have provided examples; they are the ones who so far have best dealt with urban semantics."[6] Turning his attention to the core of the Paris as a case in point, Barthes argues that, in structural terms, "the center city is always experienced as the space of gathered subversive forces, disruptive forces, ludic forces [. . .] the privileged place of 'the other', and where we ourselves are 'other.'"[7] Barthes' Paris signifies a playful, Dionysian site of disorder, a privileged field of semiotic transference, slippage, and contestation where people are no longer subject to constraining modes of identity; rather, it is in this center that becoming "other"—or rather un-becoming—is central to Barthes' notion of the possibilities of urban space. Central Paris thus represents a site of liberation. The center cannot hold; indeed, it is encouraged not to hold, for the city here in structural terms represents a paradoxical sense of freedom beyond control.

In 1904 George Russell (A.E.) invited Joyce to write something innocuous for the provincial newspaper *The Irish Homestead*. Joyce responded by writing "The Sisters," and declared in a letter to Constantine Curran his intention for the stories that were to follow: "I am writing a series of epicleti—ten—for a paper. I have written one. I call the series Dubliners to betray the soul of that hemiplegia or paralysis which many consider a city."[8] Thus Joyce's first look at the capital from within—his survey of the island—was predicated on the notion that Dublin was a diseased organic entity. In this chapter I consider in rather broad terms Barthes' urban semantics in relation to Joyce's "naïve" representation of human space as it appears in *Dubliners*. In keeping with Barthes' provocative paradigm,

Joyce constructs a semantic field in which the topographical features of the physical city combine with the mental landscapes created by its inhabitants to create a complex—and paradoxical—world of signification.[9] Unlike Barthes' theorization of postmodern Paris, however, the narrative mode Joyce employs in *Dubliners* constitutes an urban semantics in keeping with contemporary developments in literary naturalism. At one level Joyce's Dublin represents a predatory urban space in which the presence of and interaction with strangers contribute to the worst aspect of urbanism: the estrangement of the individual from the self and from the city. At the same time, Joyce's naturalistic vision poeticizes the entropy of Irish life, and in so doing creates a space of where life and art combine to both celebrate and resist the city.

A CULTURAL GEOGRAPHY OF *DUBLINERS*

Hugh Kenner, one of the first critics to identify the centrality of the city in Joyce's fiction, noted early on that *Dubliners* was "less a sequence of stories than a kind of multi-faceted novel [. . .] not an agglomeration of residents, but a city."[10] As Kenner points out, in the same way that we should read *Dubliners* as Joyce intended it—as a novel, but more importantly as part of a larger history—so too does Joyce present more than just a narrow cross-section of *fin de siècle* Dublin urbanites masquerading as a *tableau histoire*. Joyce claimed that his stories chronicled the life of Dublin in human terms, with four stages of life—childhood, adolescence, maturity and public life. Thus, more than the division of a literary text into subdivisions based on the ages of the characters involved, or mere chronology, the city itself is inextricably bound up with the oppressed, down-at-heel and imprisoned figures we experience across the public and private spaces of the metropolis. In writing *Dubliners*, Joyce defined his moral history of Dublin as a step on the road to liberating Ireland.[11] But he did not ally himself with the Irish Literary Revival's mythic and romanticized notions of rural Ireland in order to chronicle the life of the nation. Rather, it was his personal experiences of contemporary Dublin centered around the lower middle-class milieu of the depressed northeast quadrant of the city that Joyce grounded the *archae* of contemporary Irish history. And yet while Joyce concluded early on that he could not write without offending people while at the same time insisting that he was not an enemy of the people, he nonetheless committed himself to a lifelong conflict with his native city, of which *Dubliners* is the opening salvo.

If, as Thomas F. Staley notes, "a number of narrative beginnings have become signatures in our memories of the literary landscape,"[12] then "The Sisters" not only fixes a chilling evocation of a particular literary landscape—the symbol of Dublin as a "house of mourning" (D 14)[13] on Great Britain Street—in our memories, but also provides literature with a landmark inscription of landscape-as-memory/memory-as-landscape in mod-

ernist art. To this end, the opening paragraph of the story, with its enigmatic trinity of words "paralysis," "simony," and "gnomon" constitutes a
menacing overture for the codes of the collection by underscoring the physical, spiritual, and religious decay of the landscape of Dublin.[14] Moreover,
if the beginning of a text is, as Edward Said suggests, "the entrance to what
is offered and the first step in the intentional production of meaning,"[15]
then "The Sisters" corroborates Joyce's stated intention to betray the
paralysis of his native city by dissecting the anatomical space of Dublin,
while at the same time establishing *Dubliners* as "one of the formative
stages in the unfolding of modern literature."[16]

In *The Poetics of Space* phenomenologist Gaston Bachelard examines
the spaces or presences (what he terms "topoanalysis") that surround and
inform our everyday lives. The house, for example, "the non-I that protects
the I," represents a site of "felicitous space," our "first universe, a real cosmos in every sense of the word."[17] In terms of Bachelard's contemplation
of domestic space, there "does not exist a real intimacy that is repellent."[18]
In *Dubliners*, however, the presence of malignant or menacing private and
public spaces is co-terminus with a landscape encrusted with the signifiers
of oppressive civic and domestic forms of architecture. And it is these
spaces—and their attendant associations of entrapment that many of the
characters at one point or another unsuccessfully attempt to escape
throughout the collection.[19] Ironically, the cold minimalism at work in
Dubliners is at odds with the sweltering conditions under which individual
stories such as "The Boarding House" and "Counterparts" were written.[20]

In "The Sisters" and "Araby" the domestic space of suburban Dublin is
emphasized as an environment in which inhabitants grope their way
through dark houses and rooms. The exteriors of these houses, meanwhile,
are synonymous with the young narrator's own home on North Richmond
Street: "detached from its neighbors in a square ground," at the "blind
end" (*D* 28). By the same token, these are homes "conscious of decent lives
within them, gazing at one another with brown imperturbable faces" (*D*
29). In keeping with the depressing physiognomy of Dublin's urban architecture, interiors are themselves equally dispiriting, providing as they often
do a melancholy backdrop for the workings out of truncated family relations. As the opening triad on childhood reveals, "The Sisters," "An Encounter," and "Araby" present fatherless homes marked by darkened
blinds, narrow staircases, decrepit little rooms, and empty fireplaces.
Dublin is a space of isolation "under observation" (*D* 10), where the
young yearn to escape the nets of family, home, and religion. As with all of
the stories, "The Sisters" begins *in medias res*, but with one crucial difference. The ambiguous first sentence, "there was no hope for him this time"
(*D* 9), not only prepares us for the physical decay overtaking Father Flynn,
but also announces by implication that the young narrator's fate is inexorably tied to the priest's. Constrained by a religious and secular trinity
combining the Catholic church, fractured family, and depressing home life,

Flynn's death provides only salutary relief for the boy's sense of spiritual and secular emptiness. The conflation, rather, of the boy's claustrophobic surroundings with the ensuing psychic conflict resulting from Flynn's passing engenders only hopelessness in the face of the boy's predestined fate. Annoyed with himself for "discovering [. . .] a sensation of freedom as if I had been freed from something by his death," Flynn's legacy—the "great deal" he had had taught the boy—is in fact an epitaph warning of the larger fate awaiting this precociously artistic boy and his embryonic attempt to detach himself from those same familiar nets that governed Flynn's paralyzed existence and final end (D 12, 13, 16).[21]

Like the mysterious sense of fear and tension generated for the reader by the opening sentences, the young boy is similarly drawn to the windows of the house of death: "every night as I gazed up at the window I said softly to myself the word paralysis [. . .] it filled me with fear and yet I longed to be nearer to it and to look upon its deadly work" (D 9). The repetitive nature of the boy's visits to see "poor James," his "disappointed" (D 16, 17) friend, allows Joyce to establish an imaginative topographical framework. In topographical terms, the narrator's mental journeying represents a series of concentric circles enclosing a nuclear core of deadening paralysis: the "idle chalice" (D 18) that lies on Flynn's corpse at the end of the story.[22] As such, the story's symbolic structure takes us first along Great Britain Street, a hegemonic signifier that frames the narrative, on to the drapery, and, finally, to the dead-room of Flynn's resting place where his corpse embraces a chalice, the emblem of the priest's fall from grace.[23] The house of mourning is a site of imprisoning pathos; it represents the urbanization of disappointment for both Father Flynn and his sisters. In the "unassuming shop, registered under the vague name of Drapery" (D 11), Flynn's economically and socially impoverished siblings have been forced to receive the debilitating legacy of a truculent apostate whose fortunes had once taken him to the Irish College in Rome.

Flynn's final death-wish is one that ends, like so many of the stories, in defeated expectation, a fact made all the more terrifying in that he is perhaps mortally (if ironically) aware of his entombment in life. As Eliza, James's sister, recounts:

> But still and all he kept on saying that before the summer was over he'd go out for a drive one fine day just to see the old house where we were all born down in Irishtown and take me and Nannie with him. If we could only get one of them new-fangled carriages that makes no noise that Father O'Rourke told him about—them with the rheumatic wheels—for the day cheap, he said, at Johnny Rush's over the way and drive out the three of us together of a Sunday evening. He had his mind set on that. [. . .] Poor James! (D 17)

Irish Town, an example of the inertia of colonial medievalism, was an area less than two miles from the city where many native Catholics were forced to live outside the city proper by ruling of the Ascendancy culture in the seventeenth and eighteenth centuries. If the Catholic church kept the priest quarantined in his little house on Great Britain Street, with his sisters as the wardens of his fate, then Flynn's inability to revisit his birthplace, yet another site of historical marginalization, is the final, palindromic failure in a "crossed" (*D* 17) life.

The shadows of the dead in *Dubliners* often betray the world of their warm-blooded counterparts. Indeed, one of the most powerful aspects of *Dubliners* is the way in which the narrative operates so as to highlight the interconnectedness between the living and the dead. In "The Sisters," for example, we learn that the perverse priest, no longer the master of his own financial estate, ended his years a pecuniary disappointment for his immediate family and a theological embarrassment for his church. Yet in "Araby" we soon discover that a trace of Flynn lives on amid the dull quietude of North Richmond Street life. With this in mind, there is something peculiar concerning Father O'Rourke's haste in making the final arrangements for his fellow priest's estate. In effect, we are told that the former tenant (Flynn), whose "useless papers" (*D* 29) still litter that deserted part of the house, "had been a very charitable priest; in his will he had left all his money to institutions and the furniture of his house to his sister" (*D* 29). In "The Sisters," however, Eliza confesses: "only for Father O'Rourke I don't know what we'd have done at all. It was him brought us all them flowers and them two candlesticks out of the chapel and wrote out the notice for the Freeman's General and took charge of all the papers for the cemetary and poor James's insurance" (*D* 16).

Like the "gratefully oppressed" (*D* 42) Jimmy Doyle from "After the Race," or Bob Doran in "The Boarding House," it seems that Flynn and his sisters have perhaps been duped. Having tantalized the ill-educated siblings with the possibility of getting "one of them new-fangled carriages that makes no noise [. . .] them with the rheumatic wheels" to carry them all to Irishtown, it may well be the case that more good advice and sound housekeeping on O'Rourke's part followed in the form of manipulating the destiny of the Flynn family in death as he does in life by siphoning off the bulk of Flynn's estate for the church, leaving only the dead man's furniture as an impoverished legacy. There is a malignant irony at work in this story: the living betray the dead, but the dead live on, haunting the living.

Much like Joyce's handling of Dublin's urban reality and its deadening sense of paralysis, the events of "Araby," "An Encounter," and "Eveline" each pivot on a burgeoning sense of anticipation only to depress and betray in actuality.[24] Dublin is an entropic landscape: terribly boring and terribly dull. Not surprisingly, characters look for adventure beyond the city where danger and predatory influences find a home just as easily as they do within the city proper. In these stories the bazaar, Pigeon House, and North Wall do not draw distinguishable lines among themselves as spaces/places of possibility versus the disillusionment synonymous with home or school life. Moreover, the narrators of these stories are fully cognizant of the soul-destroying inertia of home and family yet find little succor in the city. Consequently, the characters are thrown back, like Eveline Hill, on lonely worlds full of "dusty cretonne" (D 36) or "familiar objects" (D 37). In the end there is little if no room for Bachelard's notion of "felicitous space" against the endemic sense of the paralysis in this metropolis.

Initially a precocious figure, the young boy in "Araby" attempts to escape the domestic claustrophobia and odorous ashpits that characterize North Richmond Street life. But from what he tells us of his garden, the memory of Father Flynn continues to haunt a new generation. While the narrator of "An Encounter" enjoys a sensation of temporary relief in Joe Dillon's back garden, there is little respite in the fallen Eden offered in "Araby"—"a wild garden" containing "a central tree and a few straggling bushes under one of which I found the late tenant's rusty bicycle-pump" (D 29). Only in "high cold empty gloomy rooms" (D 33) does the boy find solace, cut off as he is from the weakened and indistinct voices of his companions far below. Like Eveline Hill, he too is a lonely figure for whom the life of the street and beyond remains indistinct; accordingly, "nameless strangers" are viewed from behind imprisoning screens of "cool glass" (D 33) that both protect and enclose familiar worlds.

Given these conditions it is not surprising that a familiar stranger such as Mangan's exoticized sister becomes the object of the narrator's burgeoning sexual life and voyeuristic intellection. "Every morning," we are told, the boy "lay on the floor in the front parlour watching her door. The blind was pulled down to within an inch of the sash so that I could not be seen" (D 31). If Father Flynn symbolizes the transition from a betrayed youth to a depressingly pre-destined adulthood, in "Araby" it is a female other, a priestess of the romantic imagination and object of the boy's tragically banal "confused adoration" (D 31). Bound up with received ideas of a sensuous, luxuriant East (a concomitant other symbolized by the bazaar) both bazaar and girl represent the possibility of a place in the boy's imagination he can escape to beyond the monotony of home and school life. However, bazaar and girl in turn are as pathetic as they are inseparable; cast in shadow, the girl's image, like the notion of the bazaar in the boy's mind, is a non-defined silhouette signifying an unfamiliar yet seemingly attainable desire. While the girl's coy behavior suggestively encourages the boy to reward her with a gift ("while she spoke she turned a silver bracelet round and round her wrist" [D 32]), the final resting place of the narrator's quest is symptomatic, as many critics have noted, of Dublin's debased commercial commonality.

As a signifying system, Joyce's city feeds on itself, producing an endless chain of signification predicated on frustration and entrapment. Despite the fact that it is almost impossible to escape the city, the narrator of "Araby" nonetheless believes that his confused religious and chivalric adoration will act as a protective screen against the city's streets, the places "most hostile to romance" (*D* 31):

> On Saturday evenings when my aunt went marketing I had to go to carry some of the parcels. We walked through the flaring streets, jostled by drunken men and bargaining women, amid the curses of laborers, the shrill litanies of shop-boys who stood on guard by the barrels of pigs' cheeks, the nasal chanting of street-singers, who sang a *come-all-you* about O'Donovan Rossa, or a ballad about the troubles in our native land. These noises converged in a single sensation of life for me: I imagined that I bore my chalice safely through a throng of foes. (*D* 31)

The boy is more than acutely aware of Dublin's degraded commercial culture in his rejection of the social discourse of the street—"the shrill litanies of shop-boys." But he finds a similar state of commercial degradation at Araby, only here the shrill calls fall from the mouths of English vendors. Housed as Araby is within a space with "the magical name" (*D* 34), the bazaar represents a space beyond the ruinous houses of Dublin. Once inside, however, the bazaar recalls rather than eschews the marketplace of Dublin; indeed, as the boy's bitter epiphany reveals, the fall of coins on salvers and words and the bargaining of common strangers are an ironic mask for the bastardization of romance and chivalry. In political terms, "Araby's" streets also provide a venue for populist expression in doggerel verse, but the larger "troubles" afflicting the nation are rejected by the boy because they are merely blocking agents to the workings of a romantic imagination the city destroys all the same.[25]

The young narrator of "Araby," like those of "The Sisters" and "An Encounter," prefigures the emotional, intellectual, and social entrapment (and ambivalence towards the city) of their spiritual cousin, Gabriel Conroy. In the case of "An Encounter" and "Araby," the boys mirror Gabriel's disconnection from the lower grade of culture of the guests at the Misses Morkan Christmas celebration: like him, they are aware of themselves as beings apart. In addition, the narrator of "Araby," like Mr. Duffy ("A Little Cloud") and Little Chandler ("A Painful Case"), feels threatened by the life of the streets. Mr. Duffy, who lives beyond the borders of the city, is a man who shuns society, preferring to reside on the margins, in Chapelizod. A suburbanite, he embodies an intellectual distaste for the city.[26] Moreover, Mr. Duffy prefigures Little Chandler, a superficial yet sympathetic effete, who similarly rejects the squalid humanity of the city's poor.

In the understated "An Encounter," a sense of "otherness" to escape to away from the labyrinthine paralysis of home and school functions, and is partially achieved, on two levels: first, by the act of reading, a form of virtual voyaging by way of the imagination; and secondly, through play, an active "spirit of unruliness" (*D* 20) induced by Joe Dillon and his Wild West games. But as the narrator—a "reluctant Indian"—admits, their anarchy remains transitory: "I wanted real adventures to happen to myself.

But real adventures, I reflected, do not happen to people who remain at home; they must be sought abroad" (*D* 20–21). But the placement of the caveat informing the reader of Joe Dillon's vocation for the priesthood (*D* 19) intimates that all attempts at escape, even for the wildest of boys, are futile. Caught between soul-destroying rebukes during the "sober hours of school" (*D* 20) and the hunger for "chronicles of disorder," partially fulfilled in their role-playing, this bitter story is underscored immediately by the conscience of the escapee suffering under the weight of coerced assimilation. In the end, guilt, disappointment and fear provide the tension and control that mark this chronicle of escape as little more than pathetic tautology.

Supposed liberation for Mahony and Dillon comes in their plan to skip school, "a day's miching" (*D* 21). The strategy is simple. The boys agree to rendezvous on the Canal Bridge and take the Wharf Road away from the city to the docks to see the sea and the big ships; from here, they then plan take a ferryboat to their final destination, the Pigeon House. As with the North Wall in "Eveline" and the marina in "After the Race," the docks symbolize the potential for real adventure: a site of release into an unknown other; a symbolic field of play in which the city is left far behind. On their way to the sea, the narrator remarks, "school and home *seemed* to recede from us and their influence upon us *seemed* to wane" (emphasis added *D* 23). Unlike the narrator's dismissive response to the streets of "Araby," the boys of "An Encounter" mistake the drudgery of Dublin's "noisy streets," "labourers," "barges," and "brown fishing fleet" for "the spectacle of Dublin's commerce"(*D* 23). But dreams of new geographical horizons, embellished as they are by the Norwegian "graceful three-master," soon give way to "confused notions" about strange, "green-eyed" foreigners, bleached, musty biscuits in grocers' shops, and the "squalid streets" of the quays. In keeping with the story's veiled valediction forbidding escape, the boys' day out is neither successful nor exciting. Exciting in theory, the narrator's actual adventure is prefaced by a restless night's sleep, enacted using "frail canvas shoes" (*D* 21), and betrayed by Leo Dillon's failure to show at the appointed hour.

The narrator's plan finally ends outside the city in the miserable streets surrounding the docks. Unfortunately, the power of domestic home rule coupled with the fear of discovery should they return home late are just too high a price to pay for their day of fun. The telling capitulation to conformity is irrevocably sealed in the dramatic denouement of the story: the meeting with the pederast—the "queer old josser" (*D* 26)—in a field by the Dodder. The narrator, playing the role of confessor to the old man's perverted catechism, now faces a quite different pair of "bottle-green eyes" (*D* 27), which pin the boy like a specimen to be dissected. In the place of playful riot and childhood disorder, the old man's fantasies, affectionate, pleading, and sadistic pleasures seal the boy's fate.

As one critic notes, the queer old josser "seems, finally, an even more dramatic and pathetic example of capitulating to a systematic conformity than Joe Dillon, who became a priest; of the eventual and seemingly inescapable stifling of imagination and the spirit of unruliness, a per-version of the spirit of carnivalesque liberality, turned around eventually into a sadistic version of authoritarian rule and conformity."[27] The stranger's suppression of the spirit of unruliness elides any chance of liberation; as a result, the narrator is thrown back into the paralyzing normalcy of Dublin life. The schoolmaster's rebuke may have awakened a prisoner's conscience, but the old man's work completes the cycle of oppression and repression. The narrator concedes, "I was penitent" (D 28), and runs home. "Eveline" marks the first installment of the volume's second division, which focuses on adolescence; however, unlike the opening triad, the narrative traces the fate of a woman trapped in stifling urban conditions. Like much of *Dubliners*, "Eveline" is a domestic drama, but in this case it is the foregrounding of a female consciousness that trenchantly calls to mind Joyce's own conception of home as the extension of a larger system of social and cultural oppression.[28]

Eveline struggles with her responsibilities as a store clerk, housekeeper, and surrogate mother to her siblings. Like many of the characters, she too suffers from a gradual wearing down of the will in yet another one of Dublin's "little brown house[s]" (D 36). When we first encounter Eveline she is staring out of a window, ruminating on the past as the shades of evening invade the street. She is a woman whose imperfect present conditions, burdened by the past, demarcate her as little more than a superannuated commodity. Ultimately dispensable at the store where she works, where "her place would be filled up by an advertisement" (D 37), and abused in her mother's place by a rakish father, the street scene before her triggers an involuntary sense of nostalgia for a younger world of friends and play where "differences of culture and constitution were waived" (D 20).

Like Mr. Kernan ("Grace"), Eveline is a victim of the destructive capacities of new money in the modern commercial city. "Modern business methods," we are told, had spared Kernan "only so far as to allow him a little office in Crowe Street" (D 154). Behind the commercial times, Kernan represents superannuated modes of business practices. Eveline, meanwhile, reflects in solitude on her suburban environment: "one time there used to be a field there in which they used to play every evening with other people's children. Then a man from Belfast bought the field and built houses in it—not like their little brown house but bright brick houses with shining roofs" (D 36). Her past has been overlaid by the urbanization of capital. If the pathos of "An Encounter" works through its defeat of potential escapees, then the tragedy of "Eveline" lies in the fact that here, for the first time, one of Joyce's characters is stricken by a moral, spiritual, and physical paralysis on the very cusp of embarking for a new life far from Dublin. "Eveline's" "everything changes" (D 37) is tragically ironic, for if there is one thing that this story teaches us about Dublin life it is that nothing changes: the past is always hauntingly present.

Frank, Eveline's own exotic "other," opens up the possibilities of a new life with his "tales of distant countries" (D 39) and promises of a new life in Buenos Ayres [sic]. Moreover, in stark contrast to her own world full of "familiar objects from which she had never dreamed of being divided" (D 37), Frank represents the closest she will probably ever come to the fulfillment of her dream to escape Dublin: in "a new home [. . .] she would not be treated as her mother had been." But like "An Encounter's" "confused notion" (D 23) or "Araby'" "confused adoration" (D 31), Eveline's "pleasantly confused" (D 39) feelings reflect a naïve concept of love; in addition, the text perhaps hints at the consequences for a relationship in which a "lass [. . .] loves a sailor." As things turn out, the home to which Eveline has devoted herself to for so long is merely the residual trace of a larger and more menacing threat that rises to close her fate at Dublin's North Wall. Not surprisingly, as she prepares to finally escape with Frank, she is paralyzed by the bittersweet emotions of memory and desire. The echolalia of the words, "her time was running out" (D 39) remind us once more of "The Sisters" and its foreboding opening sentence ("There was no hope for him this time" [9]). A terrifying *deus ex machina*, in the form of her mother's dying words, now denies her the freedom she desperately desires: "as she mused the pitiful vision of her own mother's life laid its spell on the very quick of her being—that life of commonplace sacrifices closing in final craziness" (D 40).

Given the rhythm of despair that governs *Dubliners*, it is no surprise that Eveline, on the verge of leaving home and family for an unknown life-to-be with Frank, gives in to the security of a familiar life. A familiar environment that killed a mother becomes, ironically, a space that imprisons a daughter: "now that she was about to leave it she did not find it a wholly undesirable life" (D 38). Eveline remembers the promise to a dying mother whose life had been one of "commonplace sacrifices closing in final craziness" (D 40), and once again plays out her mother's tragedy with the refusal to join Frank at the boat. Unable to escape the weight of the past, Eveline passes through various stages of distress to a literal state of paralysis before the signifying presence of an unknown other—an abyss—symbolized by "the black mass of the boat." As the "seas of the world tumble about her heart" (D 41), the very idea of freedom becomes a death knell, with Frank yet another man waiting to oppress her: "she set her white face to him, passive, like a helpless animal. Her eyes gave him no sign of love or farewell or recognition" (D 41). Eveline erases all thoughts of a future for herself beyond the debilitating conditions of a home and city that became her mother's grave (D 38), and thus condemns herself to her mother's fate: a death-in-life existence.

THE CITIES OF *DUBLINERS*

Europe of the nineteenth century symbolized an age of capital and an age of imperial cities as metropoli underwent rapid urbanization under the aegis of unprecedented industrial expansion. In architectural terms, London became the embodiment of global economic and political empire; Paris, meanwhile, the "capital of the nineteenth century," was lauded as a monument to cultural sophistication. Dublin, in contrast to the social, economic and political developments transforming the cities of metropolitan Europe, progressively declined in the wake of its widely acknowledged and envied former Georgian splendor. Revisionist arguments have largely relegated a direct correlation between the 1800 Act of Union with Great Britain and the adverse economic consequences for nation that followed to the realms of nationalist myth.[29] Nevertheless, taken together the whimper of Irish political devolution to Westminster and the consequent flight of a newly created absentee nomadic elite to the British mainland remain significant factors in the cultural and municipal decay of Dublin. If, as political economists inform us, money follows power, then the city's progressive political and civic demise was inversely proportional to the political and cultural changes transforming her European metropolitan counterparts.

In economic terms, the 1800 settlement did adversely affect Dublin industry by further degrading the already diminishing returns of an eroding industrial and economic base. As a consequence, the city looked toward the relief provided by its casual labor pool, especially service industry occupations. For Dublin's working-class in particular, this economic shift constituted a significant factor in an already negative colonial equation. The move to a dispensable workforce not only exacerbated the impoverished social conditions of a proletariat trapped in decaying, pre-industrial slums by century's end, but also fatally compromised the city's economic viability as a whole. Yet as social historian Joseph V. O' Brien points out, Victorian Dublin was unique precisely because of its degraded urban, political, cultural, social, and economic valency.[30] For example, add to deficient material progress a lack of population expansion, endemic unemployment, and depressed housing the status of Dublin as a colonial satellite of imperial Britain entrenched in racial, political, and religious schisms, and the Irish capital is both singular and of vital historical importance in the pantheon of contemporary European cities.[31]

In response to Joyce's authorial pronouncements regarding *Dubliners*, critics have declared that the collection represents a state of material and spiritual paralysis. After all, in the writing of *Dubliners* Joyce variously claimed that he was betraying Dublin, revolting against the city's social mores, exposing its class system, and excoriating its religious order. From a critical perspective, therefore, the prevailing attitude is that *Dubliners* "is *no more* than its mechanical parts, each embodied in the life of a separate character, and the resulting environment controls these lives which work within material limits (emphasis added)."[32] Nevertheless, despite Joyce's well-documented turbulent relationship with Dublin, the city remained an abiding obsession. In fact, Joyce viewed Dublin as equal to the influences of London, Paris, Berlin, or Rome.[33] Moreover, against the opinions of English and Irish publishers alike, Joyce saw himself as the city's most recent discoverer, its latest advocate, and its most ardent defender.

In October 1905 Joyce contacted London publisher Grant Richards concerning the possible publication of *Dubliners*, and announced the warrant for the collection as follows:

> I do not think that any writer has yet presented Dublin to the world. It has been a capital of Europe for thousands of years, it is supposed to be the second city of the British Empire and it is nearly three times as big as Venice. Moreover, on account of many circumstances which I cannot detail here, the expression 'Dubliner' seems to me to have some meaning and I doubt whether the same can be said for such words as 'Londoner' and 'Parisian' both of which have been used by writers as titles.[34]

Often quoted in terms of Joyce's stated intentions toward the text, the letter also provides the reader with an opportunity to re-examine, in quite different terms, an alternative and perhaps more apposite sense of Joyce's native city as it presented in *Dubliners*.[35] In other words, Joyce's elevated notion of Dublin as he presents it for the London publisher is radically at odds with the representation of the city we are treated to in the stories. In particular, Joyce's rhetoric claims ownership of a superannuated legacy belonging to the inertia of an enduring eighteenth-century city that was the preserve of a select portion of the city's inhabitants: Ascendancy Dublin. Furthermore, the contradistinction drawn among the grandeur of the Anglo-Irish metropolis and London, Paris, or Venice is anachronistic; if anything, the boast recalls the faded civic splendor of Georgian Dublin as beautified by Thomas Cooley, James Gandon, and the Parke brothers (the Custom House, Four Courts, and King's Inns, respectively), not to mention the Dublin of paved and lighted thoroughfares brought about by the 1774 Commissioners for Opening Wide and Convenient Streets (especially Lower Sackville Street, now O'Connell Street).

While the architectural remnants of an older and certainly grander Dublin were certainly present at the time of writing, the spirit of Joyce's incongruous view of the city as it was experienced by the Catholic majority is clearly the product of a generous reconstructive memory.[36] And while we are cataloging the faded elements of the city beautiful (some of which the Lumière brothers themselves captured on film in 1901 as the first filmic artifact of the metropolis), we would do well to specify Joyce's letter further by adding the beauty of such architectural spaces as Merrion, Mountjoy, and Rutland Squares, aristocratic club houses, the Rotunda gardens, St. Stephen's Green, the Parliaments of Flood and Grattan, and the architectural and political imprimatur of Anglo-Protestant power, Dublin Castle. If anything, the anachronistic sense of Dublin Joyce parades here comes closer the description of the city offered in the 1797 edition of the *Encyclopedia Britannica*, which emphatically declared Dublin, grown fat on the economic prosperity of the mid-eighteenth century, to be the "second city in His Majesty's [George III] dominions."[37]

In more realistic terms, Joyce's letter and its attendant allusions to Dublin's place in European architectural and social history invokes the self-possessing prose we find in the 1844 *Parliamentary Gazeteer of Ireland*. Dividing the city into four quarters separated east from west along Capel Street, and north from south by the "Irish Styx" (the River Liffey), the government report laid claim to that section of Dublin that embodied colonial rule in Ireland:

> The South-east and North-east [. . .] form the real boast of the city, and vie with each other in the numerous features of urban brilliance and attraction; the portions nearest the other quarters and the quays are the abode of the wealthiest classes of trades-people, and the theatre of as proud arrays of shops and fashionable warehouses as any in the world; and the other and far larger portions are the stated residence of about two thousand families in circumstances of opulence, the home of not a few families connected with the learned professions and the fine arts, and the occasional retreat of a number of noble families, and of some 15 or 20 members of the House of Commons.[38]

The city Joyce celebrates in his letter to Richards is clearly not the Dublin we experience in *Dubliners*. If Joyce is being ironic toward the Irish capital (or at least its perception) as a municipal jewel in a colonial ruler's crown, how then should we interpret Joyce's stated intentions toward Dublin and *Dubliners*? Given Joyce's penchant for universalizing the particular, it is the "some meaning" of the letter attached to the word "Dubliner," which, "on account of many circumstances," cannot be detailed that invites further commentary, speculation, even suspicion. In terms of a parallactic vision of the city and its inhabitants, an ironic perspective betrays quite a different conception of Joyce's Dublin and its Dubliners. Let us suppose for one moment that in place of the proud Irish citizen we substitute the Joycean staple of a middle- to lower-class inhabitant, the product of a despised class cut off from Ascendancy society.[39] In contrast to the civic augustness of Joyce's urban vision as it appears in the letter, the cultural and historical legacy of our new subaltern and her world now recalls a radically different urban environment more in keeping with the realism of *Dubliners* and the city as Joyce experienced it.

As John Joyce's personal and professional fortunes declined, his family became themselves itinerant tenement dwellers. Moving from prosperous home in fashionable Blackrock to rented accommodation to the squalid slums of the Monto district, Joyce experienced the demographic and geographic physiognomy of Dublin on a subjective level hitherto the objective preserve of governmental or charitable institutions' reports. This subjective experience of the city may also account for the way in which Joyce chooses to close the letter by stating the marketing strategy by which he felt the book would succeed: "From time to time I see in publishers' lists announcements of books on Irish subjects, so that I think people might be willing to pay for the special odour of corruption which, I hope, floats over my stories."[40]

Moreover, the Dublin of 1905 that Joyce advertises in the letter to Richards is also at odds with the cultural and social blight the city was actually experiencing on a massive scale. In spite of the exponential demographic increase between the census of 1901, which recorded a population for Dublin of 290,000 and that of 1904, when the population was estimated to be somewhere between 350,000 and 400,000, the human geography of Joyce's "second city" of the Empire remained in a peasant class next to the seven millions of imperial London.[41] Early twentieth-century Dublin within the boundaries of the Canals retained its quadripartite division, but three areas continued to suffer from the flight to the southeast quarter: the old impoverished core centered at the Liberties; an equally depressed area extending west of Capel Street to the Royal Barracks; and, the northeast, the worst hit as a consequence of the middle-class removal.[42] It was this third of Dublin northeast of the Liffey between the Canals that Joyce claimed.[43] At its furthest degree, life in the eighteenth-century tenements devoid of water and sanitation no doubt contributed heavily to the worst urban adult mortality rate in the British Isles, which was was the fifth highest in the world, a statistic beaten only by cities like Trieste and Rio de Janeiro. (Dublin's high mortality rate did not decrease until well into the twentieth century.) In addition, surveys conducted before 1914 documented 25 percent of Dublin families living in one-room tenements occupied by more than four people, with at least 16, 000 families living below the poverty line.[44]

Nearly three quarters of a century after the 1844 *Parliamentary* report, the formation of Dublin's Town Planning Association, alongside the Civic Exhibition of 1914, prompted a new civic survey in order to raise public consciousness regarding the pressing needs of the city in the form of an international design competition. Published a decade later by the Civics Institute, the survey clearly refutes Joyce's boastful conception of Dublin as an imperial capital. If anything, the survey contextualizes the municipal decay against which the characters of *Dubliners* negotiate the city in its lamentable and sobering picture of a city in crisis:

> Our civic problems, physical and administrative, cry out for immediate solution. In a progressive capital the want of modern educational facilities; the need of proper forms of juvenile recreation; indifference to historical associations, so valued elsewhere; the stagnation of industry and commerce; the inconvenience and costliness of transport, and the wretched habitations of the masses of the poor, cannot be allowed to re-

main as they are in Dublin. [. . .] As compared with the historic but modernised capitals of Europe, Dublin is 100 years behind the times in civic progress. It has become obvious that the ordinary measures are totally inadequate to deal with the situation [. . .] Dublin of to-day presents to the visitor a lamentable picture! [. . .] The city's unkempt appearance is not confined to the poorer quarters. Citizens of all classes frequently endeavour to evade the byelaws framed under the Public Health Acts, and the building codes of the local authorities are obsolete. [. . .] Great tracts of Dublin are practically inaccessible hinterlands, hopeless and forbidding! Dublin of to-day needs a great awakening, a freedom from political and religious controversy, a subordination of the individual for the general good as well as a disregard of the sanctity of vested interests.[45]

Joyce may well have confessed to Richards that *Dubliners* was almost synonymous with the filth and corruption of everyday life, but he was was in fact advocating the commercial benefits of publishing a series of stories based on the northeastern quadrant of the city, an area Joyce felt represented not only the nation but also the condition of urban modernity.[46] And applying a rigorously means style—or a low tone for a higher purpose—thus became the means by which Joyce attempted to create a renewed sense of consciousness for Irish culture.[47]

Joyce of course was by no means the first to speak the cultural legacy of the Irish capital in realistic terms.[48] As social historian Maurice Craig points out in his historical study of Dublin between the Stuart Restoration and the middle of the Victorian age, before Joyce's Dublin there had existed other "architectural," "literary," and "political" Dublins: "Ormond's Dublin," "Swift's Dublin," and "Grattan's Dublin."[49] Two centuries previous, Jonathan Swift, a Dublin-loving Jeremiad (and the city's first Juvenal), similarly prefigured Joyce's "odor of ashpits and old weeds and offal" in *Description of a City Shower* (1710): "Sweepings from Butchers' Stalls, Dung, Guts, and Blood, Drown'd Puppies, stinking Sprats, / all drench'd in mud, Dead Cats and Turnip-Tops come tumbling down the Flood."[50]

Nor was Joyce the first to capture the glum environs of the city in prose. In Edith Somerville and Martin Ross's collaborative novel *The Real Charlotte* (1894), which chronicles an Ascendancy culture in decline, a typical Sunday afternoon in a Protestant quarter of the north side of Dublin is proleptic of the pathos of Joyce's representation of North Richmond Street life:

> An August Sunday afternoon in the north side of Dublin. Epitome of all that is hot, arid, and empty. Tall brick houses, browbeating each other in gloomy respectability across the white streets; broad pavements, promenaded mainly by the nomadic cat; stifling squares, where the infant of unfashionable parentage is taken for the daily baking that is substitute for the breezes and the press of perambulators on the Bray Esplanade or the Kingstown Pier. Few towns are duller out of season than Dublin, but the dullness of its north side neither waxes nor wanes. [. . .] So at least it ap-

pears to the observer whose impressions are only eye-deep, and are derived from the emptiness of the streets, the unvarying dirt of the window
panes, and the almost forgotten type of ugliness of the window curtains.[51]

The Real Charlotte's power to arrest the eye and ear and so envelop the
reader in the stifling morbidity of life in this section of the city lies in the
novel's ability to create an Irish landscape as a realistic framework on
which to hang a startlingly socio-political reconstruction of late Victorian
Dublin. Joyce, however, supersedes his literary predecessors by envisioning
the physical scope of the metropolis in both general and particular terms
well beyond a dedicated section of the city. [52] From the topographical details provided in *Dubliners* alone we experience Dublin as an intercon-
nected urban artifact circumscribed by the arterial Royal and Grand
Canals and the North and South Circular Roads. Beyond these boundaries,
the stories encompass the country that runs to Kingstown and Bray to the
south, as well as the northward curve of the bay to Howth, not to mention
the city's fluvial spine, the Liffey river, which meanders between Chapelizod and the "fifteen acres" of Phoenix Park. At the same time, just as
Joyce's organic conception of the stories expands—childhood through maturity—so too does the contiguous geographical horizon of the stories
gravitate away from the core of the city. For example, while "The Sisters"
fixes our attention on a little house in Great Britain Street, in "The Dead"
the focus on metropolitan Dublin gives way to "the mutinous Shannon
waves" (*D* 223) of the central plain, and the final symbolic coda of the
West of Ireland.

Concurrent with this linear movement away from the city is a contrapuntal movement that insistently draws our attention to the ways in which
the material presence of the city symbolically overlays and draws us back
toward the center. In "The Sisters," for example, the young narrator ritual-
istically returns to house of mourning in order to watch for the candles in
the window that will declare the priest's death. In the same way that the
boy wills (and comprehends) a sense of release for himself in these signs,
the city he perceives in the morning sunlight following Flynn's death becomes an ambivalent text in which we read the boy's impending fate in-
scribed in his exterior environment. In "The Dead," meanwhile, the quiet
pressure of the falling snow covering the country at large is counter-balanced by the contrapuntal image of the Wellington monument, which becomes the focal point of Gabriel's consciousness at several points during
the story. It is impossible, in other words, to disconnect Joyce's textual
symbolism from the realistic details of the city proper: the King's Inns in
the north eastern part of the city; the Custom House on the Liffey to the
east; Rutland Square; the Rotunda north of the river; the Castle; Kildare
Street; and Westland Row Station south of the river. It is against these enduring historical signifiers of oppression that the rhetoric of *Dubliners*' realism unfolds.

DUBLIN: A CITY OF LOSS

Enclosed within the third division of *Dubliners* ("maturity") "A Little Cloud," "Counterparts," and "A Painful Case" extend the theme of urban alienation introduced in "An Encounter" and "Eveline."[53] The stories, moreover, recapitulate the familiar Joycean theme of Dublin as a city in decline. In particular, the presence of strangers not only negates the ability of Dubliners to entertain new thoughts and identities beyond their own *milieu*, but also highlights the alienation of Dubliners from their fellow citizens. "A Painful Case" takes the idea of estrangement one stage further with its *a priori* assumption of a fundamental disconnection and rejection of the city *per se* as "mean, modern, and pretentious" (D 107). In "A Little Cloud" and "Counterparts" in particular, central Dublin plays host to encounters in which the presence of exoticized strangers reinscribes the rigid parameters of an oppressive colonial hegemony that dictates Ireland to be a cultural wasteland.

Returning to Dublin from London, Ignatius Gallaher plays the part of "Eveline's" Frank to Little Chandler. With his ribald continental tales, Gallaher, like the cars and characters that race along the Naas Road's "channel of poverty" (D 42) in "After the Race," excites in the law clerk the desire to "play fast and loose for the names of great foreign cities" (D 45). Innocent before the experience of Gallaher's Gibbonesque snapshots of European corruption, Chandler envies the sacred ("—And is it [Paris] really so beautiful as they say?") and profane ("—Tell me he [Chandler] said, is it true that Paris is so [. . .] immoral as they say?"[D 76, 77]) of Gallaher's debauched Parisian adventures over the monotonous life of "jogalong Dublin"(D 79). Gallaher seductively betrays Chandler's failure on two levels: first, in contrast to the so-called "brilliant figure on the London press" (D 71), Chandler has failed to develop the artistic aspirations of his youth by gaining recognition as a poet of the "Celtic School"; and secondly, compared with Gallaher's apparent material success and rakish existence, Chandler feels keenly the shame of a conventionally circumscribed life of domestic emasculation.

At the same time, while Chandler notices the "new gaudy manner"(D 77) of his irreverent acquaintance, the fascination with what Gallaher symbolizes remains. Moreover, the events surrounding the interview with Gallaher also throw into relief the degree to which Chandler's inability to respond imaginatively to Dublin is in fact a function of his own failure as a poet, husband, and citizen. Chandler's soul is not a poet's soul; consequently, the people of decaying, autumnal Dublin are categorized as either "untidy nurses and decrepit old men," or "grimy children" (D 71). Like the books of poetry that line the walls of his home, the enjoyment of which he denies both himself and his wife through a congenital "shyness," Chandler denies the humanity that surrounds him: "Little Chandler gave them [street children] no thought. He picked his way deftly through all that ver-

min-like life under the shadow of the gaunt spectral mansions in which the
old nobility of Dublin had roistered. No memory of the past touched him,
for his mind was full of a present joy" (D 71–72). Chandler's journey home
from the King's Inns through the streets of his native city is, in architectural
terms, "a recapitulation of Ireland's decline."[54]

At the same time, Chandler courts the very dangers of the metropolis he
fears in self-tormenting ways:

> It was his habit to walk swiftly in the street even by day and whenever he
> found himself in the city at night he hurried on his way apprehensively
> and excitedly. Sometimes, however, he courted the causes of his fear. He
> chose the darkest and narrowest streets and, a he walked boldly forward,
> the silence that was spread about his footsteps troubled him, the wander-
> ing, silent figures troubled him; and at times a sound of low furtive laugh-
> ter made him tremble like a leaf. (D 72)

Unlike Stephen Dedalus, who agonizes, swoons, and shouts with joy before the streets of Monto, Chandler's furtive experience of the street is very
much a bourgeois one. Safe and controlled, Chandler polices his own desire to the point where he has lost all connection with the real world
around him. Consequently, in Chandler's "sober inartistic life"(D 73) the
city is nowhere intimate; separated from the external reality of his office,
the streets of Dublin, Corless' bar, and his own home, he dwells in the
inner world of a second-rate imagination. Disconnecting himself from his
city, the "scene and thought of life" (D 71) remains as ugly as it is menacing. Thus Chandler revolts against the inelegance of his city, hating others
with the same bile he reserves for himself. He pities the "poor stunted
houses" that, like a "band of tramps," lie "huddled together along the
river banks, and can give "no thought"(D 73) to the dispossessed children
of the streets.

The degree to which Chandler connects with Dublin's historical past in
the form of "the gaunt spectral mansions in which the old nobility of
Dublin had roistered"(D 71) is symptomatic of a failed historical sense. By
contrast, Gallaher and London fuse together in Chandler's mind as signifier and signified, forming a point of light that trembles "on the horizon of
his [Chandler's] mind" (D 73). Chandler still believes that he can fulfill his
artistic credo, and even possibly escape from Dublin. Echoing the narrator
of "An Encounter," Chandler concludes: "There was no doubt about it: if
you wanted to succeed you had to go away" (D 73). Chandler's "present
joy" in rushing to meet Gallaher betrays a hatred for the city, and highlights the degree to which his own self-hatred and insecurity are intimately
bound up with his recoil from the life of Dublin: "For the first time in his
life he felt superior to the people he passed. For the first time his soul re-
volted against the dull inelegance of Capel Street" (D 73). Indeed, "every
step brought him nearer to London, farther from his own sober inartistic
life." Likewise, Mr. Duffy, in attempting to live apart from the city also

lives apart from himself. He shuns the crowd, preferring to by live in Chapelizod, "as far as possible from the city of which he was a citizen"(*D* 108), a man without companions, friends, church, or creed. In Duffy's case, the failed romance with Mrs. Sinico represents a failure to love, and lessens the possibility of being loved: "He [Duffy] thought [. . .] the soul's incurable loneliness. We cannot give ourselves, it said. We are our own" (*D* 111).[55]

Joyce uses Chandler's reflections to expose the parochial nature of his sentimental artistic aspirations. In trying to "weigh his soul to see if it was a poet's soul," a timid trinity is revealed: "Melancholy was the dominant note of his temperament, he thought, but it was a melancholy tempered by recurrences of *faith and resignation* and *simple joy*" (emphasis added *D* 73). Compared with the glamorous corruption of London and Paris, or Gallaher and his profession, Chandler, even at the height of his delusions regarding his critical worth, consoles himself by constructing a dramatic sense of self: "If he could give expression to it in a book of poems perhaps men would listen. He would never be popular: he saw that. He could not sway the crowd but he might appeal to a little circle of kindred minds" (*D* 74). Given Chandler's disconnection from Dublin, it is no surprise that Corless' bar is an inaccessible site of culture and privilege he mistakenly believes he can experience intimately. Consequently, Chandler pathetically attempts to gain acceptance to the interior space of this sophisticated simulacrum; however, the psychic stimulation of "the light and noise of the bar held him at the doorway for several moments. He looked about him, but his sight was confused by the shining of many red and green wineglasses"(*D* 74). Framed as the encounter with Gallaher is by an overwhelming feeling of entrapment, Chandler returns home only to implicate the domestic space of his home and wife with a debilitating city. As one critic notes, "having defined himself as a prisoner of Dublin, he makes his wife a jailer."[56]

While Gaston Bachelard examines the phenomenology of "felicitous space" in order to determine "the human value of the sorts of space that may be grasped, that may be defended against adverse forces, the space we love,"[57] Yi Fu Tuan similarly details a semantics of space in terms of place as an informing system of emotional and psychological transference as follows:

> In experience the meaning of space often merges with that of place. 'Space' is often more abstract than 'place.' What begins as undifferentiated space becomes place as we get to know it better and endow it with value. Architects talk about the spatial qualities of place; they can equally well speak of the locational (place) qualities of space. The ideas 'space' and 'place' require each other for definition. From the security of and stability of place we are aware of the openness, freedom, and threat of space, and vice versa.[58]

For Tuan the limitlessness of space represents possibility (and desire), while place (achievement or frustration of that desire as signified) is a singular point invested with value by human agency. Farrington's odyssey across Dublin in "Counterparts" parallels that of Little Chandler's sense of alienation as he [Farrington] proceeds from office to public house to home.[59] However, Farrington's estrangement is more desperate and terrifying than that of Little Chandler's, for while the latter is suffocated by his own fear of life, he has not yet become the former, a man who does not possess the ability to move beyond pathological anger and violence. (Farrington, in other words, is perhaps Chandler's future in the same way that Gabriel Conroy represents the young boy of "The Sisters.") In "Counterparts," the pub, complete with its resident cronies, is the only intimate space/place that Farrington possesses (neither office nor home providing emotional security): "The dark damp night was coming and he longed to spend it in the bars, drinking with his friends amid the glare of gas and the clatter of glasses" (*D* 89). But even this space betrays him, as the failed attempt to attract a woman with "a London accent" (*D* 95) in Mulligan's bar (sexual humiliation) and the arm-wrestling fiasco with Weathers (physical humiliation) reveal. Sober, penniless (financial humiliation), and "full of smouldering anger and revengefulness" (*D*96), Farrington returns home a defeated man to bully his wife; however, finding her gone, beats her child in her place. Farrington's house is neither hearth nor home: his wife is away, the kitchen is empty, and the fire is out. All that burns is the rage of his self-loathing.

DUBLIN: THE BEAUTY OF ENTROPY

From Joyce's critical writings we know that the self-exiled Irishman had fully immersed himself in a wide range of intellectual developments beyond Anglo-Ireland prior to shaking the dust of Dublin from his boots in 1904.[60] One such example culled from the heterogeneous mass of continental artistic styles and credos that can be traced throughout Joyce's early writing is literary naturalism (and by extension realism), a predominantly French movement that dominated various strains of European literature from approximately 1870 to 1890. Yet despite the large body of criticism devoted to the European background of Joyce's fiction, the longitudinal view of the connection to naturalism in Joyce's early writing in particular rests along a stunted continuum stretching from the mildly dismissive to that of tacit evocation.[61]

In critical terms, it is generally acknowledged that the founding texts of French literary naturalism that firmly established a naturalist poetics were *Germaine Lacerteux* (1864) by the Goncourt brothers, Zola's *Thérèse Raquin* (1867), and the so-called Bible of Naturalism, Flaubert's *L'Education Sentimentale* (1869).[62] So entrenched and revolutionary, however, was Zola's enduring influence, that Yves Chevrel notes that between 1880 and

1910 the European novel was under the influence of a codified naturalist aesthetic, which derived from a method that, as Zola wrote, "affects form itself."[63] In the 25 March 1879 issue of *Le Voltaire* (later incorporated into *Le Roman Experimental*) Zola remonstrated against critics who had committed the error of identifying naturalist writers with those "who deliberately choose the most disgusting objects, in the lower classes and in bad places."[64] By contrast, Zola contended that naturalism was a question of method, not of rhetoric. And he himself, as the heir and chief polemicist of the tradition, was a critic studying his time by utilizing a form of practical sociology which chose all kinds of subjects, as the generational *Les Rougon-Macquart* had shown. For Zola this new method of investigation in turn gave rise to a new conception of the novel: determinism enabled the novelist to relate and express the unity of life through a logical narrative pattern that attempted to isolate a prime cause.[65] Even as outspoken a critic of the experimental novel as Edmund Gosse admitted: "it is to Zola, and to Zola only, that the concentration of the scattered tendencies of naturalism is due. It is owing to him that the threads of Flaubert and Daudet, Dostoyevsky and Tolstoy, Howells, and Henry James can be drawn into anything like a single system."[66]

According to Lynn Pykett, resistance to naturalism throughout the period inevitably carried itself over in the discussion of the New Fiction and the naturalistic drama of Ibsen in the nineties. In particular, this New Fiction was seen in some quarters as the direct heir of naturalism (via the French decadents), and was frequently discussed in connection with "Ibscenity," thus revealing a very real pan-European anxiety concerning the effects of literary representation.[67] In particular, questions of aesthetic representation—who or what might be represented in fiction, in what manner, by whom, and for whom—were entrenched within debates about political representation, and, in part, the organization of the booktrade, censorship, and questions about cultural and political authority and control.[68] Hugh M. Stutfield's "The Psychology of Feminism" (1897) is representative of the way in which recycled discourses in the nineties opined against the "super-subtlety," "microscopic self-examination," and "morbid pessimism" of the New Fiction, which "expresses itself in the worship of ugliness, the minute and almost exclusive delineation of what is gloomy and squalid in life."[69]

Richard Lehan, for example, has returned to the Joyce-naturalism dialectic in order to define in negative terms modernism's relationship to the city. For Lehan, literary modernism is an essentially privileged moment that eschews the commercial city, by "moving either towards aestheticism [. . .] or towards an upper-class kind of experience that excluded the trials of the middle-class and below."[70] Put another way, modernism constitutes a cultural and intellectual move away from a world of social degeneration toward an exquisitely degraded Prufrockian *milieu*. In stark contrast, Lehan contends that "a harsher look at the modern city" was left to the naturalists, "who not only took the lower class as their subject but also the transition of modern life from an agrarian to an urban base, the movement of the masses from the land to the city, and the workings of the city as a self-enclosed mechanism."[71] Furthermore, Lehan corners the alleged intentional exclusivity of canonical modernism as a literary, cultural, and critical practice, and actively interrogates received ideas regarding modernism's preclusive Euro-centric catalog of names and techniques. As with other critics who have actively challenged culturally monistic conceptions of modernist art, Lehan's point is well taken; the so-called age of modernism does not lie solely along a privileged Euro-American metropolitan axis, and arguments against the preservation of a putatively comprehensive canon rightly challenge the myth of modernism as the product of a "preeminently bourgeois and optically white"[72] First World civilization.

At the same time, what Lehan's argument points toward but never quite reaches is that, far from eschewing the city as a phenomenon to be dissected at all levels of experience, the plurality of literary modernisms—even those of an "optically white" brand (which Lehan does not object to)—as urban forms of artistic expression actively interrogate the city in relation to a heterogeneous set of classes and social groups. In defense of a more pluralistic literary modernism that is to come, therefore, we would do well to remember that while many executors of the tradition remain marginalized, to argue that the modernism embraces "an upper-class kind of experience" in singular terms is problematic, at least insofar as the ways in which modernist writers from various social classes explore the metropolis as a polyvalent phenomenon.

Ironically, the by now widely accepted disintegration of the modern city in literary terms may well provide us with a cultural framework for the reintegration of marginalized writers into a more inclusive canon. As Michael Long points out, "we are used to the idea of modernism as an art of disintegration; and to the idea that its typical location, the scene and the cause of the disintegration it records, is the city."[73] We could even go as far as to say that the fragmented city is the transcendental signifier of modernist art. But while it can be argued that literary modernism remains a predominantly privileged one, the typical inhabitants of the metropolis are more often than not are the liminal, the insignificant. A rather obvious case in point, T. S. Eliot's *The Waste Land* (1922) has become the modernist imprimatur defining the polluted wilderness of the modern city as an analogue for a degraded modern consciousness. Eliot easily falls into Lehan's prescriptive analysis; indeed, given his recoil from the city as a way of saving the self (a gesture subsequently taken up by "the English, largely Leavisite, adoption of Eliot as the great prophet of traditionalist, anti-urban values") it is possible to demarcate the ways in which the privileged eye of modernist art easily lends itself (or is co-opted) as part of larger so-called educational, social, or ideological projects.[74]

Lehan has a somewhat harder task of solidifying his argument when it comes to the cultural, social, and literary plurality of Joyce's fiction, for the latter's moral history does not retreat from the city.[75] While there is certainly cause for recoil from the drink-sodden theocracy of Dublin, from *Dubliners* through the "Telemachia" of *Ulysses* and beyond, the dissonance and decay of the urban scene for Joyce is an urgent warrant demanding a re-envisioning and re-structuring of urban modernity. As with contemporary naturalist and realist writers, Joyce similarly presents a rigorously controlled representation for his audience to gaze upon. And, in eliminating, like naturalist writers, what is outside the frame while at the same time determining the accuracy of the framing mechanism, Joyce's fiction links naturalist fiction with modernist art. One answer to the problem of defining an accurate frame (as in Zola's *Les Rougon-Macquart*) was the model based on the natural and social history of a group of individuals bound together by common origins."[76] In many ways, it can be argued that Joyce's "style of scrupulous meanness" builds on the "odour of corruption" common to literary naturalism; indeed, in the same way that Zola argued for a narrative method with which to scrupulously represent objective reality,[77] Joyce too saw his own style of writing as source of spiritual liberation. Thus *Dubliners* offers both the rigors of particularization common to modernist art as well as the vivisective eye of the detached naturalist observer.

Defining the organizing principles operant in naturalist works of fiction such as Zola's, David Baguely argues:

> In attempting to enumerate its [the naturalist novel] principal features, one would first mention the dominant tendency of the naturalist novel to deal with a scientific or sociological topic, frequently the disorders of some aspect of neurotic or hereditary pathology, along with the exposure of the shame of some aspect of the hidden side of contemporary society. The tracing of the workings of the one along with the unmasking of the other provide the naturalist text with a principle of organization and a utilitarian purpose that differentiate it from other forms of fiction, like the bourgeois novel, structured as it is around the affirmation of a moral law, or the heroic novel, determined by purposive action, or even the realist novel in general, directed towards the revelation of the ways of the world. Running counter to this utilitarian function, there can be discerned in naturalist fiction a constant tendency to take on a poetical, pictorial, decorative aspect, one that hardly seems consonant with the often sordid and banal happenings and decor, but that clearly serves to aestheticize, transfix and transform into static verbal pictures the disintegrating reality that is being depicted.[78]

Baguely's definition of the naturalist text as an uncompromising dialectic comprising utilitarian function coupled with poetic expression is suggestive of Joyce's own method in *Dubliners*. Joyce not only appropriates the naturalist method to expose in realistic terms the urban decay of Dublin as a series of "epicleti," but also modifies the aesthetic functions of literary naturalism so as to poeticize his subject even as he castigates it. The paradox of Joyce's art has even larger implications; for example, in the process of poeticizing Dublin, the text of *Dubliners* constitutes a site of intellectual and cultural resistance. Given Joyce's critical pronouncements regarding the collection, an authorial reading of the text points to a vision of the city as a paralyzed entity; consequently, the stories themselves provide us with a symptomatic reading of the cultural and political histories and tensions of metropolitan Dublin at the turn of the century.[79] *Dubliners* is all the more effective as a naturalistic biography of a city because it was designed to reflect the lives of an otherwise indifferent public. Indeed, it was these same people, Joyce believed, who were willing to pay for the corrupt vision the collection ably supplies. In keeping with naturalist aesthetics, therefore, Joyce's poetically degraded vision of Dublin actively confronts urban crisis, engaging with the themes of moral and social entropy common to naturalist literature.

As Terence Brown points out, "critics have been so intent to demonstrate in David Lodge's terms that '*Dubliners* is not a work of wholly traditional nineteenth-century realism' that they have to some degree obscured how much it provides one of the principal pleasures of realism—a richly detailed, exactly evoked physical milieu."[80] For the most part, anti-realist critics blame a simplistic critical acceptance of the stories as faithful representations of objective reality in keeping with Joyce's stated intentions for the collection. By extension, skeptical readings of *Dubliners* variously conclude that the title is a patent misnomer, that in fact Dublin at the time was not the center of cultural and social paralysis Joyce claimed it to be.[81] But the blindness of such culturally inert readings aside, reading Joyce writing the physical milieu of *Dubliners* enables gives us insight to the symbolic nature of Joyce's moral history. More importantly, the realism of the stories is part of a literary continuum in late nineteenth-century fiction that attempts to isolate and document the sordid and banal particulars of urban experience as a function of metropolitan estrangement and alienation—or, to use Joyce's term, "paralysis."

There are of course those critics who swear to the absolute importance of Dublin for Joyce's life and work.[82] However, within these debates the geopolitical significance of Dublin for Joyce as a fading minority Ascendancy culture coexisting alongside a displaced but burgeoning Catholic Nationalist majority remains critically contentious. The valency of this geopolitical duality is important both in terms of Joyce's representation of Dublin as metaphor for Ireland as well as a synecdoche for the city as a colonial artifact. All in all, so entrenched are polarized positions regarding Joyce's warring hatred and love of Ireland that they have become institutionalized features of the critical landscape.[83]

The nearly decade-long negotiation with recalcitrant publisher Grant Richards over the publication of *Dubliners* recirculates many of the same issues concerning censorship that contemporary naturalist writers also faced in their own assault on the cultural and political authority and control of European publishing houses. For example, just as Zola defended himself against critics by defining the moral and didactic parameters of naturalist fiction, it was during the summer of 1906 that Joyce, faced with Richards' growing consternation over the moral and political shortcomings of certain stories in *Dubliners*, similarly found himself defending his own aesthetic vision.

Joyce had entered into publication negotiations with Richards by advancing the commercial viability of his stories on the back of two conjoined principles: the rejection of contemporary Irish writing as artistically inferior, and the fact that English novelists were terribly uninteresting.[84] And Joyce's principles remained firm to the extent that, as relations with Richards worsened, the adamant Hibernian repeatedly informed the London publisher that he could not alter what he had written in his conception of Dublin.[85] Ironically, Joyce was also a more astute censor by design than either Richards or his printer, and even went so far as to identify potentially scandalous stories they had missed, explaining on what grounds they would in all likelihood be attacked—and by whom—should the collection ever come before the bar of public opinion.[86] Given the climate of the times, however, Richards was necessarily cautious, fearing as he did the inquisitorial gaze of a public supported by coercive judicial powers. Joyce, meanwhile, had already steadied himself against the nets of the English legal system by rejecting class-ridden British public opinion as a travesty of its European counterpart.[87] All the same, the epistolary struggle between Joyce and Richards continued, with the latter becoming increasingly alarmed concerning the legal ramifications of publishing the Irishman's chronicle. If anything, Joyce welcomed the scandal as a unique way of marketing the book above and beyond the formulaic endorsements trundled out by reviewers of the day.[88] At the height of their heated correspondence, an exasperated Joyce appealed to Richards on the grounds that *Dubliners* represented a spiritual people, and that to refuse publication would inevitably retard the course of Irish civilization.[89] The only concession Joyce offered was that critics would identify him as the Zola of Irish literature, hardly a cause for real concern.[90]

Dubliners: Subject Position Paralyzed?

Taking his cue from David Lodge, Herbert Schneidau contends that Joyce's early fiction is predominantly transitional within the context of the general development of modernist writing:

> As we all know in Joyce's later writings Dublin, including the associated themes of betrayal and paralysis, remained the 'subject' while the aims of the portrayal were universalized in almost unprecedented ways. Consequently the notion of 'subject' mutates almost beyond recognition; no one

had ever used a city in such ways before. In the *Dubliners* stories Joyce had been willing to risk severe attenuation of apprehensible plot, story, action. Obviously he anticipated with some relish complaints that these stories were not 'about' anything. He knew what they were about. But even Joyce's friends were nervous. Ezra Pound felt himself obliged to come to the defense of 'Araby' as 'better' than a story: 'it's vivid writing.' In *A Portrait* and *Ulysses*, subjects are specifically much more in evidence, but Joyce is so evasive about climaxes, 'big' scenes, and other standard developments as to make convention-minded readers very uneasy. The hesitant and patronizing reader's report on *A Portrait* by Edward Garnett is probably typical.[91]

Joyce, as we are reliably informed by Frank Budgeon, commented long after the publication of *Dubliners*, *Portrait* and *Ulysses*, that he wrote about the particulars of Dublin in order get to the universal heart of all the cities of the world. For Schneidau, this last comment is particularly troubling in that while carrying "the Western theory of representation as far as it will go," Joyce's words remain "misleading." According to Schneidau, the claim to render Dublin universal "fails to reach into the heart of the modernist strategy of particularization," so that in the case of *Dubliners* the collection remains a stage in progress on the outskirts."[92]

While for some critics Joyce's vision of Dublin in *Dubliners* may well lie beyond modernist strategies of particularization in formal terms, for others Joyce's conceptualization of the modern city conjures up something quite different.[93] On the whole, critics agree that Joyce's metropolis constitutes a break with a received literary tradition as handed down by earlier urban commentators. There are those, however, who claim that Joyce's Dublin is very much the prototype of the modern city as Oswald Spengler envisioned it: the deadening "Megalopolis," at once "particular and universal, place and no place, real and imagined [. . .] a fully conceived cosmos."[94] Unlike Spengler, however, Joyce's vision of the city is ultimately a recuperative one; Dublin may well be a necropolis, but civilization has a future, and the future lies with the city. *Dubliners*, like Joyce's fiction as a whole, argues that the modern city is the center of modern consciousness, and that modern consciousness is an urban consciousness. Arguing that *Dubliners* lends itself suggestively to a naturalist reading of the city may even help explain why critics find it so hard to define the collection. For while Joyce predicates his vision of Dublin on the very particular claim that Irish culture is paralyzed, the paradoxical nature of this urban representation paralyzes the critic as much as it does the inhabitants the text, in fact, seeks to celebrate, liberate, even consecrate.

CHAPTER THREE

Grave Memories
The Epitaphic Consciousness of "The Dead"

The dearest of all things in Ireland is the memory of the past.

~ Stanislaus Joyce, *My Brother's Keeper*

IMAGINING "THE DEAD"

The great cities of civilization, Rainer Maria Rilke once remarked with
Rome in mind, are burdened by "an abundance of [. . .] pasts."[1] More particularly, as the broad domain of human history records, there has always
been an immemorial sense of patrimony given over by civilizations in a variety of architectural, cultural, social, and spiritual forms to the reverence—and placation—of the dead. Speaking in the broadest cultural and
historical terms, urban historian Lewis Mumford contends that, beginning
with the ritualistic practices of the earliest human settlements, the city over
time has come to symbolize the ceremonial meeting place that serves as the
goal for pilgrimage: "a site to which family or clan groups are drawn back,
at seasonable intervals, because it [the city] concentrates [. . .] certain spiritual or supernatural powers, powers of higher potency and greater dura-
tion, of wider cosmic significance, than the ordinary processes of life."[2]
Consonant with the magnetic pull of "the city of the dead [as] the forerun-
ner, almost the core, of every living city"[3] is the assertion that the origins of
language itself can also be traced back to the pre-alphabetic signs of ancient burial sites as well as later alphabetical inscriptions engraved on funeral monuments located at the heart of ancient settlements. Yet while
epitaphs manifest themselves in many forms beyond engravings or hiero-
glyphs on tombs or gravestones, as acts of commemoration their shared
sources of feeling solemnize our human points of origin and tendency *sub
specie aeternitatis*. Inseparable therefore from civilization as we have come
to know it, epitaphs speak to that liminal space separating the living and

the dead: they have the power to reconcile our belated claims on life while reminding us, ultimately, of that final journey we must ourselves one day make beyond the world of the living.

The modern city James Joyce presents in *Dubliners* constitutes a signal shift in urban ideology. The idea of the spiritual city, founded on a consecrated burial place with a centrally located sanctuary, has given way to the vision of a rationally organized metropolis radiating out from the Duke of Wellington Monument, the heart of imperial and commercial Dublin. But Joyce's secular city is more than the sum of its turn-of-the-century mercantile and colonial parts, for in the midst of this modern community of souls a vestige of the sacred cities of the past remains alive in the symbiotic relationship between Dublin's living and dead. While Joyce's representation of Dublin invites a range of fertile associations with Mumford's urban-historical paradigm, in this chapter I restrict my remarks to a consideration of the appropriately titled "The Dead" as a text subsumed in elegy, and in particular William Wordsworth's notion of the epitaphic mode, a language and logic of feeling and expression used by the poet throughout his poetry and prose to mediate competing conceptions of historical consciousness. What is unique about "The Dead" is the way in which, in keeping with the parameters of Wordsworthian epitaph, Joyce braids into language a consolatory sense of historic space or doubling of consciousness that holds in creative tension the complex realities of the organic city of the living with the inorganic and encroaching community of Ireland's dearly departed. By the same token, Joyce's use of epitaph neither compromises his own personal attachment to Dublin, nor displaces the vivisective tenor of *Dubliners* as a naturalist history of a city and culture in crisis. As "The Dead" brilliantly dramatizes, Joyce's epitaphic framework dramatizes the tensions underpinning the narrative by challenging contemporary nationalist pastoral narratives that demarcated the cultural and spiritual locus of the nation to lie beyond, and often in opposition to, metropolitan Dublin. An act of imaginative pilgrimage, finally, "The Dead" thus enabled Joyce to return once more to his native city, condensing and reiterating in manifold terms the paradox of Dublin as a vital phenomenon circumscribed by the past, the dead, and their enduring significance for the living.

ROME: *URBS AETERNA*

Conceived in the "funerary reality"[4] of the disastrous sojourn in Rome from 1906 to 1907, "The Dead," as Richard Ellmann eloquently notes, not only forced Joyce to re-evaluate himself as an artist, but also spurred him to reconsider the artistic and spiritual possibilities of his own past in relation to the haunting palimpsest of Dublin.[5] Unlike the enervating effect of Rome on artists such as Rilke, Byron, and Shelley, or even Freud's triumphant entry into the city in 1901, Joyce reacted virulently to the modern metropolis almost as soon as he arrived there from Trieste. And as his first and last letters to Stanislaus from the city record, this antagonistic relationship to Rome, Romans, and their ruins remained constant.[6] Joyce's quarrelsome conversation with the Eternal City was grounded for the most part in personal spite and professional frustration, and his tenure there was punctuated by quarrels with all things Italian, ending finally in alcohol-induced dissolution. To make matters worse, at night he was haunted by the sepulchral architecture of the city in the form of nightmares comprising violent deaths and assassinations in which he was principally involved.[7] Joyce's waking hours, however, brought little relief; in fact, he lamented to Stanislaus that he was plagued by fellow bank clerks, who either complained about their anuses or genitals, or harried him with their anti-liberal political diatribes.

Yet Joyce's response to Rome stands in stark contrast to the sense of relief a move to Rome initially elicited when, in June 1906, life in Trieste was taking a turn for the worst. In Trieste, Joyce's teaching position at the Scuola Berlitz vanished overnight with the Director Bertelli's decampment with a large portion of the school's funds; the wrangling with Grant Richards over *Dubliners* continued, as the obdurate London publisher, fearing legal action against his firm over the content of certain stories, pressed for extensive revisions; and, work on *Stephen Hero*, long lain aside as *Dubliners*, teaching and family had grown, ground to a halt. From the vantage point of a moribund existence in Trieste, therefore, Rome presaged a new horizon of possibility beyond the merely geographic. The first leg of the journey, which consisted of the passage spent sleeping on the deck of the night boat from Fiume to Ancona *en route* to Rome, was somewhat bearable; Ancona itself, however, prefigured their final destination in Joycean style, with Joyce likening the city to rotten cabbage.[8] Be that as it may, the Joyces—James, Nora, and their son Giorgio—arrived in Rome by train on 31 July 1906. However, unlike Ibsen's comfortable exile in the city forty-two years before, Joyce, after seven turbulent months in the *Urbs Aeterna*, returned to Trieste and Stanislaus in March 1907 in the same state in which he left: penniless and in debt. Caesar's Rome, Joyce later acceded, must have been a fine city, but tea-slop impressions of the kind produced by Henry James about Italy and Italians were as bad as the papal city itself.[9] At one point Joyce vehemently complained that Rome existed by selling the bones of its dead to willing tourists.[10]

Yet while the historicity of Rome weighed on Joyce's mind, as a "priest of eternal imagination" he was nonetheless determined as an artist himself to eternalize his own past by transmuting, as he would in *A Portrait of the Artist as Young Man*, "the daily bread of experience into the radiant body of everlasting everyday life" (*P* 221). In Rome "the obtrusiveness of the dead affected what he thought of Dublin, the equally Catholic city he had abandoned, a city as prehensile of its ruins, visible and invisible. More particularly, Joyce's head was filled with a sense of the too successful encroachment of the dead upon the living city; there was a disrupting parallel in the way that Dublin, buried behind him, was haunting his thoughts."[11] But it was also in Rome that Joyce was transfigured. In paradoxical terms, the anxiety of the city's influence stirred Joyce to commit himself further to the past, the role of memory, and the act of remembrance in all their complex and ambiguous forms, a transformation that liberated his latent artistic and spiritual sense of self from the weight of his own past and present.[12]

CRITICIZING "THE DEAD"

"The Dead" has been read and reviewed both as the last story of a unified collection of stories well as a separate story in its own right.[13] Not surprisingly, much of the criticism has focused on the story's preternatural ending. Beginning with such critics as Allen Tate and Kenneth Burke, responses to "The Dead" have typically migrated among the poles of formalism (the literary work as an autonomous object) and criticism that attempts to place the work in the context of cultural, historical, biographical, and socioeconomic contexts. More recently, as deconstructive formalism has receded, critical emphasis has returned once more in force to historical and literary contexts.[14] Feminist studies have also focused on "The Dead" in order to assess Joyce's view of women and heterosexual relationships (and heterosexuality),[15] while theoretical analyses influenced by deconstructionist and psychoanalytical models using Joyce's texts have also impacted critical studies in new and exciting ways.[16]

While early *Dubliners* critic Gerald Gould hailed "The Dead" as the product of a "man of genius,"[17] the collection itself received scant attention in the reviews of the time. In a 1922 essay, for example, John Macy, while praising the realism and subtle irony of *Dubliners*, predicted that "'The Dead' is a masterpiece which will never be popular."[18] In spite of the fact that early critics such as Macy acknowledged something "different" or "expansive" about the final story, it was not until the advent of New Criticism (during the 1950s and 1960s) and the investigation of the symbolic aspects of Joyce's fiction that critics began to overturn Macy's rather peremptory dismissal, and *en masse*.[19] Subsequent approaches to "The Dead," however, have remained polarized across a wide range of issues. There remains, however, one constant: responses to "The Dead" are now as general across the central plain of literary criticism as the snow that falls on Joyce's living and dead.

On the one hand, it has been suggested that "The Dead" is a discrete achievement in the short story tradition; at the same time, critics have argued that the symbolic trinity comprising Gabriel's epiphany, the spirit of Michael Furey, and the snow-covered Oughterard cemetery, with snow falling on all the living and the dead, collectively mark the story as the culmination of the collection.[20] Even those who view "The Dead" as a summative coda are split over the symbolic importance of the story's final scene. Generally speaking, questions begged of "The Dead" gravitate around Gabriel's epiphany as a moment of self-awareness and recognition of humanity (where the significance of the snow is especially important).[21] Critical approaches to the validity of Gabriel's transformation constitute as curious—and certainly as voluminous—a history as the publication history of *Dubliners* itself.[22] Indeed, so entrenched are debates concerning the story's enigmatic conclusion that Donald Torchiana asks, "When will the arguments end on how we are meant to take Gabriel at the end of 'The Dead'?"[23]

Despite the diverse range of criticism, the weight of Richard Ellmann's biographical approach, like the ghost of Michael Furey itself, continues to exert an expansive hermeneutic influence.[24] On the question of Gabriel's epiphany, Ellmann concludes that the final scene, like the story as a whole, is marked by a sense of "mutuality"; moreover, there is an endemic "melancholy unity between the living and the dead" that allows Gabriel to experience "a kind of bondage, of acceptance, even of admiration to a part of the country and a way of life that are most Irish."[25] Alan Tate similarly praises the story as an example of Joyce's success in attributing symbolic value to naturalist, objective detail, and identifies the snow as representative of "Gabriel's escape from his own ego into the larger world of humanity, including 'all the living and the dead.'"[26] Kenneth Burke's Aristotelian analysis divides the story into a series of tributary stages that end, ultimately, at a "stage of 'generosity.'"[27] The snow, symbolic of "the mythic image [. . .] standing for the transcendence above the conditioned," releases Gabriel's identity from the paralysis of social convention, elevating it to an "ideal sociality beyond material divisiveness."[28] Even Florence L. Walzl, herself a generous commentator on numerous aspects of *Dubliners* and "The Dead" in particular, continues to exert her own insistent pressure. Walzl argues for the significance of Gabriel's epiphany in terms of "illumination" or "enlightenment" in keeping with an empathic realization that he is ineluctably connected to humanity.[29]

For Walzl the snow motif is of crucial semantic and symbolic importance in terms of the reader's own response to the story. As the attention paid to this element reveals, the snow is the hemeneutic crux of the narrative, with some critics advocating its symbolic importance in terms of annihilation and death, while others counter that it represents transcendence and spiritual life. Walzl, however, in keeping with her own spiritually redemptive reading, views the snow and the story's final images as inherently related and life-affirming: "the recollections of Christ's passion in the spears and thorns are reminders that sacrifice of self is the condition of revival." While acknowledging the ambiguity in Gabriel's so-called "escape," redemptive critics generally conclude that in Gabriel there is a transcendent sense of "annunciation and new life"[30] consonant with an increased awareness of humanity. This transformation ultimately marks the story as an affirmative reading of the fundamental connection between the living and the dead.

Although many critics contend that "The Dead" is a poetic condensation of preceding themes as well as a story in its own right, a general air of skepticism abounds concerning the notion of transcendence that has been attached to the story's final scene.[31] Vincent Pecora's sustained and articulate oppositional reading, for example, rejects any notion of transformation.[32] For Pecora, "Gabriel in no way overcomes or transcends the conditions of his existence; rather, he merely capitulates them unconsciously in this self-pitying fantasy."[33] In contrast to most stances on "The Dead," Pecora hacks away at the cornerstone foundation of the Christian paradigm of self-annihilation—the premise of redemptive readings—by arguing that the reader, caught in the same ideological labyrinth as Gabriel, desires to escape just as much from his or her own sense of paralysis. As a result of this interpretation, many readers symptomatically misread the conclusion of the story in order to stave off a reality that is otherwise too much to abide.[34] In other words, in reading "The Dead" we find ourselves locked within a Burkean Manichean dialectic comprising transcendent self-knowledge as truth (achieved through loss and sacrifice) versus material existence (the paralysis of social convention), in which the reader, like Gabriel, becomes the victim of misguided feelings of adoration and sympathy. Pecora admonishes us further that it is the "desire for escape at all costs that is the most difficult response to come to grips with, for it inevitably clouds our understanding of the characters' actions and once again stimulates a confused adoration, this time on our parts."[35] In the act of reading, the tears we might shed over Gabriel's reconciliation with both the present and the past are a testament to our own flawed or deluded connection to the world.

Surveying the field of "Dead" criticism, Pecora correctly points out that critical responses to Gabriel's epiphany have indeed become an institutionalized phenomenon. Yet Pecora dismisses the bipolar nature of these perennial debates: in the first instance, those critics who reason that Gabriel's newfound understanding of himself and others is a transcendent move beyond the paralysis of his surroundings, as well as those who contend that Gabriel's symbolic westward journey is merely an act of resignation, indicating the mutability of life and the inevitability of death. According to Pecora, such conclusions—and the discussions that lead to them—are "irrelevant" because regardless of the critical roads taken, critics remain torn between an either/or reading comprising the promises of resurrection versus the possibility of a more painfully authentic relationship with the world.[36]

In its largest sense Pecora's reading of "The Dead" is not only an acid test designed to expose the ontological underpinnings of the Western philosophical tradition, but also a disconcerting re-evaluation of one of the most celebrated works of fiction in the English language. All the same, we would do well perhaps to keep in mind Joyce's explanation of *Dubliners* to Georg Goyert that the stories did not describe the way "they're" like in Dublin, but the way "we're" like.[37] In Pecora's estimation, the dangers of reading "The Dead" as a transcendent act of reconciliation are many; in particular, "threatening" and "unsettling," the story "finds its meaning in confusion and duplicity, for like much of Joyce's fiction it is "full of mirrors— cracked, duplicitous."[38] According to Joyce, in reading *Dubliners* we read ourselves; for Pecora, in ascribing an affirmative meaning to "The Dead," we purposely misread and so lose ourselves. What seems to be at issue in both cases (Joyce on *Dubliners*, Pecora on "The Dead") is the ambiguous nature of representation and, in turn, comprehension. In particular, what is called into question are the ways in which both the reader and Gabriel attempt to attain an understanding of their own selves freed from the shackles of egotism and the material conditions of social mores.[39]

By extension, Pecora argues that Gabriel's "assumed generosity of spirit" serves merely as an "ideological repository"[40] for what we most for ourselves (let alone Gabriel) desire: "our own need for transcendence [. . .] mirrored in Gabriel's conceptual recirculation."[41] Here as elsewhere, Pecora is at pains to suggest that entering into "The Dead" is tantamount to a psychic and emotional eternal return predicated on the tragedy of bourgeois history and culture. In the mess of critical inroads through "The Dead," reading Pecora reading "The Dead" is both exciting and unnerving; we are presented with a menacingly articulate analysis that races beyond the borders of Joyce's fiction and into the very act of reading and interpretation. Yet in reading the paralysis that we are so often told is synonymous with *Dubliners*, do we in fact misread our own fates as Joyce inscribes them within his purposely squalid representation of Dublin life?

If we compare Pecora's general position with Joyce's opening caveat in "The Sisters"—"It filled me with fear and yet I longed to be nearer to it and to look upon its deadly work" (*D* 9)—then there may well be an annihilating, palindromic finality to *Dubliners* (even more so should we elect to read the final story as an intentional coda for the collection). The hypnotic power of Joyce's opening valediction is certainly a menacing key signature for the stories that follow. Also, in the same way that Gabriel's final reflections continue to generate debate, Joyce, in writing *Dubliners*, may well be arguing that transcendence, even in the act of writing, is just as ambiguous a state as life itself—one that demands re-reading. Joyce could not, after all, bring himself to write his stories as Richards urged him, that is with the expectations of the public in mind.[42] Moreover, if, as Pecora contends, "The Dead" is *Dubliners* "most disturbing example of the way these conditions provide at the same time the inescapable materiality of one's imprisonment and the means with which one produces (or in Ellmann's evolutionary fashion, 'a kind of bondage, of acceptance, even of admiration'")[43], then what is to be made of *Dubliners*? If we take the part for the whole, as Joyce often exhorts us to do, should we be profoundly anxious concerning the way Joyce lures us into an ambiguous admiration for Gabriel's so-called transformation?

Of course Pecora's analysis of "The Dead" has yet to be fully scrutinized, but even at this stage he does not have all the shouting to himself. Indeed, John Paul Riquelme has penned a lively response to Pecora, in which the former takes issue with the latter's view that the self in "The Dead" dissolves into exhaustion and nothingness. In particular, Riquelme points out that Pecora attributes thoughts to Gabriel that might be more adequately assigned to the narrator himself.[44] Elsewhere, Christopher Ames, while finding Pecora's reading of "The Dead" particularly compelling (especially Pecora's analysis of the use of the word "generosity" throughout the story), voices a reservation worth noting. For Ames, Pecora's claim that the reader is caught in the same ideological nets as Gabriel in fact ironically betrays that which Pecora works so hard to deny, that is that "'The Dead' is fundamentally different from the other *Dubliners* stories."[45] In the end, we are inevitably thrown back into the web of ambiguity that marks the story's genius.

"The Dead," like Rilke's sense of Rome, is burdened by its own abundance of pasts and meanings that render any attempt to categorize and reduce its textual palimpsest to a single, unifying plain problematic. In fact "The Dead" challenges readings that render their own meanings—or ours—absolute; consequently, the text continues to entice us to look upon it and to marvel at its deadly work. Despite Pecora's compelling argument otherwise, we can and do identify with Gabriel in complex and compelling ways: as a discrete figure within the confines of the narrative; as an extension of many of the characters from the preceding stories; and, as a representation/projection of Joyce himself. Not surprisingly, the hermeneutic quest for meaning has much to do with how Joyce manifests, and we perceive, Gabriel throughout the narrative. But as I hope to suggest, embracing "The Dead" as an extension of the nineteenth century's obsession with death and the burden of Wordsworth provides for a more complex—and perhaps even liberatory—reading. In particular, Joyce's incarnation of Wordsworth's epitaphic mode transplants the provincial contours and scenes of nineteenth-century debates concerning death to the modernist city. And it is within the confines of the city that the mode presents us with a radical reconsideration of the axiomatic relationship among the shifting signs of memory and mortality, life and death, as they relate both to "The Dead" and to Joyce himself.

"THE DEAD" AND THE INCARNATION OF LANGUAGE

An epitaph is not a proud writing shut up for the studious: it is exposed to all—to the wise and the most ignorant; it is condescending, perspicuous, and lovingly solicits regard; its story and admonitions are brief, that the thoughtless, the busy, and indolent, may not be deterred, nor the impatient tired: the stooping old man cons the engraven record like a second horn-book;—the child is proud that he can read it;—and the stranger is introduced through its mediation to the company of a friend: it is concerning all, and for all:—in the churchyard it is open to the day; and the sun looks down upon the stone, and the rains of heaven beat against it.

~ William Wordsworth, *Essay Upon Epitaphs* (1810)

In typological terms, Richard Lehan notes that from F. Scott Fitzgerald to T. S. Eliot, the "funereal moment" in modernist literature is a common staple denoting that "one's fate in the city often starts or ends with the grave."[46] But literary modernism's fascination with death masks a hidden history, the roots of which can be traced back to the shared discourses of nineteenth-century theologians and creative writers concerning the four last things: death, judgment, heaven, and hell. Michael Wheeler, for example, has shown in his investigation of religious experience, belief and language in Victorian Britain, that despite the wide range of contemporary responses to the subject of death there was in fact a "shared vocabulary" common to imaginative literature and theological discussions that constituted "a Victorian cult of death."[47] Central to these discussions on death on the part of theologians and preachers, poets, novelists, and painters was the difficulty in coming to terms with what Wordsworth in *The Excursion* (1814) termed "death and its two-fold aspect":

Death and its two-fold aspect! wintry—one,
Cold, sullen, blank, from hope and joy shut out;
The other, which the ray divine hath touched,
Replete with vivid promise, bright as spring.[48]

According to Wheeler, "these conflicting ideas and emotions associated with death in its two-fold aspect or paradoxical nature—as the first of the four last things, as terminus and point of departure, or as loss and gain—often focused upon two *loci* in the nineteenth century: the deathbed and the grave."[49] From a literary and critical perspective the epitaphic mode is centrally associated with Wordsworth's three essays collectively entitled "Essays Upon Epitaphs."[50] Surveying a range of epitaphs composed by "modern Writers," the essays attempt "to determine what a sepulchral inscription ought to be" with regard to "taste and judgement."[51] Basing his argument upon the authorities of nature and ancient burial practices, Wordsworth characteristically isolates the soothing efficacy of a traditional "parish-church, in the stillness of the country," as a "visible centre of a community of the living and the dead,"[52] in contrast to the "busy, noisy, unclean, and almost grassless churchyard of a large town."[53] But as critics Frances Ferguson and Alan Liu have discovered to varying degrees and in radical contexts, the collective value of "Upon Epitaphs" can be viewed as something more than contributions to a larger cultural, aesthetic, and even religious debate. In fact, Wordsworth's exegesis of the epitaphic mode provides for provocative statements on poetic language while also highlighting the mode's more penetrating and self-reflexive application.[54]

Although Wordsworth ostensibly uses the epitaphic mode for occasional verse commemorating those individuals who have passed away—what Liu refers to as "Wordsworth's version of the return of the dead [. . .] from a transformed world"[55]—in generic terms the mode actually constitutes "a ubiquitous, multi-form presence"[56] throughout the poet's poetry and prose that enables Wordsworth to renegotiate the bonds between the past and present in all their infinite guises. In Book II of *The Prelude*, for example, the mode typically manifests itself whenever Wordsworth speaks of his present state of consciousness in relation to a former "self" thus:

> so wide appears
> The vacancy between me and those days
> Which yet have such self-presence in my mind
> That, musing on them, often do I seem
> Two consciousness, conscious of myself
> And of some other Being. (27–33)[57]

Wordsworth's use of epitaph allows the consciousness of the poet to turn back upon itself "across vacancies almost as wide as those between the living and the dead"[58] in order to locate and/or recall dramatically the traces of former selves adrift in the continuum of space and time. The result in poetic terms is a spiritual autobiography grounded in "self-epitaphic history."[59] Furthermore, in keeping with the rhetoric of Wordsworth's romantic landscapes as a function of space and place, the mode mediates competing conceptions of historical consciousness between the poet and his relationship with rural northern England, the chosen venue for his use of the mode. In nature, therefore, Wordsworth cons the engraven image of his own soul.

The triduum that constitutes "Upon Epitaphs" resonates with Mumford's own identification of the concentration of "spiritual or supernatural powers" of ancient cities as having higher powers than the "ordinary processes of life" associated with organized, living cultures. Moreover, in same way that Mumford's numinous city privileges a necropolis at its core, so Wordsworth's historical sense similarly underscores the cultural, social, and religious importance of epitaphs for protecting and memorializing the corporeal remains of a culture's dead. In historical terms, Wordsworth notes that,

> Almost all Nations have wished that certain external signs should point out the places where their dead are interred. Among the savage tribes unacquainted with letters this has mostly been done either by rude stones placed near the graves, or by mounds of earth raised over them. This custom proceeded obviously from a twofold desire; first, to guard the remains of the deceased from irreverent approach or from savage violation: and, secondly, to preserve their memory.[60]

The first requisite in an epitaph, Wordsworth advises, is that it "should speak, in a tone which shall sink into the heart, the general language of humanity as connected with the subject of death—the source from which an epitaph proceeds—of death, and of life."[61] Yet as Wordsworth notes emphatically, epitaphs take their being not so much from the conjunction of "the principle of love" or the "faculty of reason"[62] intrinsic to humankind but from the "faith that Man is an immortal being."[63] There is a compelling "intimation or assurance within us," Wordsworth continues, "that some part of our nature is imperishable."[64] By extension, at the heart of Wordsworth's obsession with epitaphs is a fixation on the power of language as "an incarnation of the thought."[65] Inasmuch as the bulk of "Upon Epitaphs" is given over to a revaluation of epitaphic writing as an expression of "the taste, intellectual power, and morals of a country," taken together the essays constitute both a theoretical and instructional discourse on the formal and aesthetic elements necessary for the writing of epitaphs. Variously chastising and praising his literary predecessors, there is much at stake in the commemoration of the dead, for "language, if it do not uphold, and feed, and leave in quiet, like the power of gravitation or the air we breathe, is a counter-spirit, unremittingly and noiselessly at work to derange, to subvert, to lay waste, to vitiate, and to dissolve."[66]

As the 1902 essay "James Clarence Mangan" attests, Joyce too committed himself at an early stage in his own writing to developing a theory of the imaginative and artistic needs of his nation. Calling for a fusion of classical strength and serenity to the intense romantic imagination, "Mangan" defines art as "an act of reverence," one that ultimately appeals to a universal "great memory." [67] At one level Wordsworth's epitaphic consciousness might well supply a skeleton key to the tantalizing logic behind Joyce's reconciliation of the paradox of Dublin as a sacred city comprising the living and the dead; at the same time, Joyce imaginatively builds on the notion of epitaph by expanding on the paradox of Mumford's ancient city as well as Wordsworth's consideration of language and death as functions of human civilization, in which "origin and tendency" are "notions inseparably co-relative."[68] Indeed, while Joyce's use of epitaph and the self-epitaphic mode as a vehicle for the consideration of language, life, death and memory is grounded primarily in the workings of Gabriel's consciousness, the story actually unearths a range of epitaphs held in suspension throughout the narrative.

Nowhere is the framework of Joyce's epitaphic consciousness more ingeniously embedded than in Gabriel's extended dinner speech, where the notions of human origin and tendency are thoughtfully negotiated. The speech, like the feast spread before the Morkans' guests, is truly one of the highlights of the story, with the theme of hospitality—that Irish quality Joyce celebrates unreservedly—the most successful subject Gabriel approaches. In the course of a polished delivery, Gabriel presents several topics: the homegrown tradition of hospitality as a "princely failing" among the "modern nations" (*D* 202–03); the relation of the past and its sense of hospitality to a present "hypereducated" and "thought-tormented age" (*D*

203); and, the "sad memories" of the past (*D* 204). Praising the past at the expense of the present, Gabriel's remarks operate at the level of epitaph insofar as the speech invokes a range of private and public memories for those present at the table. But rather than drawing Gabriel as the narrator of the epitaph into the consciousness of the group, his evocations of the past merely serve to highlight an entrenched sense of social, cultural, and emotional disconnection from the gathering.

Prior to delivering his speech, Gabriel seemingly withdraws from the party on the grounds that he wants to be alone: "Now that supper was coming he began to think about the [Robert Browning] quotation [. . .] and retired into the embrasure of the window." Secluded from the company, his thoughts subsequently turn away from his fellow Dubliners: "How pleasant it would be to walk out alone. [. . .] The snow would be lying on the branches of the trees and forming a bright cap on the top of the Wellington monument. How much more pleasant it would be there than at the supper table!" (*D* 191–192). Moreover, as the time for dinner draws closer, Gabriel further worries about his imminent "failure," given the "grade of culture" of the guests, to comprehend his literary allusion, especially "the lines from Robert Browning." He admonishes himself because in his mind, "He would only make himself ridiculous by quoting poetry to them which they could not understand. They would think that he was just airing his superior education. He would fail with them [. . .]" (*D* 179). And yet despite his feelings of alienation, the toast to the Morkans' hospitality is the most genuinely energetic moment of the evening, providing as it does the only point at which everyone at the party feels "in unison" (*D* 205).

The memories of the living aside, at the core of Gabriel's speech lies the foreboding presence of the dead: "the past, of youth, of changes, of absent faces we miss here tonight" (*D* 204). Gabriel's epitaph, however, unlike the centripetal force of the company's earlier memories concerning the old days of Dublin's "legitimate opera" (*D* 199) and its bygone singers, is one to which the narrative registers no response. Eschewing commemoration as something fit only for morose sentimentalism, Gabriel declares: "I will not linger on the past. I will not let any gloomy moralising intrude upon us here tonight" (*D* 204). Gabriel's rhetorical maneuver fails because his incarnation of the past has no direct effect upon the members of his audience, whose own memories and desires concerning the shades of the past define their present thoughts and experiences. Perhaps one reason for Gabriel's failure here is that he does not possess, in spite of his generous nature, an epitaphic sense capable of bearing the weight of the past. From a Wordsworthian perspective, we might even go as far as to say that Gabriel's epitaph fails because "only epitaphic historical consciousness, in sum, can lay the past to rest with acceptance of loss because it lays to rest the present—with all its hopes and fears—as well."[69]

Running counter to Gabriel's use of epitaph is Aunt Julia's rendition of "Arrayed for the Bridal," a lyrical memorial performed to music. The song recalls Aunt Julia's musical past, and is a virtuoso performance that generates romanticized passions—and dangers—within the borders of the text. Aunt Julia's age, however, belies the possibility of ever acting her part in the romantic Nationalist narrative she continues to sing. But her captive audience is able to believe and join in the sense of excitement that her song creates: "To follow the voice, without looking at the singer's face, was to feel and share the excitement of swift and secure flight." So enticing is her performance that even Gabriel himself "applauded loudly with all the others at the end of the song" (*D* 193). If, as the text implies, Aunt Julia is yet one more of Joyce's symbols for Ireland, then we might also take her song to be an epitaph for Nationalist Ireland: an old woman with "a vague smile of reminiscence playing on her face," who "wouldn't be said or led by anyone" (*D* 194); an old woman unable to recognize the reality of her past. Joyce may well be warning us against romanticizing a history of servitude and betrayal in Aunt Julia's rendition, but the lyricism of her performance—unlike Gabriel's literary eloquence—is the first communication of the evening to invoke a sense of passion and communion between performer and audience alike.

It is left to Miss Ivors, who most fully embodies the ethos of the Nationalist movement, to call into question Gabriel's political and cultural disconnection from Irish life. In the first instance, she unnerves him by revealing her knowledge of his literary contributions to the Unionist *Daily Express*, a conservative publication opposed to the Nationalist cause. She also criticizes Gabriel's attendant refusal to join in the cause of his "own land [. . .] own people, and [. . .] own country" (*D* 189). Gabriel, however, responds with antipathy to such calls to duty: "—O, to tell you the truth, retorted Gabriel suddenly, I'm sick of my own country, sick of it!" (*D* 189). But Miss Ivors returns with an ideological taunt that rankles Gabriel for the rest of the evening: "—West Briton!" (*D* 190). The situation is made all the more frustrating for Gabriel because he "wanted to say that literature was above politics," but could not risk "a grandiose phrase" (*D* 188) with a woman who is his intellectual equal. Gabriel's subsequent rejection of his wife's entreaty to join Miss Ivors and her nationalist friends on a "trip to the West of Ireland" (*D* 191) is still another call Gabriel refuses to consider; and, as the narrative suggests, the manner of Gabriel's refusal seems unnecessarily harsh.

It is not until the closing scene in the Gresham Hotel, when Gabriel learns of the tragedy of Gretta's past in the West of Ireland, that he finally realizes the extent to which her latent desires are determined by a past to which he has no authentic connection. Indeed, Joyce takes full advantage of the moment to underscore one of the core imperatives of the story: destiny is a function of, among other things, geography. In the wider provinces of the story, the desires and passions associated with the West of Ireland constitute a phantasmagoric backdrop intimately bound up with the life histories of Gretta, Michael Furey, and Gabriel. If anything, Gretta's remembrance of Michael Furey's death betrays Gabriel's bourgeois pretensions by re-exposing his cultural antagonisms to the life of Ireland beyond the city. As a result, because he places himself in a position from which he cannot perceive, much less penetrate, any part of Gretta's consciousness of the past that is distinct from his own, he cannot comprehend her present passions, let alone her sense of self-epitaphic history.

Like Gabriel, Joyce also turned to the continent in order to distance himself from the calls of Nationalist Ireland. Joyce also wrote periodically for the *Express*, a choice he felt "did not necessarily make him pro-English."[70] But Joyce's reasons for escaping Ireland were quite different from those of Gabriel. In exiling himself from Ireland, Joyce made it patently clear that he was not rejecting his nation in favor of its colonial overlord. Rather, Joyce attempted to transcend the debilitating English-Irish binary by turning to a broader, more inclusive frame of reference: Europe. As the omniscient narrator Joyce manipulates the valency of this radical disconnection—Gabriel/Ireland versus Joyce/Ireland—in order to betray Gabriel's bourgeois pretensions at the expense of galvanizing his own moral history. One instance of Joyce distancing himself from his epitaphic narrator is Gabriel's focus prior to the dinner on things particularly English: the iconographic symbol of English imperialism in the form of the Duke of Wellington monument (a civic memorial commemorating an Irishman who became an English hero; and, English poet Robert Browning (whom Joyce blamed for Irish poet James Clarence Mangan's neglect).

In *Dubliners* Joyce consciously chose to turn his looking-glass for the Irish people in the direction of the city; consequently, he challenged the "dreamy dreams"[71] of the Literary Revival which, in Joyce's opinion, wallowed in a degraded romantic conception of Ireland's brutal past and present rural-urban realities. As Declan Kiberd has shown, stock cultural stereotypes such as the music hall Paddy, taken from the vaudeville repertoire of nineteenth-century British cultural discourses, were in time internalized, and indeed sentimentalized, by an emergent indigenous Irish social formation: the Irish Catholic middle-class.[72] Moreover, this bloc "installed the landless peasant, the superannuated aristocrat, and the urban poor as the new bearers of an updated mythology."[73] Too late perhaps, the culmination of this cultural turn inwards was, as many Irish writers later discovered, nothing short of "a fake nostalgia for a pastoral Ireland [. . .] the false consciousness of the peasant periphery."[74] Joyce, who was writing even as this aestheticization of country people was being codified on the part of nationalists and their sympathizers, outlined in "Mangan" a conception of history in direct opposition to that promoted by the revivalists thus: "History or the denial of reality, for they are two names for one thing, may be said to be that which deceives the whole world".[75]

In Joyce's mind, a romanticized vision of history obscured the reality of the nation's oppressions; "The Dead," as a consequence, can be read as a form of self-epitaphic history that exposes the dichotomy between the (rural-urban) myth of romantic primitivism embodied in the West of Ireland and the culture of metropolitan Dublin. Furthermore, "The Dead" also highlights the fact that in *Dubliners* Joyce is clearly attempting to negotiate what "Ireland" and/or "Irish" might possibly mean for anyone, let alone himself. But having disconnected himself from his nation in the first fourteen stories so as to betray the realities of Irish life all the more clearly, Joyce nonetheless felt that his picture of Ireland had been "unnecessarily harsh," and that he had not given a faithful account of the "ingenuous insularity" and "hospitality" of the Irish people.

Critics often point to the letter written to Stanislaus from Rome dated 25 September 1906 prior to the composition of "The Dead" to suggest that Joyce intended the final story to cast a more indulgent view of Ireland over the collection. Striking a confessional pose, Joyce states:

> I have often confessed to you surprise that there should be anything exceptional in my writing and it is only at moments when I leave down somebody else's book that it seems to me not so unlikely at all. Sometimes thinking of Ireland it seems to me that I have been unnecessarily harsh. I have reproduced (in *Dubliners* at least) none of the attraction of the city for I have never felt at my ease in any city since I left it except in Paris. I have not reproduced its ingenuous insularity and its hospitality. The latter 'virtue' so far as I can see does not exist elsewhere in Europe. I have not been just to its beauty: for it is more beautiful naturally in my opinion than what I have seen of England, Switzerland, France, Austria or Italy. [76]

The tone of the letter is certainly disarming. Yet as the decade-long publication battle with publishers Grant Richards, Joseph Maunsel Hone, and George Roberts to wrest authorial control over the stories from the censoring hands of publishers and printers alike attests, Joyce was "more than conscious of the ways in which the representation of his intentions could be easily transformed by intentional structures beyond his control."[77] Indeed, Joyce foregrounds an awareness of this point in the very same letter by immediately following his admission of failure with a restatement of his own critical distance thus:

> And yet I know how useless these reflections are. For were I to rewrite the book as G. R. [Grant Richards] suggests 'in another sense' (where the hell does he get the meaningless phrases he uses) I am sure I should find again what you [Stanislaus] call the Holy Ghost sitting on the hump of my pen."[78]

The irony of Joyce's position is that, in trying to portray his native city and its culture with less ironic distance (the admission of having been "unnecessarily harsh" and the subsequent writing of "The Dead") Joyce rejected Richards' injunction to write "in another sense." It is precisely this harshness that Joyce used to create the symbolic Irish landscape of *Dubliners*, a sense of critical irony in the service of artistic honesty that kept the Irish writer intellectually faithful to his stories as moral histories.

As the well-documented nostalgic tone of his correspondence to Stanis-laus from Rome reveals, this remove often came at the cost of isolating himself from the passions of his countrymen. In many ways, reconceptual-izing Irish life and culture in "The Dead" allowed Joyce to recapture that sense of his former self he believed self-exile and progressive artistic dimin-ishment had taken from him. Writing "The Dead," meanwhile, enabled Joyce to attempt a more tempered conception of his native city and its en-during significance for his life and work. In a larger sense, therefore, "The Dead" constitutes a national countercultural discourse that allowed Joyce to reevaluate the origins and tendencies of what he had earlier outlined in "A Portrait of the Artist" (1904) as "the word [. . .] the masses [. . .] and the nation that is to come."[79]

At the end of "The Dead," the two-fold paradox of death that so trou-bled the Victorians in their many deathbed and graveyard scenes is once again recuperated to devastating effect by Joyce's appropriation of Wordsworthian epitaph. Failing to turn Gretta's will to his own present physical needs, Gabriel's attempt to undermine her commemoration of Michael Furey (*D* 219) serves only to reinforce further the pathos of her epitaph. Instead of triumphing over the living and the dead, Joyce makes it abundantly clear that Gabriel is shamed: "Gabriel felt humiliated by the failure of his irony and by the evocation of this figure from the dead, a boy in the gasworks. While he had been full of memories of their secret life to-gether, full of tenderness and joy and desire, she had been comparing him in her mind with another" (*D* 219).

In turn Gretta's memorial for Furey opens up a space of contemplation and reflection for Gabriel, as she lies physically and emotionally exhausted on a bed saturated with memory, desire, and loss. At this critical juncture Gabriel's sense of paralysis in the face of Gretta's confession is com-pounded by Joyce in two ways. First, the narrative confines Gabriel to res-ignation: "It hardly pained him now to think how poor a part he, her husband, had played in her life" (*D* 222). At the same time, Joyce follows on quickly with a vision of Gabriel's latent bitterness masquerading as pity as we are told that "a strange friendly pity entered his soul. He did not like to say even to himself that her face was no longer beautiful but he knew that it was no longer the face for which Michael Furey had braved death" (*D* 222). Yet Joyce's moral distance toward Gabriel is also dissipated some-what by the latter's self-epitaphic confession of his own failings: "He [Gabriel] saw himself as a ludicrous figure, acting as a pennyboy for his aunts, a nervous, well-meaning sentimentalist, orating to vulgarians and idealizing his own clownish lusts, the pitiable fatuous fellow he had caught a glimpse of in the mirror. Instinctively he turned his back to the light lest she [Gretta] might see the shame that burned upon his forehead" (*D* 220).

In his mind Gabriel now foresees Aunt Julia's death with himself, "sit-ting in that same drawing-room, dressed in black, his silk hat on his knees. [. . .] Aunt Kate would be sitting beside him, crying and blowing her nose and telling him how Julia had died. He would cast about in his mind for words that might console her, and would find only lame and useless ones" (*D* 222–223). The pathos of this premonition is rendered all the more complex at this point, in that Joyce presents Gabriel as seriously conflicted. On the one hand, these lines give the impression that Gabriel is concerned more with the burden of once more having to lend significance to the ritual of death through his own formal incarnation of language as opposed to responding emotionally (authentically) to Aunt Julia's passing. At the same time, the passage also intimates that Gabriel is more than ever aware of his over-reliance on language as a way of mastering and/or deceiving reality. Yet this unsettling disjuncture may well, as Pecora contends, have to do with Joyce's use of free indirect discourse, in that "language in Joyce, even in *Dubliners*, is often *dispossessed* discourse—thought, feeling, or inner speech that never completely belongs to the speaker."[80]

"The Dead"'s famous coda ends as follows:

> The time had come for him [Gabriel] to set out on his journey westward. Yes, the newspapers were right: snow was general all over Ireland. It was falling on every part of the dark central plain, on the treeless hills, falling softly upon the Bog of Allen and, farther westward, softly falling into the dark mutinous Shannon waves. It was falling, too, on every part of the lonely churchyard on the hill where Michael Furey lay buried. It lay thickly drifted on the crooked crosses and headstones, on the spears of the little gate, on the barren thorns. His soul swooned slowly as he heard the snow falling faintly through the universe and faintly falling, like the descent of their last end, upon the living and the dead. (*D* 223–224)

Despite Joyce's reservations concerning Gabriel, it might well be argued that in the "lyric peace"[81] of this closing moment the former creates a link between his own aesthetic vision and the masses through the latter, who first recognizes the veiled power of romantic passion, and then transcends the bounds of his self in order to identify with the *archae* of that passion: the specter of Michael Furey and the ghostly Oughterard cemetery. Lying alongside Gretta's prostrate body on the bed, Gabriel's symbolic resting place collapses the boundaries separating deathbed, grave, and beyond as he prepares for his own journey westward toward the hosts of the dead.

Given that the highest form of presence in "The Dead" is absence in the form of the past and the dead, Gabriel's final epiphany naturally has ramifications far beyond his connection to the world of the living. Looking westwards, we are told that Gabriel's "soul had approached that region where dwell the vast hosts of the dead. He was conscious of, but could not apprehend, their wayward and flickering existence. His own identity was fading out into a grey impalpable world: the solid world itself which these dead had one time reared and lived in was dissolving and dwindling" (*D* 223). As this passage reveals, the power of Furey's spectral presence, like a sentinel from beyond the world, engenders a kind of supernatural absorption (colored over as it is with Gabriel's "generous tears" [D 223]), in which Gabriel's sundered soul figuratively dissolves out into the collective presence (and memory) of the grateful departed. In the heart of metropolitan Dublin, Gabriel thus embarks on a metaphysical journey toward that community of souls beyond the living: the dead.

EPITAPH: RECONCILING LIFE AND DEATH IN "THE DEAD"

Gabriel's westward gaze, it has been argued, is merely one final instance of "the social *ricorso* that eventually traps all who remain in Joyce's Dublin"—as if the city itself is the site of some "grand repetition compulsion by which the conflicts that trouble its inhabitants are constantly evoked and rehearsed, but never worked through."[82] I would like to argue the opposite. If anything, "The Dead" presents us with a narrative structure that evokes, rehearses, and works through the historicity of Dublin's past and present in keeping with *Dubliners* as a spiritual autobiography. By the same token, Joyce, as narrator of the epitaph, purposefully evokes, rehearses, and works through his own sense of self-epitaphic history in the writing of "The Dead." In doing so, Joyce turns his consciousness back upon variegated points of origin and forward toward their approximate tendencies through the eyes of Gabriel, an epitaphic narrator the reader by design is required to scrutinize. In Wordsworth's case, the use of epitaph often exists in opposition to the very real deaths of the individuals memorialized, for as Wordsworth notes, the writer of an epitaph "performs his act of remembrance "by the side of the grave."[83] *Dubliners*, in keeping with Wordsworth's dictum, similarly commiserates with very real people by exposing and poeticizing in fictional terms the diachronic realities of Irish life that have engendered a death-like state of cultural paralysis.

There is also a concentric beauty to the logic of Wordsworth's use of the epitaphic mode, particularly the way in which the mode moves beyond specific characters and communities to embrace, meditate upon, and commiserate with the deceased at a universal level. According to Wordsworth, the rationale for moving beyond immediate passions is "so that what was peculiar to the individual shall still be subordinate to a sense of what he had in common with the species, [and] our notion of a perfect epitaph would then be realized."[84] In commiseration, therefore, Wordsworth aims to defuse an affective response; the universal affections of the writer are their own justification, and thus an appeal to the reader's affections is avoided. Yet as incarnations in language, Wordsworth's epitaphs nonetheless radically implicate the consciousness of the reader, for as Liu pointedly remarks, "*self*-epitaph [. . .] allows the reader to pick up the bones of the dead in a different way. The nature of the self-epitaph is to trigger further stages of self-epitaphic consciousness in the reader."[85] Consequently, a complex of interacting relationships or living consciousnesses arises comprising the poet, reader, and the deceased (through the poet) through which "the stranger is introduced [. . .] to the company of a friend."[86] A similar system of informing relationships is also apparent in Joyce's use of epitaph. In reading "The Dead," we invariably reach the terminus of Wordsworth's own sense of the epitaphic mode, for "out of the discontinuities of both language and life" Joyce, like Wordsworth, brokers "a poetry of memory."[87]

As the dramatic framework supporting Gabriel's epiphany unravels, the consciousness of the reader is inevitably drawn into a series of reciprocal relationships mediated by Joyce as the writer of the epitaph as follows: Joyce and Gabriel; Gabriel and Gretta; Gabriel and the guests at the party; Gretta and Michael Furey; Furey, the hosts of the dead, and Gabriel; and, finally, the reader and all of the above permutations. In the course of these interdependent relationships, the use of epiphany is a necessary component in the process of representing "reality" as the thing-in-itself, as revealed "truth." And yet as Joyce's use of epiphany affirms, the incarnation of language-as-epiphany does not necessarily correspond to Gabriel's, Joyce's, or even the reader's own transfiguration. One reason for this state of indeterminacy is that the danger with incarnation is that it is not always absolute. The epitaphic mode enhances this state of ambiguity precisely because it triggers further stages of self-epitaphic consciousness within the reader. In other words, Wordsworth's epitaphs necessarily throw the burden of consciousness back upon the reader in order to remind us that, in the process of linguistic incarnation, "language is not a salvation for the complexities of individual consciousness," and that "the life of language in poetry, like the life of the individual, is radically implicated with death."[88] All the same, "The Dead" is as much the first cry of a newborn spirit as it is the last gasp of a dying soul. What we are left with perhaps is Joyce's guarded confession that the artist and the common people can only meet through their passion on a spiritual rather than a political plane. Yet even in this final point lies the irrevocable pathos at the heart of all forms of epitaph, Joyce's included: "the incarnation into language comes always ex post facto, too little and too late."[89]

CHAPTER FOUR

The Metropolitan Consciousness of *A Portrait of the Artist as a Young Man*

It will interest you that for a long time now I assert in my lectures: each major intellectual epoch has had a central concept whose position has thereby determined that it characterizes the highest reality and, at the same time, the highest value: for the Greeks the concept of Being, for Christendom that of God, in the 17th and 18th centuries that of Nature and now that of 'Life' appears to have entered in this position.

~ Georg Simmel, Letter to Hermann Keyserling, 30 March 1911

Welcome, O life! I go to encounter for the millionth time the reality of experience and to forge in the smithy of my soul the uncreated conscience of my race.

~ James Joyce, *A Portrait of the Artist as a Young Man* (1916)

THE ARTIST *AND* THE CITY

In the slipstream of continental theoretical approaches to literature such as structuralism, deconstruction, and poststructuralism, the general trend in Joyce criticism in the past two decades has been away from the New Critical presumption of organic unity, away from symbolic interpretation, and away from biography. The critical landscape readers now find themselves engaging is one characterized by a "a close analysis of style, a re-examination of the social and political context of Joyce's work, an intense theoretical examination of the implications of Joyce's writing project, and a questioning of previous interpretations of the entire modernist movement."[1] As complex as the Joyce "system" has become, however, readers of *A Portrait of the Artist as a Young Man* still respond imaginatively to the enduring human drama of the novel: the realistic portrayal of the young Stephen Dedalus' struggle for "Life" against the oppressive cultures of home, church, and state, and of his transfiguration by the search for a transcendent idea of beauty.[2]

Debates concerning Stephen's personality continue unabated, especially Joyce's own attitude or distance from his protagonist.[3] On the one hand, there are the majority of critics who, building on the work of Harry Levin, read the novel as a portrayal of artistic genius. They variously sympathize with Stephen's rejection of the imprisoning, ossified forms of Irish society, approve his aesthetic theory as Joyce's own, and endorse Stephen's self-imposed exile as a faithful quest for a mode of existence whereby his artistic spirit might express itself (and thus the conscience of the Irish race) in unfettered freedom.[4] At the same time—and with equal fervor—are those critics, influenced primarily by Hugh Kenner (and in their extreme form termed "Stephen haters"), who take the position that, despite careless readings to the latter, "Stephen does not become an artist at all."[5] Kenner, though having softened his approach somewhat in his later criticism, has been especially aggressive in bemoaning the novel's juvenile neo-platonic aesthetic. He has even gone as far as to dismiss Stephen's attempt to transform himself into a "priest of the eternal imagination" (P 221)[6] as "indigestibly Byronic."[7] Given that the dramatic energy of Portrait emanates almost exclusively from Stephen's imagination, it is no surprise that critics continue to scour the terrain of the novel for clues to the Joyce-Stephen dynamic. Yet however much Dedalus sympathizers, haters, and undecideds privilege their own attitudes in their respective hermeneutic quests, Portrait continues to offer new and exciting surprises concerning the cultural and social forces transforming both the Irish and their metropolis at the turn of the century.

Criticism of course has long been sensitive to the importance of Dublin for Joyce's fiction. More recently, however, it has been suggested that Portrait in particular is not only a representation of the modern city as a singular outgrowth of aesthetic modernism but also a symptom of modernity itself.[8] In this chapter, I build on the fertile possibilities embedded in this hypothesis by proposing that Stephen's own consciousness is itself symptomatic of a particular kind of metropolitan consciousness as identified by German sociologist Georg Simmel in his landmark study titled "The Metropolis and Mental Life" (1903). Although there is no documented link connecting an intellectual exchange and/or appropriation on Joyce's part of the pioneering theoretical work of Simmel (certainly nothing to suggest an authorial intention on Joyce's part to frame his novel in sociological terms), the larger sociological imagination of Joyce's urban fiction nonetheless allows room for the consideration of aesthetic and thematic analogies on the part of these writers with regard to their co-relative readings of the city.

One of the major theorists to emerge in German philosophy and social science at the turn of the century, Simmel investigated some of the most pressing issues and cultural contradictions of the modern world: the function of money; the fear of the outsider that pervades Western culture; and, the fate of individual identity in city life. [9] By linking Joyce's literary representation of Dublin with Simmel's theoretical analysis of Berlin as representative examples of modern urban experience, I investigate ways in which it is possible to comprehend the figure of Stephen as the embodiment of a particular form of artistic urban consciousness. The larger aim of my discussion, therefore, supports a dual focus: the reading Joyce's urban fiction alongside the urban sociology of Simmel illuminates in thematic and non-linear terms how these writers blur the epistemological and disciplinary distinctions separating their aesthetic and critical practices.

As David Frisby notes, it has been the fate of "The Metropolis and Mental Life"[10] to lead a life of its own "far away from [its] original context."[11] For example, the essay has often been anthologized and analyzed as a virtuoso piece, of which perhaps the most famous example occurs in *The City* (1925), where Chicago School theorist and Simmel pupil Louis Park describes the essay as "the most important single article on the city from the sociological standpoint."[12] "Metropolis" first appeared in a volume of the Gehe Foundations proceedings in 1903, and was based on a series of lectures given in the winter of 1902–1903 in connection with an exhibition of the modern metropolis in Dresden.[13] Though never explicitly stated as such, the metropolis that Simmel has in mind is clearly his native capital Berlin: the seat of the Prussian economy, commercial interactions, and social distractions; the premier location of metropolitan culture and state bureaucracy; and, in keeping with Prussian militarism, a site of military presence and prowess. Like the positive public exhibition itself, the tone of Simmel's essay runs counter to the long-established tradition of cultural pessimism associated with urban life (*Gemeinschaft*) in German intellectual thought. Simmel's analysis presents no negative contrast with past forms of urban existence; rather, metropolitan life, with its power to both level and inspire, is our present and our future.[14]

As the title of "Metropolis" suggests, Simmel was acutely aware of the phenomenological relationship between the city and human consciousness.[15] For Simmel, the centripetal and centrifugal stimuli generated by the conditions of city life—"modernity"—resulted in an almost unmanageable assault on the sensory capacities of all individuals regardless of class. Moreover, the nature of this incursion on the psyche was characterized by illogical juxtaposition and unpredictable paradox as scintillating to the human senses as it was debilitating. "Metropolis" opens with a bold yet enigmatic statement: "The deepest problems of modern life derive from the claim of the individual to preserve the autonomy and individuality of his existence in the face of overwhelming social forces, of historical heritage, of external culture, and of the technique of life."[16] It is the task of the sociologist, apparently, to isolate the soul of urban culture by first solving that formula which the city sets up between the individual and external life. The metropolitan formula that Simmel sets out to solve is one variously defined as the center of the money economy; dominated by the multiplicity and concentration of economic exchange; subject to the negation of the individuality of phenomena; and, focused on objective measurable achievement, in keeping with the idea of the city as a capitalist web or network of production and consumer-oriented intersecting spheres.

Yet despite the fact that Simmel here is obviously describing a particular type of social environment, that is a capital city, the ecology of industrial metropolis is not of specific interest to him. Of greater importance is the idea of the city as a web of social groups and individuals, a dynamic intersection of intellectual, social, and cultural circles consonant with the protean nature of the ever-expanding metropolis.[17] In particular, Simmel is most concerned with quantifying the metropolis as the primary location of the development of diversity and contradiction, as the place where a new "quantity of consciousness" and a new "rhythm of sensual-intellectual life" emerges.[18]

In *Portrait*, Stephen's burgeoning subjectivity and artistic development are caught in the inseparable tension between what can only be described as a sacred and profane relationship with the composition and consciousness of Dublin. One consequence of this dialectic is that Stephen's being, like Simmel's metropolitan individual, is burdened by an abundance of urban sensations the young artist must negotiate in order to preserve his own consciousness. In the course of his struggle to master and/or contain exterior reality (the "nets" of nationality, home, and religion), Stephen is thrown back on the necessity to protect the interiority of his artistic self— what Joyce refers to in the essay "A Portrait of the Artist" (1904) as "that ineradicable egoism which he [Stephen] was afterwards to call redeemer,"[19] or what Gary Leonard terms "the protected space of aesthetic contemplation."[20]

THE ART AND THEORY OF MODERN LIFE

Even as Joyce was forging an authentic Irish imagination within the context of European art and self-exile, Simmel too was fighting to define his own brand of sociology within the social sciences. Moreover, as Joyce was defending his moral history of Ireland before the censoring hands of publishers and printers alike, Simmel's own professional travails were taking place within the heated context of debates, in which the disciplinary terrain of the social sciences was being aggressively contested in academic and intellectual circles.[21] In the midst of competing claims in the human sciences, notably among psychology, political science, economics, sociology, and history, Simmel maintained that it was only by abandoning the idea of society as a hypostatized and totalized object that sociology could develop successfully as both an academic and theoretical practice.[22]

A closer examination of Simmel's life and work reveals a shared community of thought linking the elder German Jewish theorist with the artistic development of his younger Irish-Catholic counterpart, especially their coextensive epistemologies of the modern metropolis. Kurt Wolff summarizes Simmel's life and professional achievements succinctly when he writes,

> Georg (Friedrich Eduard) Simmel was born in Berlin on March 1, 1858, of Jewish parents, both of whom had already converted—his father to Catholicism, his mother to Protestantism. He was baptized a Protestant but left the church during World War I, without, however, embracing Judaism. After graduating from the gymnasium he studied at the University of Berlin, beginning with history under Theodor Mommsen, moving to psychology, especially *Volkerpsychologie* (Moritz Lazarus), then to ethnology (Adolf Bastian), and at last to philosophy (Eduard Zeller, Friedrich Harms); he minored in Italian, specializing in Petrarch [. . .] As his dissertation he submitted a paper on 'Psychological-Ethnographic Studies on the Beginnings of Music' [. . .] it was rejected; he obtained his doctorate instead (in 1881) with an essay for which he had received an academic prize two years before, *Description and Assessment of Kant's Various Views on the Nature of Matter*. On the basis of a second essay (again on Kant) and a 'test' lecture, 'On the Theory of Assessment of Ideas' [. . .] he was appointed *Privatdozent* in 1885 at the University of Berlin, a post he held for the unusually long period of 15 years, after which he was promoted to *Ausserordentlicher Professor*. In 1914, almost as long again, he became an *Ordinarius* at the University of Strasbourg, four years before he died (September 26, 1918).[23]

From the early essay "What Is Society?" (1896) through *The Philosophy of Money* (1900) to the summation of his sociological investigations in *Sociology* (1908), Simmel attempted to establish sociology as an independent discipline, devoting much of his investigations to the life-world of individuals as the key to understanding the larger concept of society.[24] By extension, in the same way that Joyce's relationship with his native Dublin remains central to evolving critical interpretations of his fiction, Simmel's own attachment to Berlin, from his central city birthplace at the corner of Leipziger and Friedrichstrasse through the city's most rapid period of expansion, reflects a unique and informing relationship linking the man, his environment, and his work.[25] Recalling his father's own words, Hans Simmel recalled, "Berlin's development from a city to a metropolis in the years around and after the turn of the century coincides with my [Georg] own strongest and broadest development."[26]

Simmel, part analyst of urban phenomena, part structural sociologist, and part investigator of the economic and social fabric of urban society, was also an astute aesthetic and cultural critic of modernity. Like his colleague, Max Weber, whose essay "The City" (1921) also attempts to trace the historical development and importance of the Occidental city, Simmel argued that cities, unlike rural communities, were by nature overwhelming. However, whereas Weber looked to the medieval cities of early modern Europe for his "ideal-typical" form, Simmel isolated the modern city as paradigmatic of the dangers and possibilities of civilization, and in doing so argued that the elements of this description should be psychological and not structural.[27] Contending that the prehistory of modernity lay in the development of the mature money economy, Simmel predicated his sociological investigations on the metaphysical principle of the fundamental interrelatedness of all phenomena. The city, like society, comprised a labyrinth of interconnecting human relationships, many of which remained occluded; it was the task of sociology, Simmel argued, to reveal these hidden connections. Siegfried Kracauer interprets the complex principle underpinning Simmel's thought as follows:

> All expressions of cultural life [. . .] stand in an inexpressible plurality of relationships to one another, none is capable of being extracted from the contexts in which they find themselves associated with others. This standpoint is one of Simmel's fundamental experiences upon which his understanding of the world rests.[28]

At the end of *The Philosophy of Money*, Simmel asserts another cornerstone principle of his work: not only are all phenomena interrelated, but they are also in perpetual flux: "In reality itself things do not last for any length of time: through the restlessness with which they offer themselves at any moment to the application of a law, every form becomes immediately dissolved in the very moment when it emerges; it lives, as it were, only by being destroyed."[29] Beginning, therefore, with what he believed were the fragments of social reality and the delicate (even invisible) threads of social relationships, Simmel attempted to distill from each of life's details the totality of a larger (and discontinuous) social meaning. As with Joyce's own project to map the moral history of Ireland based on an intimate reading of Dublin, Simmel also attempted to connect the particular strands of everyday life in order to gain access to a universal understanding. But in Simmel's case he ultimately aimed to typify the results of his investigations in keeping with his sociological tendencies.[30]

According to Simmel, while the location of modern experience is the metropolis and the mature money economy, it is ultimately the development of the latter that accounts for the origins of modernity. Like Marx, Simmel viewed the development of the capitalist money economy as the *archae* of modernity (with money, at the aesthetic level, the symbol). In time, Simmel's investigations of the consequences of the money economy contributed to a larger theory of cultural alienation as the basis for the tragedy of modern society: the inevitable conflict between subjective experience and objective culture.[31] Within this paradigm, society's worst version of itself is often played out in the city. It was here that the impersonality of life, the faceless nature of bureaucracy, and rational market processes converged on people so that all they could do to defend themselves was to behave in nonemotional, reasoned, and functional ways.[32]

Simmel was so taken with this condition of urban existence that a major portion of "Metropolis" is given over to the contention that, in order to survive the city its inhabitants by necessity reduce all life to an objective and devalued level. This "technique of life" as Simmel stylistically terms the negotiation of modernity, is inevitable. Characterized by its almost Pavlovian features, the technique is carefully described as a necessary form of protection against the inescapable excesses of psychic stimulation that hallmark the modern city. At the same time, Simmel's theory of culture also concedes that it is possible for the individual to escape the debilitating consequences of the modern labyrinth. Indeed, Simmel's description of the psychological mechanism he identifies closely with metropolitan existence is grounded in the concept of a selfhood capable of protecting itself against external reality. But this self, this emotional being, is not an insulated, otherworldly sphere that can survive untouched by the defense mechanisms it establishes in response to the city. Rather, the process of constructing such a defense system against the city inevitably influences the identity of the individual.

The subtlety of Simmel's paradoxical concept of urban consciousness thus does not reduce the connection between the life of the city and the life of the individual to a single form. In other words, there is no necessity for alienated spirits to arise in people whose day-to-day lives are functional and impersonal; moreover, the inner lives of individuals need not suffer because they have little outlet in ordinary affairs. According to Richard Sennett, for Simmel the banal nature of the bulk of human relations within the metropolis is precisely what drives people to search for a more authentic—even transcendent—emotional and intellectual connection with themselves and their environments. And Sennett goes on to note, "there is something ironic in a persecuted Jewish intellectual giving this most Christian of ideas its first modern form in terms of city life."[33]

The full range of human experience, from the minutiae of everyday life to vast economic systems and mass society, is central to Simmel's theoretical speculations.[34] But it is the investigations into the two sites of modernity—the mature money economy and the metropolis—in relation to the individual that most fully provide for a sociological and psychological study of the consequences of urban life.[35] So drawn was Simmel to the importance of the individual that he declared: "The pessimism with which the majority of more profound thinkers seem to view the contemporary state of culture has its foundation in the ever-wider yawning abyss between the culture of things and that of human beings."[36] Simmel's metropolis is not Spengler's industrial city "beyond good and evil," but rather a city like Joyce's Dublin, a city of the petty bourgeoisie, a thoroughly modern city of commercial consumption. By extension, Simmel's prototypical city dweller is not Marx's alienated worker, but Baudelaire's flâneur, a walker in the city in search of the fortuitous moments that constitute the eternal flux of modern experience.

One commentator has noted that, "if the two great subjects of modern literature are the artist and the city, then the one great subject has to be the controlling sensibility of the artist in the city."[37] In *Stephen Hero*, we are told that Stephen comes to realize that certain fixed moments illuminate the meaning of a city—that Dublin, or London, or Paris is an essence that reveals itself in its accidents, that is its mechanical expressions. Thus for Stephen "an inchoate, trivial conversation overheard revealed the essence of urban love, and this made him think of collecting together such moments together in a book of epiphanies."[38] Joyce's use of epiphany, so central to his artistic and intellectual vision, is the key that unravels the mystery that is the city, illuminating the city as a web of human connectedness in all its ordinary and extraordinary wonder.[39]

For Simmel too the key to contemporary society lay not in society or its institutions as constitutive of a monolithic social system *per se*, but in the particles of everyday life, "the invisible threads" and "fortuitous fragments of reality" that were to be viewed as examples of eternity.[40] In the particular was contained the universal. Simmel, furthermore, openly rejected the idea of society as a totality in favor of a conception of social totality as the sum of its interactions, ultimately "a constellation of individuals."[41] The object of Simmel's study was determined not merely by a particular mode of viewing modern life but by the new mode of experiencing a new social reality itself. Yet as the preface to *The Philosophy of Money* makes clear, this approach does not exclude access to social totality: "the unity of these investigations lies [. . .] in the possibility [. . .] of finding in each of life's details the totality of its meaning."[42] So strong in fact was Simmel's aesthetic interest in literary and aesthetic modernism that his work is evocative of something more than mere social theory or even sociology.[43]

Consonant with the larger goals of Simmel's investigations, "Metropolis" also makes room for a Weberian acceptance of rational capitalism, in that the essay causally connects the transformation in human identity— what Simmel terms the shift from a "subjective spirit"[44] to an intellectual, "objective spirit"—to the larger mechanisms of the money economy and the division of labor. In particular, it is the impersonal nature of the city brought about by capitalist society and its attendant system of relations that engenders in humanity a *sui generis* defense mechanism Simmel identifies as the "blasé attitude."[45] Simmel's theory of city life may well be founded on the claim that the preservation of the personality is ultimately "bought at the price of devaluating the whole objective world, a devaluation that in the end unavoidably drags one's own personality down into a feeling of the same worthlessness."[46] At the same time, this analysis of urban consciousness is also somewhat of a paradox, in that the same conditions that engender alienation (and thus self-protection) also intimate liberation. For Simmel the condition of modernity is contained in the fact that the individual is not only bound to society but by definition also has to shield himself or herself against its effects. In "The Day of the Rabblement" (1901), Joyce also outlines the dangers facing the urban artist when he writes, "no man [. . .] can be a lover of the true or the good unless he abhors the multitude; and the artist, though he may employ the crowd, is very careful to isolate himself."[47] While the smoldering tone of Joyce's dramatic outburst against the culture of metropolitan Dublin is certainly dramatic, it nonetheless resonates with Simmel's conception of the challenges that confront the urban individual.

THE ARTIST IN THE CITY

A Portrait "is," as one critic notes, "not because Stephen thinks but because Stephen perceives."[48] Stephen's unique sensory impressions of Dublin and his place in it are born out of the agony and ecstasy of a precocious subjectivity. Examining the valency of Stephen's perceptions, therefore, from his schoolboy days in Clongowes to the suburban quietude of Blackrock and beyond to the noisy streets of Dublin, is central to understanding Joyce's own conception of metropolitan consciousness as represented within the space of the novel. At the start of the novel Stephen's Saussurean engagement with the world is symptomatic of a burgeoning consciousness. In his geography book, he locates himself at the center of a universe radiating out from his own earth-bound existence to infinity:

> Stephen Dedalus
> Class of Elements
> Clongowes Wood College
> Sallins
> County Kildare
> Ireland
> Europe
> The World
> The Universe. (*P* 15)

This platonic/christian conception of the universe, in which the city of Dublin has yet to play a part, finds its correlative in Stephen's reverence for the simple life and order of the peasants of the village of Clane, whose identity is bound up with a simplistic sense of awe for the mysteriousness of religion, rural life, and the ways of the rural Irish.

The people of Clane are "holy peasants" (*P* 18), inhabitants of a romantic landscape that becomes increasing unstable, even problematic, as the novel progresses. This same natural world beyond the civilizing boundaries of the school engenders in turn sentimental reveries: "It would be lovely to sleep for one night in that cottage before the fire of smoking turf, in the dark lit by the fire, in the warm dark, breathing the smell of the peasants, air and rain and turf and corduroy" (*P* 18). Mediated by Stephen's consciousness, the peasants of Clane lack clear identities; rather, they exist as disembodied figures, or as objects in a receding landscape typically viewed by Stephen and his friends as they pass to and from the railway station. On the whole, while rural Ireland exists beyond the borders of the text, its muted yet enigmatic presence serves to enrich and define Joyce's concept of the culture of metropolitan Dublin in distinct and informing ways.

In chapter V, for example, as Stephen and Davin—"the peasant student" (*P* 180) and ardent nationalist—walk "through the dark narrow streets of the poorer Jews" (*P* 181), Davin recounts a tale of near seduction by a peasant woman at whose isolated house he stops late one night in search of rest and refreshment. As Stephen walks along the street (the location for much of his frustrated disquisitions on classical and modern aesthetics), Davin's peasant is taken up by Stephen's imagination as yet another of Joyce's equivocal symbols for Ireland:

> The last words of Davin's story sang in his memory and the figure of the woman in the story stood forth, reflected in other figures of the peasant whom he had seen standing in the doorways at Clane as the college cars drove by, as a type of her race and his own, a batlike soul waking to the consciousness of itself in darkness and secrecy and loneliness and, through the eyes and voice and gesture of a woman without guile, calling the stranger to her bed. (*P* 181)

The suspicion attached to this myth of rural Ireland is again rehearsed toward the end of *Portrait* as Stephen prepares to quit Dublin. At this point the narrative structure gives way to entries taken directly from Stephen's diary:

> 14 *April:* John Alphonsus Mulrennan has just returned from the West of Ireland. (European and Asiatic papers please copy.) He told us that he met an old man there in a mountain cabin. Old man had red eyes and short pipe. Old man spoke Irish. Mulrennan spoke Irish. The old man and Mulrennan spoke English. Mulrennan spoke to him about universe and stars. Old man sat, listened, smoked, spat. Then said:
> —Ah, there must be terrible queer creatures at the latter end of the world.
> I fear him. I fear his redrimmed horny eyes. It is with him I must struggle all through this night till day come, till he or I lie dead, gripping him by the sinewy throat till [. . .] Till what? Till he yield to me? No. I mean him no harm. (*P* 251–252)

According to Simmel, the psychological basis of the metropolitan type is environmentally determined, and is the result of "the intensification of nervous stimulation which results from the swift and uninterrupted change of outer and inner stimuli."[49] Although Stephen's urban subjectivity is shaped over time with his removal from Blackrock to Dublin proper, there are intimations of the encroaching influence of the metropolis from the beginning of the novel. Not surprisingly, Stephen's sense of shock in response to Dublin is all the more intense given that he is himself a migrant to the city.

In Simmelean terms, the shock of the city invades Stephen's senses before he registers its presence in geographical terms. Following on from the fading socio-economic fortunes of his father Simon, "baby tuckoo" (*P* 7) is forced to quit the reveries of his rural childhood for the "new and complex sensation" (*P* 66) of Dublin. As a child Stephen constructs a semantic bridge to the world around him by creating a lexicon based on the memorization of what he perceives to be the denotative and connotative meanings of words: "Words which he did not understand he said over and over to himself till he had learned them by heart: and through them he had glimpses of the real world about him" (*P* 62). At the same time, the move to Dublin naturally coincides with a psychic shift in the way Stephen becomes inducted into his new environment: "The hour when he too would take part in the life of that world seemed drawing near and in secret he began to make ready for the great part which he felt awaited him the nature of which he only dimly apprehended" (*P* 62). Even at an early stage of the novel, it appears that Joyce is patiently formulating his own sense of that equation the city sets up between the individual and external life.

Confronted by the new and unfamiliar labyrinth of Dublin, an environment made all the more threatening by his own "dissatisfaction [. . .] embitterment and intuition or foreknowledge of the future," Stephen at first contents himself with "circling timidly round the neighbouring square or, at most, going half way down one of the side streets" (*P* 66). But driven by the embers of his own discontent and the hope of a chance encounter that will transfigure his existence, he feels compelled to move through "the gloomy foggy city." It is here that he searches deeper into the arterial structure of the commercial city, passing "unchallenged among the docks and along the quays," where he wonders at "the vastness and strangeness of the life suggested to him by the bales of merchandise stocked along the walls or swung aloft out of the holds of steamers [. . .] "(*P* 78).[50] Yet the more Stephen journeys abroad in search of his urban "Mercedes" the more he becomes estranged from both the city and himself: "A vague dissatisfaction grew up within him as he looked on the quays and on the river and on the lowering skies and yet he continued to wander up and down day after day as if he really sought someone that eluded him" (*P* 77). Indeed, the progressive effect of "the dull phenomenon of Dublin" (*P* 78) continues to disquiet Stephen's soul to the extent that, coupled with the increasingly squalid conditions of home life, his new mode of urban existence fills him always "with unrest and bitter thoughts" (*P* 78).

In a later and much-heated conversation with Davin, Stephen openly rejects an oppressive life bounded by the trinity of "this race and this country and this life" (*P* 203). In all their abstract and concrete forms, these forces remain central in Stephen's search for his own artistic soul, and are nowhere more apparent than in his relationship to Dublin, the essential ground of Stephen's experience of modernity. However, while Joyce's representation of Dublin lends itself to an examination of the metropolis and mental life, it is actually in the city of Cork that *Portrait* provides us with a powerful instance of Simmel's psychological portrait of urban consciousness.

Following Stephen's return from Cork, Joyce informs us that "the letters of the name Dublin lay heavily upon his mind, pushing one another surlily hither and thither with slow boorish insistence" (*P* 111). But it is in Cork, the scene of his father's final and irrevocable financial dispossession from middle-class Irish life, that Stephen is inexorably pushed "beyond the limits of reality"(*P* 92). Stephen, disgusted by the vulgar shock of the "foetus" incident at the University, which acts as a kind of moral barometer for the "monstrous images"(*P* 90) of his own riotous imagination, is further sickened by the trite details of his father's rakish youth, the details of which are paraded before Stephen as they visit old haunts and converse with old cronies. Caught between the chaos of his inner life and the weight of external reality, Stephen fumbles for a center of meaning within a fog of thought. But in a cold epiphanic moment, he symbolically breaks with his father, assuming in the process the characteristic features of Simmel's metropolitan consciousness:

> He could scarcely interpret the letters of the signboards of the shops. By his monstrous way of life he seemed to have put himself beyond the limits of reality. Nothing moved him or spoke to him from the real world unless he heard it in an echo of the infuriated cries within him. He could respond to no earthly or human appeal, dumb and insensible to the call of summer and gladness and companionship, wearied and dejected by his father's voice. He could scarcely recognize as his own thoughts, and repeated slowly to himself:
> —I am Stephen Dedalus. I am walking beside my father whose name is Simon Dedalus. We are in Cork, in Ireland. Cork is a city. Our room is in the Victoria Hotel. Victoria and Stephen and Simon. Simon and Stephen and Victoria. Names. (*P* 92)

Back in Dublin, and flush with capital accrued from his scholarship money, Stephen establishes a domestic "commonwealth," an economic "breakwater of order and elegance against the sordid tide of life" (*P* 96). It comes as little surprise that the "swift season of merrymaking" (*P* 98) fails to shore up the financial ruins of the eroding Dedalus household. In the wasting fires of his "loveless lust"(*P* 96), Stephen returns once more to his impulsive wanderings; however, this time he does not follow the quiet avenues of suburban Blackrock in search of his childhood Mercedes, but rather traces a path through the "dark slimy streets"(*P* 98) to the brothels of Dublin. The obsessive quest for religious and spiritual enlightenment fails because Stephen refuses, finally, to "merge his life in the common tide of other lives" (*P* 151). In its place, rather, a "spiritual dryness"(*P* 152) consumes him, a state of being that erodes all resistance to the temptations the city affords.

In offering a brief reading of *Portrait* alongside Simmel's sociological analysis of metropolitan life, I am not suggesting that in order to understand Joyce's fiction one needs to read contemporary sociological studies. The complex and dynamic relationship that has always existed between the novel and sociology is well beyond the scope of this study, but the possibilities for such an undertaking are endless. If anything, the city remains the greatest subject for both modern artists and urban theorists. [51] However, in terms of the larger history of urban writing, sociologists and novelists, though often separated by the barriers germane to their respective disciplines or divided by different forms and genres of writing common to their respective pursuits, have always worked in close intellectual proximity.[52] Sociologists, for example, have long regarded novelists as incisive social observers.[53] This acknowledgment alone allows us to position *Portrait* outside a circumscribed literary context in favor of a more inclusive tradition of urban writing (both literary and theoretical), and in doing so rethink the outlines of that history.

In nineteenth-century Europe the development of sociology, as Wolf Lepenies has shown, took place within a dynamic and conflicting interaction between "literary" and "scientific intellectuals" over the forms, genres, and discourses that were best equipped, and therefore most authorized, to represent modern society. Lepenies goes on to note that, "from the moment of its inception sociology became both a competitor and a counterpart of literature. [. . .] When sociology desired to be sociography it came into conflict with above all with the realistic novel over the claim to offer adequate reproduction of the 'prose of everyday circumstances'; when, on the other hand, it claimed to be social theory it incurred the suspicion of degenerating into a 'closet science.'"[54]

In the context of European, Russian, and American literature, Joyce's work stands, on the one hand, alongside such names as John Dos Passos, Jack London, Upton Sinclair, John Steinbeck, William Faulkner, and, on the other, DeFoe, Balzac, Flaubert, Maupassant, Hugo, Thackeray, Dickens, Zola, Gorky, Chekov, and Dostoyevsky, names that evoke the tension between country and city as well as their attendant phenomena: migration, industrialization, urbanization, and modernization. In historiographical, terms this body of literature presaged the birth of formal sociology, played a major role in the development of the social sciences, and, by extension, contributed to the development, most notably in the United States, of the sociological novel.[55]

The social consequences of the industrial revolution raised important philosophical questions about the condition of humanity, for example, how the massing of people in cities would affect the social order. It was thus the growth of the Western industrial city, as well as the wider economic changes transforming the world, that fostered the development of sociology, and urban sociology in particular. Urban sociology in particular emerged at the end of the nineteenth century at a time when sociology itself was achieving a greater measure of distinction within the social sciences. However, urban social science, as William G. Flanagan notes, has never been completely successful in defining its object of study. One reason for this state of disciplinary indeterminacy may well have to do with the fact that no formal efforts have been made to define clearly "the macrological and micrological concerns of sociology." [56]

Building on the work of classical urban sociologists, more recent theoretical trends, and subdivisions within sociology (for example, urban ecology and urban political economy) have contributed to an increasingly specialized field. Furthermore, "add to this the fact that researchers and theorists in other disciplines—anthropology, geography, history, political economy—are often engaged in work that is indistinguishable from the interests of urban sociologists"[57] and it soon becomes clear that urban sociology remains a heterogeneous mix of issues, methodologies, and perspectives. The fact remains that while the questions that engage the attention of urban sociologists are broadly divergent—from the experience of the individual to structural analyses of broad-scale political and economic analyses—cities themselves constitute a socially defined environments that inform the choices people make, choices that create and alter those same environments in ever-new and demanding ways. As a consequence, while there has been a significant expansion in the scope of urban sociology in recent times, the central question of how the shifting ecology of urban environments influence human behavior remains a dominant concern.

For the most part, sociologists working in the first half of the twentieth century on theories of city life emphasized the alienating aspects of the urban environment. For example, between 1900 and World War II classic urban writers fall into two distinct schools: in the first instance, between 1900 and 1925 there was the German caucus located in Heidelberg and Berlin, and comprising Max Weber, Georg Simmel, and Oswald Spengler. Beginning in the 1920s and building on the work of their German counterparts, University of Chicago investigators Robert Park, Louis Wirth, Ernest Burgess, and Robert Redfield conducted their own sociological studies on human behavior in the urban environment, and analyzed city life at the level of the individual as well as in terms of the larger community.

James Donald correctly identifies Simmel's "metropolitan man" as having "two main aspects to his personality. In the first instance, the blasé attitude protects against the shock of exoribitant external stimuli. The other aspect, in a specifically modern way, is more expressive, in that it identifies a form of conduct or an exercise of liberty that manifests itself in an urban aesthetics of self-creation."[58] Nowhere is this desire for transformation and transcendence more passionately stated than in Stephen's ardent self-questioning before the bourgeois culture of Irish life: "How could he hit their conscience or how cast his shadow over the imaginations of their daughters, before their squires begat upon them, that they might breed a race less ignoble than their own?" (*P* 238). Stephen's growth from innocence to experience, his religious conversion and inevitable fall, and his deliverance into the beauty of mortal conditions lends itself suggestively to Simmel's bifurcated notion of the metropolitan individual's search for beauty and order at the heart of the city.

CHAPTER FIVE

Ulysses and *Manhattan Transfer*
A Poetics of Transatlantic Literary Modernism

So now we come to Joyce. What was the main thing that Joyce did in this work? You know more or less what *Ulysses* is about: it's 700 pages of description of a day in the life of a man who solicits advertisements for an insurance company [sic]. The whole day is described from beginning to end. What exactly did Joyce do? He took one character, one person, one event and looked at it under an incredible microscope. Ordinarily you could describe a day like that in three or four pages. He began to examine all the details under the microscope, that is, he completely unfurled everything that you see at that moment [. . .] One subject merges into another, one word into another.

(From the audience: Dos Passos does that.)

Don't ever draw parallels [. . .] That just confuses things. It's disgraceful what critics are doing, linking Joyce with Proust or whomever. Don't make that mistake.

The most ridiculous aspect of criticism of Joyce is that when they deny the question of the usefulness of studying Joyce and when they write about learning from Joyce they keep viewing learning as slavish copying. Whether they say that it isn't necessary to learn or it is necessary, they always look at learning as copying. But learning is not copying but understanding what the particular process consists of; not in borrowing the external form, but in understanding the principle and making it one's own, and then there will be one's own representational form.

~ Sergei Eisenstein, Lecture on James Joyce at the State Institute of Cinematography, November 1, 1934[1]

The creative power of the cult of experience is almost spent, but what lies beyond is still unclear. One thing, however, is certain: whereas in the past, throughout the nineteenth and well into the twentieth century, the nature of American literary life was largely determined by national forces, now it is international forces that have begun to exert a dominant influence. And

in the long run it is in terms of this historic change that the future course
of American writing will define itself.

~ Philip Rahv, "The Cult of Experience in American Writing" (1940)

Rereading Urban Modernism

As the broad and highly contested field of contemporary scholarship reveals, the history of American modernism, like its European counterpart, is
an elusive and complex phenomenon as disparate in its polemics and man-
ifestos as it is rich and evocative in its artistic productions.[2] While theories
of modernism have traditionally focused on the work of a small cadre of
predominantly white Anglo-Saxon males working in major European and
American cultural centers during the opening decades of the twentieth century, revisionist readings have progressively challenged such exclusive conceptions so as to include writers from a variety of ethnic and cultural
groups.[3] The increasing urgency of these re-readings of modernism seeks
not so much to diminish the importance of canonized artists or cultural
events taking place in cities like Paris, London, and New York; rather, the
collective aim has been to increase the circle of understanding regarding
what all too often has been a restricted terrain of artistic and intellectual
inquiry. As Richard Poirier has ably argued, the major achievement of such
reassessments in recent years has been "the effort to break down the co-
herencies that have passed for literary history," with the result that we now
"see that the very cult of modernism is in itself a demonstration of the arbi-
trariness and impertinence by which literary history gets made and re-
made."[4]

In the same way that the term "modernism" engenders contentious debates among a wide range of critical schools, any attempt to isolate the definitive origin of modernism independent of the claims of antecedent events
and ideas is as unwise as the assumption that the modernism itself can be
tied solely to any one particular geographical region or national culture.
Virginia Woolf, however, famously disagreed. In response to the London
exhibition of postimpressionist art, Woolf claimed from her European vantage point that, "on or about December, 1910, human character
changed."[5] On the surface, Woolf's claim to have isolated the moment of
modernism seems a little extravagant in terms of its cultural and temporal
specificity. But her remarks are nonetheless symptomatic of feelings felt by
her contemporaries, who likewise concurred that they too were living
through a period of immense cultural and social change. In Henry Adams'
case, the shift occurred in the Gallery of Machines at the Paris Exposition
of 1900, where his "historical neck" was broken by the "irruption of
forces totally new."[6] For Adams the rupture transcended the merely technological; the "break," rather, was an epistemological one that called into

question the ontological relationship between the individual and history, one that inspired him to formulate his "Dynamic Theory of History."[7]

Conflicting reports concerning the birth, alleged death—even the existence—of modernism aside, Woolf's declaration and Adams' meditation speak to a larger claim that, in historical terms, the international moment of modernism marked a point at which the inertia of nineteenth-century social, cultural, and economic formations both enabled, and collided with, the forces of the new century in ways never before experienced. What resulted, in general terms, was the parturition (though by no means innocent or unique to Western culture) of a revolutionary sense of modernity—an historiographical emphasis in the arts on the present and the "new" as opposed to the overburdening structures of tradition, the past, and history.[8] But while the discontinuities implied in Woolf's radical rethinking of human awareness and Adams' belief in the end of history were both grounded in their experiences with European artistic sensibilities and technological advancements, nowhere was the international impact of modernism anticipated more zealously, desired more earnestly, felt more profoundly, or participated in more fully than in the United States, a nation whose relationship with European cultural formations has long influenced the shaping of American urban identity.

In this chapter, I investigate the ways in which Joyce's *Ulysses*, *the* quintessential literary city of modernism, and Dos Passos' *Manhattan Transfer*, an experimental narrative that takes as its subject *the* quintessential material city of modernism, New York, are paradigmatic examples of a transatlantic system of competing yet mutually informing urban aesthetic philosophies and critical ideologies. In *Ulysses*, a novel written, edited, and revised across the face of Europe in cities as diverse as Dublin, Pola, Trieste, Rome, Paris, and Zurich during a period of violent historical transformation, Joyce constructs an internationalist vision of Dublin in interlocking and recursive ways. The novel demarcates Dublin in naturalistic/realistic terms as a quantified and knowable Edwardian object in paradoxical terms: *Ulysses* is a reading of modernity grounded not in a modernist culture-capital but in a city of moral, cultural, and social destitution. At the same time, Joyce's Dublin transforms the topos of the metropolis into an imaginative urban vision of the city in universal terms.

For Dos Passos the precariousness of modern American history—"a restless industrial world of joyless enforced labor and incessant goading war"—also found its locus in the modern city. *Manhattan Transfer*, Dos Passos' third novel and gateway to the panoramic *U.S.A.* (1930–1936) trilogy, isolates the city of New York, set on the granite rock of Manhattan, as a symbol for this phase of history: the embodiment of a "sanitary civilization of a scientized New World Order," a world that had enslaved itself to a debilitating "industrial system, offering little succor, except in the hectic pleasures of suffocating life in cities."[9] Dos Passos' novel supports the premise that the totality of the modern city, like the totality of American history itself, had grown beyond human comprehension. More particularly, America under the presidency of Woodrow Wilson had become a "malignant Colossus trampling out the hope of the Western world."[10] Unlike Joyce's Dublin, however, Dos Passos' New York is a massive urban palimpsest riveted by industrial imagery and criss-crossed by the multiple frenetic rhythms of intersecting lives. But while *Manhattan Transfer* lends itself to a collectivist vision where individuals are less the central concern than the city itself, Dos Passos' New York also reveals the beauty of this nascent megalopolis in the opening decades of the century through evanescent moments of epiphany.

JOYCE AND DOS PASSOS: AN EMERGENT POETICS

Even before the postimpressionist exhibition that had so profoundly affected Woolf was unveiled in New York in 1913 as the famous Armory show, American poetry, fiction, and indeed all the arts in cities such as New York and Chicago had been radically informing, appropriating, and transforming for their own homegrown purposes the artistic influences and movements emanating from European metropoli from the mid-nineteenth century onwards.[11] So extraordinary was the period that critics now commonly refer to the 1920s as a Second Renaissance in American literature, because it rivaled in the form of Hemingway, Faulkner, and Fitzgerald the outpouring of classic texts by Emerson, Hawthorne, Melville, Thoreau, and Whitman during 1850s. Modernist artists, however, caught in the interstices of a society entrenched in the genteel backwaters of a belated American Puritanism and the vision of a nation as culturally triumphant as its emerging industrial order, nonetheless felt a deep sense of ambivalence with regard to America's ability to foster and sustain a cultural front.

At the furthest extreme of action, Gertrude Stein, Ernest Hemingway, and Ezra Pound were the first generation following Henry James to choose expatriation as one way of forging an authentic American consciousness far from the shores of the New World.[12] However, terms such as the "Jazz Age" and "Lost Generation" remain easy critical and historical constructs that delimit the extent of the radical disjunction many American artists felt toward the cultural aspirations and social tendencies of the by now well-documented intellectual diaspora of the 1920s. As Marcus Klein notes, the case that a so-called generation's exile (metaphorical and literal) can be blamed upon disillusionment with a nation's lost idealism and grubby commercialism is dubious at best; if anything, "the sheer business thrust of American civilization had been more blatant in the years of the robber barons, prior to the turn of the century."[13] More particularly, artists working in the twilight of the nineteenth century often felt that, while post-Civil War bourgeois society had achieved an extraordinary level of wealth and apparent social stability envied the world over, the cultural heart of the nation under Reconstruction remained a "bumptious, conservative adolescent, coercive in its smugness and unreceptive to change."[14] The preceding generation's antagonism toward American society might well have challenged the privileged discourse of the 1920s, but the cultural mythology of this golden literary age of American disillusionment, lost idealism, expatriation, and classic fiction remains tied to the cultural heritage of the emerging nation.

Just as T. S. Eliot's "historical sense"[15] both defined and marketed a poetic-historical paradigm for European sensibilities," so American artists working in America and Europe attempted to stamp their own cultural authority on emerging representative forms of art. From Henry James to Gertrude Stein, and from e. e. cummings to Hart Crane, what American writers progressively called for was not so much a remedy for the state of the nation's cultural mediocrity as the shattering of a tradition of fossilized forms and poetic sentiments. In a typically Whitmanesque call to arms for an internationalist art predicated on the lifeblood of American culture, John Gould Fletcher's essay "It Is Time to Create Something New" is indicative of a larger aesthetic conversation concerning what e. e. cummings termed the "New Art":

> There is much to be learned from the precursors I have mentioned [Blake, Matthew Arnold, Whitman, Samuel Butler]. There is a great deal to be learned form the French poets—Parnassians, Symbolists, Whitmanites, Fantaisistes—who have, in the years 1860 to 1900, created a new Renaissance under our nose. But above all, what will teach us the most is our language and our life.[16]

Writing from England in 1912, Ezra Pound, energized by his own manifest project to wed the English movement Imagism to American poetics, predicted the beginnings of an "American Risorgimento [that] will make the Italian Renaissance look like a tempest in a teapot!"[17] Unfortunately, when Pound visited America he "found no writer and but one reviewer who had any worthy conception of poetry."[18] Like Pound, Mencken also lamented that America lacked "a genuinely first-rate poet."[19] It seemed as if the American poetic impulse first corralled by Harriet Monroe's *Poetry: A Magazine of Verse* (1912) had, by 1919, spent itself. Disaffected by what he saw as a retrograde movement in the arts, Mencken could find comfort in the fact that only "America's commercialized technology showed the sole form that American ingenuity could take."[20]

Whereas modernism as a visual art began in Europe, the increasing association of science and technology with art in America following World War I defined an image of modernism (and modernity) for American artists and critics as very much an American way of life.[21] In his first public essays titled "A Humble Protest" and "Against American Literature" (both published in 1916), Dos Passos explained both the purpose and nature of modern American life in the industrial age ("A Humble Protest") as well as the national literary aesthetic ("Against American Literature"). The concrete questions posed by "A Humble Protest" constitute a proletarian stance best summed up as a poetics of repudiation that highlights the theoretical and aesthetic intersection of modernism and proletarianism. For example, Dos Passos asks "what is the goal of this mechanical, splendidly inventive civilization of ours? and "how do [thought and art] fare under the rule of [. . .] industrialism, and Mechanical Civilization?"[22] In addition, Dos Passos ponders how this twentieth-century culture—a "human pyramid where the few at the top are in the sunlight while the rest seat in the filthy darkness of meaningless labor?"[23]—could possibly reconcile the accomplishments of science and industrialization with the method of its achievement. (Dos Passos' mature fiction, with its admixture of art and politics, is clearly tied to the formative statements expressed in these essays.)

Though sophomoric pieces, "A Humble Protest" and "Against American Literature" cemented Dos Passos' conviction that the defining tenet of American democracy was the principle of individual liberty, a standard he would spend the rest of his life defending.[24] In tandem with this protest the rhetoric of "Against American Literature" counters that the nation at large lacked an American idiom capable of sustaining a belief in the primacy of the individual: "Our books are like our cities: they are all the same."[25] Moreover, vilifying the urban bourgeoisie for its fidelity to an empty tradition tied to the "'niceness' of the middle-class outlook,"[26] Dos Passos declared: "no wonder it is a relief to us Americans to turn from our prim colonial living room of thought, where the shades are drawn for fear the sun will fade the carpet Puritan ancestors laid there, to the bizarre pains and passions, to the hot moist steppe-savour of a Russian novel."[27]

In Sinclair Lewis' landmark 1926 review of *Manhattan Transfer*, America's foremost writer lauded Dos Passos' controversial novel as a new and vibrant strain of fiction rivaling the best that Europe had to offer. He also took the opportunity in the course of his review to measure Dos Passos' achievement against contemporary transatlantic developments in the novel. Though airing his dissatisfaction with the state of the novel in general, Lewis' remarks are clearly an extension of the broader conversation in American *belles lettres* concerning the demise of American aesthetics. In particular, Lewis bemoaned the tired formulas being trundled out by young novelists on both sides of the Atlantic:

> In America and in England alike, these young aspirants write, again and again, the same story in the same way, and this is the chart of their tale: A young man is (a) on a farm, (b) in the household of a father zealously given to finance and to scorn for Art, (c) on a newspaper with a cruel city editor, or (d) in a university, preferably Yale or Harvard, Oxford or Cambridge. Wherever he is, he discovers with bleating dismay that he is a genius. And there is a conversation about socialism and sex. Well, never mind. There is a girl—And so at last he writes a poem or a novel, and immediately it is great poem or novel, and sanctified critics with goat

whiskers proclaim him the real right thing, and he gets divorced from the Girl, and marries the other one, and is equally unappreciated by her and, as the novel ends in the gray-blue twilight by the North River, the Thames, or the Chicago drainage canal, he is preparing to marry the third.[28]

Taking on the literary establishment of the day, Lewis' review (written while savoring the comfort—and safety—of the Hotel Bermuda in the Bahamas in 1925) presents the reader with a candid persona characterized by ironic detachment, jocular spleen, and stalwart defensiveness of the "new" fiction. In typological terms, *Manhattan Transfer* for Lewis represented a break with a homogenous novelistic tradition incapable of capturing the spirit of the age. Yet as Raymond Williams points out in his analysis of the relationship between the modern city and the emergence of modernist art forms,

> Although modernism can be clearly defined as a distinct movement, in its deliberate distance from and challenge to more traditional forms of art and thought, it is also strongly characterized by its internal diversity of methods and emphases: a restlessness and often directly competitive sequence of innovations and experiments, always more immediately recognized by what they are breaking from than by what, in any simple way, they are breaking towards.[29]

Twenty years earlier and half a world away in Rome, Joyce, by now a self-exiled artist with *Dubliners* almost completed and *Stephen Hero* in the process of transforming itself into *Portrait*, was similarly engaged in casting a myopic eye across the terrain of the contemporary novel. While in Rome (1906–1907) Joyce committed himself to becoming a voracious reader and a pointed critic to the extent that "the whole idiom of twentieth-century fiction was established in his mind by 1906."[30] But what he read in Oscar Wilde's *The Picture of Dorian Gray* (1890), Thomas Hardy's *Life's Little Ironies* (1894), George Gissing's *Demos: A Story of English Socialism* (1886), George Moore's *The Untilled Field* (1903), and *The Lake* (1905) failed to impress.[31] Moreover, whereas an English writer of Hardy's stature merely bored the Irishman, Irish writers fared no better; if anything, Moore's *The Lake* was absurd.[32]

Much has already been written about the European cultural influences that informed Dos Passos' technique and style;[33] however, much more can be learned from Dos Passos' own critical analyses concerning Joyce's larger influence on the development of modernist art. In the retrospective essays "Contemporary Chronicles" (1960) and "What Makes a Novelist?" (1967), for example, Dos Passos outlined the rampant influence of *Ulysses* during a period when "artistic styles, like epidemics and popular songs, [were] borne in the air. They cross[ed] the wildest oceans, the most tightly barred frontiers [. . .] spreading across the world."[34] Having allied himself with socially committed artists who had also returned from the trenches of

Europe, Dos Passos identified a shared moral imperative: to "describe in colors that would not fade, our America that we loved and hated."[35] Unlike John Milton, who attempted in *Paradise Lost* to "justify the ways of God to man," Dos Passos' secular odyssey into the consciousness of modern America aspired to justify "the ways of machinery to man"[36] in a novelistic form he variously defined prospectively as "a contemporary chronicle," "a chronicle of the present," "a chronicle of protest," "a simultaneous chronicle," and "a novel full of snapshots full of life like a documentary film."[37] As an aesthetic artifact, *Manhattan Transfer* embraced in its formal structure the tendency of American modernism, approximating in textual terms the energy and geometry of urban experience.

Dos Passos records had read *Portrait* and *Dubliners* while a student at Harvard, and later excerpts from *Ulysses* published in the *Little Review*. But Dos Passos' experience of Joyce's leviathan urban novel in its published form occurred during the spring of 1922, as he returned to America on the *Aquitania* after having traveled extensively in the Near East:

> I had read James Joyce's *Ulysses* on my way home from Europe laid up with a bad case of flu in a tiny inside cabin down in the third class of a Cunarder. It's a marvelous way to read a book. *Ulysses* got linked in my mind with Sterne's *Tristram Shandy*. They are both subjective novels. My interests were the opposite: I wanted to write objectively. [. . .] I dreamed of using whatever I'd learned from all these methods to produce a satirical chronicle of the world I knew. I felt that everything should go in: popular songs, political aspirations and prejudices, ideals, hopes, delusions, crackpot notions, clippings out of the daily newspapers.[38]

While "Contemporary Chronicles" and "What Makes a Novelist?" remain important statements of philosophy, Dos Passos' 1932 introduction to a reissue of *Three Soldiers* (originally published in 1921) constitutes a core articulation of methodology, especially the significance of Joyce as an ideal example of the modernist configuration of art. Dos Passos' selection of Joyce as a model for vigorous writing served to highlight the dissolution of contemporary aesthetic standards brought about by the feminized, pulp-sodden machinery of literature:

> What I'm trying to get out is the difference in kind between the work of James Joyce, say, and that of any current dispenser of daydreams. It's not that Joyce produces for the highbrow and the other for the lowbrow trade, it's that Joyce is working with speech straight and so dominating the machine of production, while the daydream artist is merely feeding the machine, like a girl in a sausage factory shoving hunks of meat into the hopper. Whoever can run the machine runs it for all of us. Working with speech straight is vigorous absorbing devastating hopeless work, work that no man need be ashamed of.
>
> You answer that Joyce is esoteric, only read by a few literary snobs, a luxury product like limited editions, without influence on the mass newspaper readers. Well give him time. The power of writing is more likely to

be exercised vertically through a century than horizontally over a year's sales. I don't mean either that Joyce is the only straight writer of our time, or that the influence of his powerful work hasn't already spread, diluted through other writers, into many a printed page of which the author never heard of *Ulysses*.[39]

The form of Dos Passos' convenient—and questionable—feminine conception of mass culture aside, the introduction clearly does not adhere to the premise that art and mass culture are mutually exclusive; rather, Dos Passos' argument supports a democratic continuum between high art and the masses. In effect, Dos Passos' refusal to bracket Joyce with the "luxury product[s]" of "limited editions" not only challenges critical conceptions of Joyce as an apolitical writer and/or obscure formalist, but also arguably aligns him with the very people he represents, that is "the mass of ordinary newspaper readers."[40]

CRITICAL APPROACHES TO THE JOYCE-DOS PASSOS CONNECTION

As Janet Galligani Casey notes in her study of representations and theorizations of gender in Dos Passos' major fiction, although "he is frequently mentioned in general studies of the period, acknowledged as an innovative narrativist, and noted as the most celebrated artistic figure of the American Left, his vision is virtually never perceived as central to an understanding of American modernism."[41] Criticized for being too experimental by his fellow proletarian artists and too political for the modernists, even his most well-known work—the 1500-page trilogy *U.S.A.*, comprising *The Forty-Second Parallel* (1930), *Nineteen Nineteen* (1932), and *The Big Money* 1936), with their respective narrative devices comprising the Newsreel, Camera Eye, Biography, and fictional narrative—has steadily fallen out of circulation because of its over-reliance on historical specificity and formal difficulties. This may in part explain why recent scholarship of *U.S.A.*, which has traditionally invited a wide variety of approaches over the years (formalist, historical, sociological, political, biographical, existential, and interdisciplinary), has moved away from historical, social and political concerns to consider aesthetic (Schloss), epistemological (Strychacz), psychosocial (Martin), and cultural (Casey) paradigms.[42] However, next to the *U.S.A.* trilogy, which remains in critical currency, since the 1980s Dos Passos' *Manhattan Transfer* has been afforded such scant criticism that it seems even less well known as we move into the twenty-first century.[43]

The most popular explanation cited for Dos Passos' critical demise following the publication of *U.S.A.* is the "convoluted history of his political opinions."[44] During the 1920s and 1930s works such as *Manhattan Transfer* and *U.S.A.*, along with Dos Passos' involvement with Leftist publications such as *The New Masses*, highlighted a broad commitment to the formalist concerns of modernism as well as to social issues and proletarian aesthetics. By the 1950s (long after his break with Communist ideology in the 1930s) Dos Passos' gradual shift to Goldwater Republicanism ensured that both the Left and the Right found reasons to denounce him as an apostate. But as Casey succinctly records, the history of Dos Passos' political odyssey should not be allowed to overshadow his importance as a radical American modernist:

> It seems that Dos Passos, as a member of both camps, was twice damned rather than twice saved: his simultaneous—and unique—occupation of differently circumscribed discursive territories is thus integrally related to his singular position in American literary and cultural history. No other American writer achieved his status both here and abroad as a representative of Marxist sensibilities (the Soviet Writer's Union even sponsored a three-day discussion of Dos Passos in 1933), and yet no other proletarian writer achieved the purely literary respect accorded to Dos Passos as a modernist practitioner of narrative experimentation.[45]

Almost immediately, the publication of *Manhattan Transfer* polarized the critical community into antagonistic camps, variously perplexing and outraging, on the one hand, those defenders of a more genteel tradition of writing, while heralding for others the beginning of a new mode and expression of writing.[46] Reviewers used such words as "impressionistic," "expressionistic," "super-naturalistic," "neo-realistic," "architectonic," "panoramic," "kaleidoscopic," and "cinemascopic" to define in typological terms the genre they felt the novel aligned itself with most completely.[47] However, despite the inevitable state of critical sclerosis surrounding *Manhattan Transfer*, the novel clearly represents a defining moment of artistic maturity. If anything, the expressionistic techniques Dos Passos employs to present his montage of New York reveal an embarrassment of artistic influences. And all of these techniques serve multiple ends: to demonstrate themes of materialism and soul-deadening conformity; to satirize political and social corruption; to delight and amuse the reader with the life of New York's urban burlesque; and, to sympathize with the ludicrousness of characters who dash hurried and confused about a city that looms larger throughout the novel than any of the individual figures.[48]

While there are of course exceptions, the majority of criticism prior to the 1980s attempts to project onto Dos Passos' fiction categories and labels such as socialism and aestheticism—what he later called literary "pigeon-holes."[49] Dos Passos is further characterized as a proletarian writer committed to Marxism and the class struggle; a Romantic and/or Harvard aesthete opposed to modern industrial America; a determinist who portrays his characters as individuals bound helplessly by hostile environmental forces; a social critic devoted to changing society; a moralist who hold his characters responsible for their actions; an impersonal realist and/or naturalist; a cultural satirist; a propagandist; a pamphleteer; a collectivist interested only in portraying the social behavior of the group; and, a writer committed to legitimating the individual within mass society. And then there are those critics who attempt in interdisciplinary ways to reconcile elements of these many and many other contradictory positions. One reason for the majority attempt to confine Dos Passos within formalist or political dimensions has more to do with the fact that critics have been unwilling to consider Dos Passos' representative fictions as discursive formations capable of straddling, or coexisting within and across, the boundaries and principles outlined by modernist art and proletarian theory and practice.

In the case of *Manhattan Transfer* in particular, more often than not Dos Passos is labeled a cultural pessimist and the text a political diatribe.[50] Edmund Wilson, for example, declared in somewhat contradictory terms that while Dos Passos "made a systematic effort to study all the aspects of America and to take account of all its elements, to compose them into a picture which makes some general sense," he allowed his politics to falsify his judgment, and thus failed in his responsibility to present in the novel a balanced view of society.[51] According to Wilson, Dos Passos' political "disapproval of capitalist society seems to imply a distaste for all the beings who go to compose it," and that "no human life under any conditions can ever have been so unattractive."[52] In a similar vein, English critic F. R. Leavis described *Manhattan Transfer* as "a work that exhibits the decay of capitalist society," and judged the novel the product of a failed propagandist who has few suggestions as to how "meaning is to be restored to the agonized vacuity that it is his distinction to convey so potently."[53] If in Leavis' eyes Dos Passos' socially constructivist vision failed because it displaced the individual in favor of the denunciation of society, Richard Chase went as far as to characterize Dos Passos as a mere pamphleteer "inspired less by imagination than by anger and zeal."[54] Furthermore, if Dos Passos' political relevance failed because he could not (or would not) propose solutions for the very problems he attacked, perhaps it was because, as Granville Hicks argued in his survey of Dos Passos' work, "there is not much politics in *Manhattan Transfer*; the book is directed against a way of life, not a political or economic system."[55]

At the same time Dos Passos' fiction was being attacked on Marxist and/or political and social grounds at one end of the critical spectrum, at the other critics like John Aldridge were turning on Dos Passos for not doing the very things that Wilson, Leavis, Hicks, and Chase accused his fiction of attempting. Preferring to bracket Dos Passos as a member of the Harvard Aesthetes and the Lost Generation, Aldridge contended that Dos Passos' work was devoid of an affirming principle; consequently, his fiction lacked a "cause great enough to impel him toward a supreme integration of his powers," ultimately coming to rest as "a mere cataloguing of disgust."[56] Yet there are those who have brokered reconciliatory critical responses that to some extent accommodate the competing conceptions of Dos Passos as a socially engaged writer as well as an *avant-garde* artist.

Malcolm Cowley tried to synthesize the opposing images of Dos Passos as a collectivist, a "radical historian of the class struggle," and as "an esthete moving about the world in an ivory tower."[57] Having originally interpreted *Manhattan Transfer* as an imperfect example of the "art novel" (a poet misunderstood by the world), and more particularly the product of an esthete-individualist, Cowley later revised his opinion that the "art novel" and the "collective novel" were not radically opposed in Dos Passos; instead, these two novelistic forms existed, "like the two sides of a coin."[58] Similarly, though in somewhat spurious terms, Alfred Kazin attempted to balance these same categories of individualist and collectivist when he wrote that Dos Passos brought to an end "a chapter in the moral history of modern American writing" by transferring "the defeatism of the lost generation [Hemingway and Fitzgerald]" from individual persons to society itself.[59]

Lionel Trilling, however, at odds with Cowley and Hicks, countered claims that Dos Passos was a radical historian, a collectivist, or a determinist. Arguing that Dos Passos' morality was an essentially "romantic morality,"[60] Trilling contended that the cultural pessimism embedded in Dos Passos' fiction was the result of a mature political perception of the failures of the Left as well as the greed and corruption of the established order. Moreover, Trilling further argued that Dos Passos held the individual just as responsible for his or her own destiny as the often hostile environments in which his characters found themselves enmeshed. In more sympathetic terms still, Arthur Mizener made cogent distinctions separating Dos Passos the realist and/or naturalist, Dos Passos the social or collectivist novelist, and Dos Passos the cultural satirist. He also maintained that in 1930s America "the form of the collective novel had been adumbrated by fashionable critics and proved in theory to be the one demanded by the times."[61] Mizener ultimately concluded that what Dos Passos was really doing in his fiction up to and including *U.S.A.* was writing a satiric comedy in the style of Jonson or Swift.[62]

Like *Ulysses*, *Manhattan Transfer* radically challenged the symbiotic relationship between form and content, a feature which had traditionally been maintained through plot. Critics, however, while identifying Joyce as a probable influence on Dos Passos' work, have been somewhat cursory in dealing with the open acknowledgment of the intellectual debt. Joseph Warren Beach, for instance, isolates *Ulysses* as among the list of possible influences that affected Dos Passos' conception of *Manhattan Transfer*.[63] In particular, Beach notes that the affective technique in *Manhattan Transfer* of not presenting a character's thoughts "formally and consecutively, but by flashes and allusions, as in actual thinking, and with free association of ideas which do not follow a steady and logical course" is "suggestive of James Joyce or Virginia Woolf," a mode of presentation "dictated by many considerations purely esthetic."[64] Likewise, John D. Brantley points out that the "Joyce touch noted by some critics is perhaps most evident in the stream of consciousness passages such as the scene of Stan Emery's suicide, or Merrivale's final musings on his successful career."[65]

In more declarative terms, Charles C. Walcutt argues that *"Manhattan Transfer* [. . .] owes a very great deal to Joyce's *Ulysses*, from which it takes the method of showing the life of a city by flash after flash of incident and personal experience. Dos Passos is more sentimentally aware of his people than Joyce: he shows their agonies and fears and defeats in passages of considerable force."[66] Meanwhile, George J. Becker, careful to situate Dos Passos' art within a larger constellation of influences, argues that the arrival of *Manhattan Transfer* as a "cross-section" novel represented the full implementation of nineteenth-century realism in the American novel, and links Dos Passos' work with Flaubert, Zola and the contemporary novels of Galdes and Joyce.[67] Isolating several literary points of connection in passing, Becker more closely compares Jimmy Herf's surrealistic courtroom scene with the "Circe" episode in *Ulysses* as an example of the contradistinction in *Manhattan Transfer* between the worlds of "actuality" and "dreams" in the novel.[68] Moreover, Becker also considers Dos Passos' appropriation at times of Joyce's verbal techniques and the occasional borrowing of actual content from *Ulysses*.[69]

The above commentaries are symptomatic of the fact that up to this point, no single critical approach has been able to accommodate adequately the literary-critical significance of Joyce's urban poetics for Dos Passos' own conception of the modernist city. Aside from identifying those narrative moments where *Manhattan Transfer* appears to be suggestively resonant of Joyce's experimental techniques, criticism has yet to analyze fully the Joyce-Dos Passos connection as central to an emerging transatlantic modernist discourse that focuses on the city as the primary site of modern experience.[70] By far the most sustained analysis to date of the artistic relationship between Joyce and Dos Passos is that presented by Marshall McLuhan.

In the course of a relatively short essay, McLuhan surveys the two writers' technical similarities, but more importantly investigates how their respective cultural backgrounds impact their respective treatments of the individual in modern society. McLuhan's premise is clearly stated at the outset:

> The reader of Dos Passos is not required to have much more reading agility than the reader of the daily press. Nor does Dos Passos make any more serious demands than a good movie. And this is said not to belittle an excellent writer who has much to offer, but to draw attention to the extreme simplification to which Dos Passos has submitted the early work of James Joyce. *Three Soldiers* (1921), *Manhattan Transfer* (1925) and *U.S.A.* (1930–36) would not exist in their present form but for *A Portrait of the Artist as a Young Man*, *Dubliners*, and *Ulysses*. It is as a slightly super-realist that Dos Passos has viewed and adapted the work of Joyce in his own work.[71]

McLuhan further contends that because Joyce's and Dos Passos' respective discontinuous landscapes are similar, the latter's fiction would not exist in its present form if he had not read the former. From a formal perspective, McLuhan argues that the impressionistic and imagistic techniques used in *Manhattan Transfer* correspond in general with "the linear handling of history as a dwindling avenue" which "concurred with the eighteenth-century discovery of discontinuity as a means of enriching artistic effect."[72] But despite Dos Passos' use of this tradition, which he weds to contemporary imagistic methods so as to create impressionist landscapes and characters that sharpen perception and define states of mind, the emotional range of Dos Passos' urban topos and its characters is limited and monotonous. There is technique but little sensibility: "[Dos Passos] is sensitive to the ugliness and misery as things meant he can see. But he is never prepared to explore the interior landscape which is the wasteland of the human heart."[73]

Moreover, surveying "the unresolved attitudes and conflicts of the milieu [everything from Walter Scott to Whitman to Frank Lloyd Wright to post-impressionism]" that Dos Passos was exposed to as a child growing up in Chicago as well as during his undergraduate studies at Harvard, McLuhan's central argument is grounded in the philosophical claim that Joyce's vision of the human condition is more profound and his characterizations more convincing. Simply put, "Dos Passos is not a thinker who has imposed a conceptual system on his material." Joyce, by contrast, accepts the presence of evil as a universal principle of all human society, and is therefore able to construct a continuous parallel between the historical past and present to make the characters of modern Dublin representatives of the human condition. In *Ulysses*, Joyce's use of discontinuous landscape is the product of a method both impersonal and analogical; the cityscape is presented using imagistic devices, McLuhan notes, "but Joyce manipulates a continuous parallel at each moment between naturalism and symbolism to render a total spectrum of outer and inner worlds. The sharply focussed moment of natural perception in Joyce floods the situation with analogical awareness of the actual dimensions of human hope and despair."[74] More particularly,

> The difference between this kind of art [Joyce's technique of cubist or overlayering perspectives, of symbolic implication] and that of Dos Passos [impressionistic/imagistic] is that between one of univocal, psychological and one of properly analogical effect. Joyce constantly has his attention on the analogy of being while Dos Passos is registering a personal reaction to society.[75]

Dos Passos' view of man, it appears, is limited, conditioned as it is by an atrophied historic sense comprising transcendental optimism and Jeffersonian idealism. Unlike Joyce, Dos Passos does not accept evil as intrinsic to human nature and therefore attributes the suffering of individuals to the mechanized impersonality of the city and to the shortcomings of central-ized government. Moreover, Dos Passos' treatment of society is not truly analogical, as is Joyce's, because Dos Passos' historic sense fails to resolve the Jefferson-Hamiltion dichotomy that exists at its core. In other words, Dos Passos' fiction foregrounds the spirit of the "Jeffersonian ideal of the farmer-craftsman economy" only to expose the moral degeneration of con-temporary America as a bastion of "Hamiltonian centralism, power, and bigness."[76]

In addition, for McLuhan Dos Passos' response to the celebrated, the obscure, the sordid, and the banal elements of the city takes its prime im-pulse from an objectification of the political and economic situation. But because Dos Passos' intention is satirical and his methods impersonal (which together limit both his emotional response to, and his ethical view of, his characters), the connection with Joyce's own impressionistic tech-nique and view of the world is, at best, derivative and, at worst, inferior. Typical of the larger pragmatic estimation of the moral and aesthetic dif-ferences separating Dos Passos and Joyce, McLuhan maintains that, "to match Joyce's epiphanies Dos Passos brings only American know-how. [. . .] Joyce contemplates things for the being that is theirs. Dos Passos shows how they work or behave."[77] The value of McLuhan's analysis clearly lies in its identification and separation out of the differences with regard to in-tention and method used by Joyce and Dos Passos, but as Allen Belkind as-tutely points out, Mcluhan "tends to judge the supposed shortcomings of Dos Passos' work on the basis of a Joycean standard of realism with its ac-companying objectivity and impersonality."[78] Not only does McLuhan oversimplify Joyce's stated intentions for *Dubliners, Portrait,* and *Ulysses,* but the essay also fails to consider the fact that Dos Passos' intentions for *Manhattan Transfer* as a synoptic text called for a different treatment of both character and environment as a function of a quite different city, an American city.

MAKING THE MODERN WORLD POSSIBLE FOR ART

Prior to the publication of *Ulysses* in 1922, Joyce attempted to outline the symbolic structure of his "damned monster novel"[79] for the first genera-tion of perplexed readers when, in 1920, he sent his Italian translator, Carlo Linati, "a sort of summary—key—skeleton—scheme" of Homeric and other parallels. According to Joyce's explanation, *Ulysses* is

> the epic of two races (Israel-Ireland) and at the same time the cycle of the human body as well as a little story of a day (life). The character of Ulysses has fascinated me ever since boyhood. [. . .] My intention is not only to render the myth *sub specie temporis nostri* but also to allow each adventure (that is, every hour, every organ, every art being interconnected and interrelated in the somatic scheme of the whole) to condition and even to create its own technique.[80]

Joyce's stated intention for the text emphasizes a synthesis of myth, style, and symbolism into a self-reflexive organic whole that simultaneously mutes the realistic aspects of the novel—"a little story of a day." On the one hand, Joyce's foregrounding of allusion and allegory (the synchronic) over "reality" (the diachronic) has subsequently contributed to the creation of a global "Joyce industry." At the same time, the introductory schema has also helped shape a dualistic international critical inheritance the roots of which can be traced back to competing American and European modernist positions regarding the place, form, and function of art.

A. Walton Litz, for example, argues that the continuum of *Ulysses* criticism can be viewed as "an extended conversation—often amiable, occasionally irritable—between the spiritual descendants" of the "two most powerful literary sensibilities of the age": Ezra Pound and T. S. Eliot.[81] Among their notable commentaries on Joyce's work in various magazines and reviews from 1917 onwards, Litz isolates Pound's "James Joyce et Pécuchet" (1922), an essay that trumpets Joyce's "realism" as an inheritance from the prose tradition of Flaubert and the Goncourts. This position is counter-balanced with Eliot's famous 1923 review of *Ulysses* in *The Dial*, titled "*Ulysses*, Order, and Myth," in which the poet of *The Waste Land* pays tribute to the author of *Ulysses* for providing the modern age with nothing less than an aesthetic framework capable of combining the past and present, myth and history.[82] Aside from the fact that Eliot's and Pound's respective critical energies and artistic tendencies were bound up with Joyce's art—and not a little anxious and/or suspicious of the Irishman in the process[83]—the Pound/Eliot conversation is especially significant because it dramatizes in critical terms what Arnold Goldman has termed "the fact/myth ambiguity" in Joyce's art.[84] More recently Michael Groden has similarly diagnosed the two predominant sides of *Ulysses'* many dualisms as "the 'novelistic' story and the 'symbolistic' pattern of parallels and correspondences."[85]

One of the central critical differences dividing Eliot and Pound is that whereas the former praises Joyce's "mythical method"[86] as that of the manipulation of "a continuous parallel between contemporaneity and antiquity," the latter contends that the novel's schema is merely an organizational device.[87] Indeed, in keeping with the tenor of much of his pronouncements concerning Joyce's fiction from 1914 onwards, Pound declares in "James Joyce et Pécuchet" that *Ulysses* is "the realistic novel *par excellence*, each character speaks in his own way, and corresponds to an external reality."[88] Ultimately, Pound's importance for Joyce criticism remains undervalued,[89] while Eliot's ultimately self-serving apotheosis of *Ulysses* retains a greater hold on the critical imagination.

The core of Eliot's argument in "Ulysses, Order, and Myth" is a *faux* spat with Richard Aldington for reading Joyce's novel as a formless "invitation to chaos."[90] In 1917 Pound himself had defended *Portrait* in a similar vein against the criticism of Edward Garnett, who dismissed the novel as unrestrained and ugly. When Pound read Garnett's comments, he suggested the writer be sent to the Serbian front. Similarly, Eliot's elitist rebuttal takes Aldington to task for his "pathetic solicitude for the half-witted," and in doing so holds up the technique of *Ulysses* as a singular art form:[91]

> In using myth, in manipulating a continuous parallel between contemporaneity and antiquity, Mr. Joyce is pursuing a method which others must pursue after him. They will not be imitators, any more than the scientist who uses the discoveries of an Einstein in pursuing his own, independent, further investigations. It is simply a way of controlling, of ordering, of giving a shape and a significance to the immense panorama of futility and anarchy which is contemporary history. [. .] Instead of narrative method, we now use the mythical method. It is, I seriously believe, a step toward making the modern world possible for art.[92]

In analogous terms, if for Eliot a central tenet of modern consciousness was a sensitivity to myth, then "it is part of the mythology of modernism that we habitually discuss *The Waste Land* and *Ulysses* as coextensive literary performances.[93] Moreover, in addition to the *imprimatur* regarding *Ulysses*, Eliot's theoretical pronouncements between 1918–21 may also be read as "covert responses to Joyce's amassing novel."[94] At the conclusion of *The Waste Land* Eliot borrows a culturally inclusive benediction taken from the coda to an Upanishad, but as Michael H. Levenson contends, this conclusion is characteristic of the way in which Eliot's poem as a whole "rejects the boundaries of the Western tradition [. . .] resists Eurocentrism [and] represents a challenge to the self-sufficiency of Europe."[95]

In contrast, however, Eliot's position as outlined in the manifesto "Tradition and the Individual Talent" (1919) presents a quite different philosophy, what with its overt "commitment to European values and the European sensibility."[96] This apparent contradiction between Eliot the poet and Eliot the critic betrays more than a conflicted sense of cultural identity. Nowhere is Eliot's assertion of the universal significance of European culture more pronounced than in his measured praise for *Ulysses*, where "European" becomes synonymous with "international":

> [*Ulysses*] is the first Irish work since that of Swift to possess absolute European significance. Mr. Joyce has used what is racial and national and transmuted it into something of international value; so that future Irish writers, measured by the standard he has given, must choose either to pursue the same ideal or to confess that they write solely for an Irish, not for a European public.[97]

As Litz's study reveals, reading Pound and Eliot reading *Ulysses*/Joyce allows for a richer understanding of the significance of the Irishman's fiction as central to the aesthetic development—and marketing—of European literary modernism. However, when we expand the boundaries of these same debates to include American responses to *Ulysses*, the larger impact of Joyce's fiction in international terms becomes readily apparent. For exam-

ple, even as the Eliot/Pound debate was unfolding on one side of the Atlantic (in the midst of vituperative attacks against Joyce's allegedly venal
and excrementous vision of Dublin), on the other side American literary
and cultural critics were similarly engaged in their own pitched battles as
to whether modern art was capable of making a modern American world
possible for art.

As with its European reception, *Ulysses* became a storm center of controversy in the 1920s and 1930s, amazing and outraging American reviewers in equal measure.[98] Once again, criticism of the novel was characterized
by allegations of formlessness and reputedly obscene content.[99] By way of
pleading the case against *Ulysses*, commentators assiduously tracked the
novel's serialization the moment it appeared in Margaret Anderson's *The
Little Review*, which published fourteen chapters of the work-in-progress
from 1918 to 1920. The strongest early objections to the novel typically
came from British critics decrying all manner of aesthetic and moral failures and transgressions; however, it was in American intellectual circles
during the 1930s that criticism of *Ulysses* mutated into a form of cultural
warfare, "with critics from opposing perspectives arguing that Joyce,
among other modernist writers, was the cause or the symptom of contemporary social problems."[100]

While European modernism reached an experimental apex with the formal appearance of *Ulysses* and *The Waste Land* in 1922, the United States
had to wait until 1925 for its own literary *annus mirabilis*, the year that
saw the publication of such novels as Fitzgerald's *The Great Gatsby*,
Dreiser's *An American Tragedy*, Loos' *Gentlemen Prefer Blondes*, Hemingway's *In Our Time*, Williams' *In the American Grain*, Lewis' *Arrowsmith*,
and Dos Passos' *Manhattan Transfer*. As this year of prodigious artistic
output revealed, to all intents and purposes the cultural climate of the
United States had changed irrevocably. To the critics now fell the task of
explaining to the general public (and to each other) the meaning of this
artistic rupture in the cultural fabric of the nation, who or what was responsible, and why. Yet even as American critics "associated formal experimentation in art with revolutionary or antibourgeois tendencies," Dos
Passos "much more than Joyce, served as their model."[101] More than any
other critic at the time, Sinclair Lewis championed Dos Passos' *Manhattan
Transfer*, a novel that both shocked and amazed contemporary reviewers
with its vision of Manhattan. Moreover, Lewis' critique galvanized the
claim that, like it or not, a new and exciting kind of American city novel
had arrived at last.

In the same way that Eliot championed *Ulysses* as a European phenomenon of international importance, Lewis seized on *Manhattan Transfer* as
an American template for a new mode of novel writing. If we juxtapose
Eliot's value claims as they appear in "*Ulysses*, Order and Myth" with
those made by Lewis in "*Manhattan Transfer*," what results is a rhetorical
echo, with each critic vying for the cultural preeminence of his respective

culturally symbolic text. In particular, Lewis' review, which originally appeared in *The Saturday Review of Literature* shortly after the novel's publication, heralded Dos Passos' super-realistic brand of fiction as a radical break with the romantic idealism of the nineteenth-century novel. The review was also very much an open challenge to both European and American literature to consider Dos Passos' method as both singular and unique.[102]

According to Lewis, it is not "the mechanics of technique" (Eliot's "method") that distinguishes *Manhattan Transfer* (though method enough there is, Lewis assures his reader) so much as Dos Passos' "passion for the beauty and stir of life."[103] So enamored is Lewis of the novelist's work as a world-shaping American *zeitgeist* that he declares in a typically boosterish tone:

> I wonder whether it may not be true that *Manhattan Transfer* is a novel of the very first importance; a book which the idle reader can devour yet which the literary analyst must take as possibly inaugurating, at long last, the vast and blazing dawn we have awaited. It *may* be the foundation of a whole new school of novel-writing. Dos Passos *may* be, more than Dreiser, Cather, Hergesheinner, Cabell, or Anderson the father of humanized and living fiction [. . .] not merely for America but for the world!
>
> Just to rub it in, I consider *Manhattan Transfer* as important in every way than anything by Gertrude Stein or Marcel Proust or even the great boar, Mr. Joyce's *Ulysses*. For Mr. Dos Passos can use, and deftly does use, all their experimental psychology and style, all their revolt against the molds of classic fiction, all their interiority, their completeness of thought. But the difference is—Dos Passos is interesting! Their novels are treatises on harmony, very scholarly and confoundedly dull; *Manhattan Transfer* is the moving symphony itself.[104]

In the words of one critic, when Lewis died in 1951 he left "a somewhat insecure reputation as a writer of serious fiction and practically none as an essayist and critic."[105] Lewis' literary reputation has certainly waned considerably over the years, but during the 1920s he attained an unparalleled popular and critical success in American literary culture. Not only did he publish to international acclaim *Main Street* (1920), *Babbitt* (1922), and *Dodsworth* (1929), but he also rounded out the decade by being the first American to win the Nobel Prize for literature. Given Lewis' lauded position and cultural authority in American letters, his trumpeting of Dos Passos' novel is all the more significant within the context of contemporary cultural debates. Moreover, in 1926 the publishers Harper & Brothers reprinted Lewis' abridged *Saturday Review* essay in full in order to do "a service to contemporary writers and critics," and went on to add the following note: "This discussion by Sinclair Lewis of John Dos Passos' novel, *Manhattan Transfer*, must take rank as one of the most remarkable tributes from one distinguished writer to another."[106]

Unlike Henry James, who had earlier assumed the role of counselor to would-be writers in his Prefaces (1907–1909), Lewis never produced a manifesto or an essay that spoke to the question of authorship—despite H. L. Mencken's hyperbolic admonition that, if Lewis "would pull himself together, translate his very sure instincts into plain propositions and put them on paper, the result would be the best treatise on novel writing ever heard of."[107] What we have instead from the Lewis archive on the question of authorship is a plethora of lively remarks scattered in essays, introductions, lectures, interviews, and reviews that together aggressively promote "American commerce and American culture."[108] Lewis certainly energized a wide interest in creative writing after World War II, but it was during the 1920s that he effectively became "the spokesman of a new renaissance in American writing [. . .] the representative American artist of his era"[109] Typical of the disillusionment with romantic idealism of the nineteenth century felt by American writers of the early decades of the new century, Lewis, in the wake of WWI, promoted the new realism by urging young writers to write about real people with real problems in real places.[110]

For Lewis, *Manhattan Transfer* more than any other novel represented a formal break with the "classic method" of nineteenth-century modes of narrative structure in its representation of Manhattan:

> I am wondering if this may not perhaps be the first book to catch Manhattan. What have we had before, what have we had? Whitman? That is not our Manhattan; it is a provincial city near the frontier. Howells, Wharton, James? A provincial town near to Bath and the vicar's tea-cups. Hughes, Fitzgerald, Johnson, all the reporters of the Jazz Age? Their characters are, mostly, but foam on the beer! O. Henry? Change Broadway to Market Street or State Street in his stories, and see whether any one perceives the change![111]

As Percy H. Boynton remarked early on, Lewis' review of *Manhattan Transfer* in fact inspired the latter to formulate his own definition of the "ideal novel."[112] Indeed, Lewis' critique recycles and recuperates a wide range of Americanist views on the novel, defining in the process a negative definition of the type of novel the new realism attempted to emulate. Dos Passos not only presented New York to the world, but in doing so created a new mode of expression that was uniquely American.

THE CITY AS COMMUNITY

If the *Futurist Manifesto* (1909) enthusiastically embraced the twentieth-century metropolis as the preeminent subject for art, futurism itself often intimates a sense of disorientation, shock, even antagonism toward the city as a cultural and social matrix. But this ambiguity is symptomatic of the larger divisions of opinion on the part of artists and theorists alike during the opening decades of the twentieth concerning the impact of urbanization on human life. In the nineteenth century, international debate over the exponential growth and perceived threat to life of cities focused on the ways urban conditions affected (and were affected) by global political and economic change, and the ways in which urban settings determined human behavior. In western nations in particular, social theorists and artists more often than not agreed that urban civilization undermined moral values and weakened social ties. For example, the deadening images of Victorian coketowns as described by Charles Dickens in *Hard Times* (1854) were matched in English literature by the social, economic, and political analyses of urban conditions by Freidrich Engels in the *Condition of the Working Class* (1845) and Alexis de Tocqueville's *Journeys to England and Ireland* (1835). Moreover, the wealth and weight of documentary evidence and parliamentary discussion concerning appalling child labor and factory conditions set the ground for widespread public concern and, in time, sweeping legislation. Similarly, Baron Hausmann's mid-century destruction and rebuilding of Napoleon III's Paris produced heated cultural and political debate, while in America the creeping threat of the European factory system was watched closely even as the social experiments by Lowell and Waltham claimed to offer alternatives to the degradation of urban life. By the turn of the century the image of the city in America and Europe had not improved much. Lincoln Steffens' *The Shame of Cities* (1904) warned of the continued evils embedded in the political power structures and money economies of American cities, while Charles Booth's *Life and Labour of the People in London* (1902) chronicled the miserable conditions of the under-classes in England.

Although outraged liberals and conservatives continued to rail against the evils of urban life with good reason, during the nineteenth century the inertia of an essentially mercantilist economic world-view still governed the terms and conditions of the capitalist city. Victorian intellectuals held fast to the idea that the traits associated with the city could be related in one way or another to society as an enclosed marketplace in which individuals or groups struggled with each other for economic gain. This closed system of competing forces that generated the social conditions of the times was commonly regarded as a shared idea; consequently, useful knowledge could be gained in discovering the good and evil of the controlling mechanism.[113] Such a mechanical conception of a market economy generating urban social conditions governed much of the work of social philosophers and theorists alike well into the early decades of the twentieth century. But a hypostatized idea of society was too simple, and reduced away the complexity of urban experience. In time, therefore, social theorists invariably moved away from challenging the rightness or wrongness of the mechanical idea of the market in favor of a theory of society that attempted to show how the economic life of the city was related to noneconomic conditions.

The modern city made possible what Walter Pater called "the quickened, multiplied consciousness," but as artists discovered the creation of this super-sensual urban consciousness was bought at a terrible price: alienation. Pater of course was not the first person to remark on the root causes of urban estrangement. With the publication of *The Girl with the Golden Eyes* (1835), Honoré de Balzac declared himself the historian of Paris, a city swimming in the wreck of empire and revolution. Classifying the French capital into social and economic categories, Balzac excavated five classes (or what he variously terms "spheres" and "circles") as a means of ordering the urban mass of the city. The categories he chose to record the life of the city comprised the proletariat, the lower bourgeoisie, the upper or professional bourgeoisie, the world of artists, and the aristocracy. Prefiguring naturalist conceptions of the modern city as a diseased organism, *The Girl with the Golden Eyes* presents Paris as a "cadaverous physiognomy" and, dividing the city into two ages of man—"youth and decrepitude"—poses one central question: "What are they [Parisians] striving for? Gold, or Pleasure?"[114] Like modernist indictments of the city, Balzac's Parisian *comédie humaine* asserted a "moral point of view"[115] in keeping with the city as a betrayal of human potential; as a consequence, he felt it was his responsibility as both an artist and a historian to expose the city.

In writing *Dubliners*, Joyce, like Balzac before him, examined the corruption of society, but modified his investigation so as lend to his vision of the city the objectivity of a social scientist coupled with the cold art of another betrayer of social mores, the dramatist Henrik Ibsen. As an undergraduate student, Joyce had praised Ibsen's "mind of sincere and boylike bravery, of disillusioned pride, of minute and willful energy" in the essay "Drama and Life."[116] In particular, it was Ibsen's impersonal manner and uncompromising attack on the tenets of nineteenth-century Western civilization that most attracted the disaffected young Irishman. In *Stephen Hero*, Joyce once again acknowledges the simultaneous meeting of minds between the Celtic novelist and the Norse poet, a conjunction which allows Joyce to define his own method of investigation as "vivisective": "The modern spirit is vivisective. Vivisection itself is the most modern process one can conceive."[117] The spirit of vivisection implied a comprehensive examination of all levels of society, that nothing which life presents should be rejected, but rather that it should be recorded in the most disinterested terms possible.

And yet while it has been argued that, "to the artist fell the duty of striking off the mask in order to show modern man his true face,"[118] social theorists writing on the city since the mid-nineteenth century argued that they too played a prominent role in attempting to identify and explain the origins and tendency of what was "new" in Western culture. Indeed, the conclusions reached by social investigators such as Karl Marx, Max Weber, Georg Simmel, Robert Redfield, and Robert Park have furnished classic generalizations for artists, theoreticians and urban investigators alike. Marshall Berman, for example, maintains that Marx was "the first and greatest of modernists,"[119] and the *Communist Manifesto* (1848) "the archetype of a century of modernist manifestoes and movements to come."[120] Marx's 1848 theory of political economy, co-authored with Friedrich Engels, identified three dimensions of modernity grounded in the sphere of circulation and exchange of commodities: the revolutionary destruction of the past; the ever-new destruction of the present; and, the ever-same reproduction of the commodity form as a barrier to a quantitatively different future.[121] At the heart of Marx's historical configuration of capitalism as a bourgeois epoch unlike all earlier forms lay the commodity form: the symbol of social relations of modernity and a central source of their origin. However, as Marx later argued, rather than people being forced to face with sober senses their real conditions and social relations, capitalist production in fact transformed these same conditions and relations into a fetishized world of commodities in which all values were transitory and all relations fleeting and indifferent.[122]

In analogous terms, in the same way that Joyce's moral outrage in *Dubliners* isolates the imprisoning culture of Dublin as a function of urban paralysis, so Marx's *Economic and Philosophic Manuscripts* (1844) locates the tragedy of modernity in the dehumanized objects and subjects of capitalist society. For Marx as much as Joyce, a deadening sense of paralysis lay at the heart of modern life. Summing up the core account of the alienation and dehumanization of the worker in capitalist relationships of production (commodity fetishism), Marx concluded: "The worker puts his life into the object; but now his life no longer belongs to him but to the object."[123] Moreover, while for Marx earlier forms of society and their social relations were simpler (transparent), under capitalism the money form concealed the products and the social character of private labor and the social relations among individual workers by making those relations appear as relations between material objects instead of revealing them plainly. When Marx and Engels wrote the *Manifesto*, the latter had already studied English industry firsthand in *The Condition of the Working Class in England*, while Marx had moved his focus of study to economic cycles. However, in setting out a party platform, the *Manifesto* calls for social reforms that would have problematic consequences; for example, "the gradual abolition of the distinction between town and country by a more equitable distribution of the population over the country."[124] In the final analysis, while Marx believed that the capitalist system was doomed to failure and the victory of the proletariat inevitable, modernity continued to remain hidden to its participants in the "bewitched, distorted and upside-down world haunted by Monsieur Le Capital and Madame La Terre."[125]

Marx's contemporary, Ferdinand Tonnies, also attempted to come to terms with the implications and possibilities of modern urban existence in his thesis *Gemeinschaft* (community) and *Gesellschaft* (society). Tonnies' categories focus on the ways in which individuals lived together in terms of social relationships, a reciprocal phenomenon comprising "expressions of wills and their forces,"[126] and were intended to classify the different forms this force field produced in and through the relationship of these wills. According to Tonnies, "the relationship itself, and also the resulting association, is conceived either as real and organic [*Gemeinschaft*], or as imaginary and mechanical [*Gesellschaft*]."[127] Despite the consequences of *Gesellschaft* for the modern world, however, for Tonnies the relationship between *Gemeinschaft* (the rural world, and real) and *Gesellschaft* (the urban environment, and imaginary and/or conceptually mechanical) was an ambivalent one. Simply put, Tonnies' work does not privilege the myth of a pastoral idyll over the life of the city; rather, his intellectual system tries "to understand how it might be possible to provide some certainty for the individuals whose lot it is to live in the unbounded and inherently reflexive milieu of the city."[128]

However, if, as Baudelaire's concept of *modernité* pronounced, modernity constituted the new, fleeting and fortuitous moments of existence, then social investigators did attempt to delineate that which was new in society but largely failed to analyze the conditions under which individuals experienced this same newness of existence within the boundaries of the city. For Tonnies, Emile Durkheim, and Max Weber the origins of modernity are located in the transition from organic to mechanical society, a shift in which people operate as individuals, on the basis of self-interest, with each person seeking to profit from interaction. Tonnies' work today appears rather simplistic, what with its descriptive statements as opposed to theoretical speculations. More importantly, the dominant motive of self-interest that guarantees individual isolation denies the possibility of a private sphere in which to cultivate meaningful social ties.

By extension Durkheim's classic formulation *The Division of Labor in Society* (1893), in which he contrasts mechanical and organic solidarity further reinforced Tonnies' binary formulation. For Durkheim, rural life was characterized by a unity of values, as the members of every peasant household experienced more or less the same cycles of existence during the course of their lives. As a result of this shared sense of existence, there was a unity of ideas expressed in a collective consciousness. Unlike the country, the city could not provide conditions conducive to a similar state of being, because dense population coupled with occupational specialization rendered social unity obsolete. In addition, functional interdependence dictated a debilitating state of dependence based on economic terms as opposed to kinship on a social, cultural or religious level.

Marx of course was not alone in his concern for a world veiled in mystifications and illusions. Friedrich Nietzsche's critique of modernity as outlined in *Beyond Good and Evil* (1886) castigated the decadence of contemporary society, with its false truths, empty historicism, and eternal recurrence of the ever-same.[129] In particular, Nietszche argued that when the modern philosopher contemplated modern culture in the form of the haste and hurry now universal, of the increasing velocity of life, of the cessation of all contemplativeness and simplicity, he almost thinks that what he is seeing are the symptoms of a total extermination and uprooting of culture. The waters of religion are ebbing away and leaving behind swamps or stagnant pools; the nations are again drawing away from one another in the most hostile fashion and long to tear one another to pieces. The sciences, pursued without any restraint and in a spirit of the blindest *laissez-faire*, are shattering and dissolving all firmly held belief; the educated classes and estates are being swept along by a hugely contemptible money economy. The world has never been more worldly, never poorer in love and goodness [. . .] Everything, contemporary art and science included, serves the coming barbarism. The cultured man has degenerated to the greatest enemy of culture, for he wants lyingly to deny the existence of the universal sickness and thus obstruct the physicians.[130]

Much like Joyce's biological theory of Irish history as a form of hemiplegia, Nietzsche's analysis was rooted in the conception of modern culture as an infected entity. Nietzsche, however, shunned the value of sociological theory on the grounds that it was an "illusory science;"[131] sociology, he believed, misunderstood its object of study and was itself symptomatic of the effects of decadence. By the same token modern art constituted both threat and promise. Nietzsche in particular vilified art's passive reflection and expression of the "hurried and over-excited worldliness" of modern life, "untiring in the constant change in excitements and titillations, as it were, the spice shop of the whole West and East, equipped for any taste [. . .] regardless of whether someone exhibits good or bad 'taste' within it."[132] But even as Nietzsche looked to philosophy and religion as an antidote, in *The Will to Power* he nonetheless suggested that art could serve as a counter-movement to the decadence of the times rather than existing merely as an escape from the sickness of the times.

While there is no clear relationship connecting Joyce, Marx, and Nietzsche, Stephen's Dedalus' famous pronouncement, "History [. . .] is a nightmare from which I am trying to awake,"[133] is resonant of Marx's view of history as "the tradition of all the dead generations that weighs like a nightmare on the brain of the living"[134] as well as Nietzsche's critique of the "malady of history."[135] Joyce, for his part, was concerned with how the novelist could imagine through art the potentiality of humankind, and in doing so transcend the confines of history and culture. Indeed, as Leopold Bloom reveals, the oppressive diachronic reality of Irish history is counterbalanced by his synchronic, timeless imagination, which gives *Ulysses* its universal historiographic weight. Like Joyce, whose fiction transforms the detritus of everyday life into dramatic art, Nietzsche affirmed the ability of history to take "a familiar, perhaps commonplace theme, an everyday melody, and composing inspired variations on it, enhanc[e] it, elevating it to a comprehensive symbol, and thus disclos[e] in the original theme a whole world of profundity, power and beauty."[136]

It has been argued that Joyce modified for his own purposes the concerns of late nineteenth-century realism and literary naturalism with the paradigm shift of contemporary human history from an agrarian lifeworld to an urban one.[137] In effect, Joyce, like Zola, Chekov, Ibsen, Hauptmann, and D'Annunzio, was "trying to do in literary terms what Marx and Engels had done in economic terms and Lenin would do in political terms, that is, attempting to come to terms with the land question, the displacement of a peasant class, the entrapment of a commercial class in a new kind of city controlled by money and commodity relationships."[138] While social science has undoubtedly enriched our understanding of the topos of the urban environment and its developing economic and political economy, the enduring legacy of Joyce's moral history of Ireland presents us with an unsurpassed paradox. On the one hand, Joyce's fiction focuses on a unique geographical locale that to all intents and purposes existed as a marginal field of study for both theorists and artists. At the same time, Joyce's Dublin and its inhabitants speak in universal terms to the sea-change in human consciousness brought about by the expanding city, the city as labyrinth, and the city seemingly beyond the scale of human comprehension.[139] Joyce's city fiction examines the dangers and possibilities of an urban polity and culture, and in doing so initiates new and enduring conversations between the present and the past about the future of the city.

Visions of the Modern City

In his major two-volume philosophy of history, *The Decline of the West* (1918–1922), German social theorist and philosopher Oswald Spengler claimed that the philosophical historian was uniquely placed to detail the past and thus best qualified to predict the shape and development of the future. Building on the claim that cultures have a functional life-cycle, Spengler contended that the West-European-American civilization of the twentieth century had reached its phase of creative fulfillment and, consequently, was now faced with a period of debilitating decline. Having based his diagnosis on a survey of eight high cultural histories (Egyptian, Sumero-Babylonian, Greco-Roman, Indian, Chinese, Maya-Aztec, and West European), Spengler reasoned further that a crucial moment arose in each of these civilizations when the intellectual faculties of man gained supremacy over the instinctual. Western and non-Western cultures alike thus formulated a "folk spirit" in their early agrarian phases, a spirit that gave the culture its particular identity. However, the growth of the massive city gradually obliterated this cultural character by encouraging in its inhabitants a sense of individuality and separateness. According to this cyclical paradigm, although mutually incomprehensible to one another, civilizations in time gained supremacy over the country, a move that subsequently engendered a period of enlightened creativity. But this cultural turn typically ended in exhaustion and mechanical repetition, confusion, and dissolution. In broad structural terms this intra-cultural relationship gave all cities a sense of sameness despite their different cultural roots. More importantly, in all cases this cultural sameness signified sickness and imminent collapse.

In its fullest sense, *The Decline of the West* constitutes a totalizing theory: the rise and fall of urban civilization has a clear pattern predicated on the principle of birth, growth, and decay. Yet Spengler's thesis has not only been roundly dismissed as the product of a cultural pessimist, but has also been termed "a metaphor without a process," and a flaccid generalization "without a clear idea of the steps by which a large city could install separatism and isolated individualism in the place of common cultural character."[140] Spengler's hypothesis is certainly as intriguing as it is irritating: "becoming and declining are two aspects of one and the same organic process: the full measure of life can only be discovered when decline and decay are perceived and assessed as clearly as beginning and becoming."[141] With this theory in mind, Spengler contended that cultures follow essentially parallel courses, with each culture transforming itself in accordance with its own guiding and sustaining ideas. Moreover, Spengler argued that his premise held for all stages of evolution, including those marked by decline. In all cases, Spengler concluded, cities of a certain size corrupted their inhabitants by over-institutionalizing the processes of human interchange, making them routine and unemotional. Casting a cold eye over the cities of his own time, he identified the mechanization of intellectual activities, the meaningless of all forms of political life, the rise of cosmopolitan metropoli and their rootless masses, and the advent of a second rather primitive religiosity as indicators that the time of the city was fast approaching its manifest end.

From the Roman historian Polybius onwards cyclical accounts of history in which the city figures in some way as a symbol of growth or decline have deep roots in Western culture. Following Spengler, American social historian Lewis Mumford similarly argued that the modern city was fast becoming a necropolis of its own making. Of the sprawling gigantism of western cities of his own time, Mumford wrote,

> As the eye stretches towards the hazy periphery one can pick out no definite shapes [. . .] one beholds rather a continuous shapeless mass [. . .] the shapelessness of the whole is reflected in the individual part, and the nearer the center, the less [. . .] can the smaller parts be distinguished. [. . .] The city has absorbed villages and little towns, reducing them to place names. [. . .] It has [. .] enveloped those urban areas in its physical organization and built up the open land that once served to ensure their identity and integrity [. . .] [Then] as one moves away from the center, the urban growth becomes ever more aimless and discontinuous, more diffuse and unfocused. [. . .] Old neighborhoods and precincts, the social cells of the city, still maintaining some measure of the village pattern, become vestigial. No human eye can take in this metropolitan mass at a glance.[142]

Echoing Spengler's diagnosis, Mumford's organic metaphor isolates the process of urban decay as a formless growth emanating from a cancerous core. Mumford's vision of ruin and decline is particularly interesting in that it not only recuperates Spengler's pronouncement on the city but also anticipates Frederic Jameson's later deconstructionist analysis (though in less misanthropic terms) of the post-industrial city: the "non-place urban realm"—a centerless suburban web in which it is impossible to orient oneself within an endemic flatness of identity.[143]

Placing the pre-ordained fate of the city within a global cultural and historical context, *The Decline of the West* is still more significant when read alongside modernist art's privileging of the modern city. In Spengler's words, "the real criterion of world-history that differentiates it with utter sharpness from man's history is that world-history is the history of civic man."[144] While for Spengler "the birth of the City"[145] entailed its ultimate death, the philosophical historian's measured denunciation of (and fascination with) the metropolis is symptomatic of the larger totality of modernism's obsession with the city, especially the plight of the urban individual. Certainly, as the mass of modernist literature affirms, "the experience of modernity in Europe and America is often described in schismatic images of a traumatic discontinuity between past and present, rooted in a series of technological, social, cultural, and historical transformations, and generating a chasm of incoherence and ambiguity."[146] Yet much of the crisis rhetoric of modernist art is equally matched by the artistry and imagination with which practitioners and commentators embraced and contested the city in multiple mediums in ways never before achieved. Twentieth-century urban consciousness demanded—and generated—new art forms and modes of expression, but it was in the novel and in poetry in particular that artists most completely attempted to represent the drama and intellectual contours of metropolitan life. As Spengler astutely notes, "the great Epic, which speaks and sings of the blood, belongs to *Pfalz* and *Burg*, but the Drama, in which *awakened* life tests itself, is city-poetry, and the great Novel, the survey of all things human by the emancipated intellect, presupposes the world-city."[147]

Dos Passos was one such artist who attempted to negotiate his own fascination-repulsion relationship with New York as a symbol of modern urban history. In chronicling the life of New York-as-civilization, Dos Passos' pronouncements on the fate of the city rest on both a synchronic and diachronic historical sense that aimed to "create characters first and foremost, and then to set them in the snarl of the human currents of their time, so that there results an accurate permanent record of history."[148] As he noted in "Statement of Belief," "the only excuse for a novelist [. . .] is a sort of second-class historian of the age he lives in. The 'reality' he misses by writing about imaginary people, he gains by being able to build a reality more out of his own factual experience than a plain historian or biographer can."[149]

Yet as the social and cultural impact of *Manhattan Transfer* and the trilogy *U.S.A.* reveal, Dos Passos' intentions for his best work enabled him to achieve "the occupation of a special kind of writer": a political writer.[150] "Using blocks of raw experience," Dos Passos' fiction consequently embodies the paradoxical thesis that the political writer "should be both engaged and disengaged. He must have passion and concern and anger—but he must keep his emotions at arm's length in his work. If he doesn't he's simply a propagandist, and what he offers is a 'preachment.'"[151] Central to Dos Passos' synoptic (and, at times impersonal) history of American society is New York as the point of convergence for a larger theory of civilization; moreover, stretching back into classical history and out into infinity, Dos Passos' metropolis carries a large load, for unlike Spengler's vision of the city "the *U.S.A.* narratives were never supposed to end."[152]

In representing the urban reality of Manhattan within the confines of an experimental narrative, Dos Passos isolates the soul of American culture by revealing—or approximating—the material reality of the American city so as to capture and record the fleeting moments of modernity. As Sharon Spencer notes in her analysis of the modern novel, the "new" or "modern" novel constructed a more complex perspective on space and time, replacing traditional narrative modes with an "architectonic" structure.[153] This mode of experimental writing, which attempted to approximate a valid representation of the way in which we perceive reality, foregrounded a heightened awareness of structure and language in the form of montage as a way of synthesizing simultaneity of action and prominence of structure. According to Spencer's definition,

> although, like many modern novels, the architectonic novel manifests an avoidance of character developed for its intrinsic interest, its essential feature is neither thematic nor stylistic, but structural. Its goal is the evocation of the illusion of a spatial entity, either representational or abstract, constructed from prose fragments of diverse types and lengths and arranged by means of the principle of juxtaposition so as to include a comprehensive view of the book's subject. The "truth" of the total vision of such a novel is a composite truth obtained from the reader's apprehension of a great many relationships among the fragments that make up the book's totality.[154]

In keeping with Spencer's interpretation of the architectonic novel, *Manhattan Transfer* underscores the declaration that in the twentieth century "the city is both massive fact and universally recognizable symbol of modernity, and it both constitutes and symbolizes the modern predicament."[155]

Unlike the village or town, which for Spengler were merely "centers of landscape," the "new Soul of the City speaks a new language, which soon comes to be tantamount to the language of the Culture itself," for it is exclusively "the city's destiny and the life-experience of urban man that speaks to the eye in the logic of visible forms."[156] Much like Spengler's city, the spatial world of *Manhattan Transfer* provides for both containment as well as the possibility of simultaneity. New York, a city-as-culture is given shape in the structure of the city's streets, thoroughfares, bridges, sidewalks, and neighborhoods, which together impose dichotomies between ethnicities and classes of people. The city is thus both a geographic locale as well as psychic location, the center of an American landscape.[157] Organic structure gives way to a new vocabulary of the senses contained within an architectonic form. But at the center of this landscape lies an elusive and threatening city of "signs." Of course the valency of Dos Passos' logic of visual form is compounded by the novel's radical questioning of the notion of an ordered urban space (as a function of civilized order), indeed the idea of an attainable "center." As one character notes, "the terrible thing about having New York go stale on you is that there's nowhere else. It's the top of the world" (*MT* 220).

The novel begins with various "arrivals" in this city of signs: "the center of things" (*MT* 4). The opening vignette in particular describes immigrants disembarking at Ellis Island: "Gates fold upwards, feet step out across the crack, men and women press through the manuresmelling wooden tunnel of the ferry house, crushed and jostling like apples fed down a chute into a press" (*MT* 3). Ellen Thatcher is conceived and born in the midst of such arrivals, while Bud Korpenning, fleeing the country, arrives in New York with dreams of a better tomorrow. "How do I get to Broadway?" Bud asks. "I want to get to the center of things." "Walk east and turn down Broadway," comes the reply, "and you'll find the center of things if you walk far enough" (*MT* 4). Unlike Ellen, whose trajectory from chorus girl to magazine editor of *Manners* constitutes an urban "success" story, Bud's "tragicomic quest for transcendence"[158] ends in suicide in the East River. Forever asking, "Is that kinder the center of things (*MT* 25), Bud mistakenly believes that he too can share in the myth of New York if he can just "git more into the center of things" (*MT* 24).[159]

In the same way that Dos Passos' novel approximates the space of Manhattan, the synoptic structure of *Ulysses* is famously grounded in the geographical locale of Dublin, defining the spatial world and boundaries of the text in relation to Joyce's own physical and mental relationship with the city. Yet while contiguity defines much of the form of Dos Passos' novel (for example, in the experience, say of James Merivale's monied experience of New York versus Anna Cohen's frustrated working-class existence), Joyce's text, which also utilizes multiple perspectives, uses the movement of characters to create a sense of continuity that links contrasting aspects of urban life.

This structuring principle, which takes precedence over any one single image, is of central importance throughout the novel in that it links oppositions (for example, Bloom's journey from Paddy Dignam's funeral in "Hades" to the birth of Mrs. Purefoy's son in "Oxen of the Sun"). Given that *Ulysses* creates a meaningful form of synthesis in the face of urban multiplicity, it is Joyce, ultimately, who most fully challenges Spengler's dire prognosis of the moment of urban culture's "waking-consciousness,"[160] "Intellect," "Geist," or "ésprit," according to Spengler, were the specific urban forms of the understanding waking-consciousness, and marked the moment of attunement when a civilization turned away from the land, becoming a world unto itself as it moved toward its ultimate death. For Spengler this intellectual spirit (the new urban individual), like the stone mass of the city itself, was short-lived: "the free intellect—fateful word!—appears like a flame, mounts splendid into the air, and pitiably dies."[161] Unlike Dos Passos, the totality of Joyce's urban fiction reconciles through art the intellectual spirit of the artist with the idea of the city, and in the process makes them both live.

As we know, Joyce had written *Dubliners* as a chapter of the moral history of Ireland, and had chosen Dublin for that scene as the center of Irish cultural and social paralysis. In *Portrait*, Joyce returned to his native city, but with the cold promise to "forge the uncreated conscience of my race" (*P* 221) by way of exile for his artist-hero, Stephen Dedalus. A succeeding chapter of moral history came into being with *Ulysses*, but this time Joyce declared he wanted "to give the colour and tone of Dublin with my words; the drab yet glistening atmosphere of Dublin, its hallucinatory vapours, its tattered confusion, the atmosphere of its bars, its social immobility."[162] Obsessed with the fate of the individual caught in the flux of history, Joyce took upon himself the lifelong responsibility of insulting rather than flattering national vanity, of shocking his compatriots into a deeper awareness of their self-deceptions. Whereas Dos Passos constructed his vision of the American city within the geographical confines of Greater New York, Joyce declared open war on the social order of Dublin as a synecdoche for Irish history by way of exile. But as a chronicler of everyday life Joyce constantly gravitated toward his native city, immersing his imagination in the streets, homes, and institutions of Dublin. By getting to the heart of Dublin as a city in history, Joyce believed he could "get to the heart of all the cities of the world."[163]

Dublin, in keeping with Joyce's polytropic conceptual framework, is a synthesis of multiple urban visions: the capital of Ireland; a symbol for all capital cities of Europe (Vienna, Paris, London, Berlin, and Rome); a figure for Odysseus's travels; and, as Leopold Bloom acknowledges, a mythical evocation of the corrupted 'sacred' cities of the past: "the cities of the plain: Sodom, Gomorrah, Edom. All dead names" (*U* 50). But Dublin is more: the prototype of the modern city, Joyce's metropolis is an expression of the radical order of postcolonial Irish life under the political, social, religious, and economic yoke of two masters: "a crazy queen, old and jealous" in the form of the imperial British state, and an Italian, "the holy Roman catholic and apostolic church" (*U* 17). In writing "The Sisters" as the first installment of *Dubliners*, Joyce outlined his intent to betray the soul of the city that was to become the universal city of his work. However, it is Joyce's paradoxical artistic credo as it appears in the early essay "Drama and Life" (1900) that best speaks to Joyce's relationship to Dublin. In the course of adumbrating the major differences between literature and drama before an adamant audience of fellow University students and faculty, Joyce announced: "Still I think out of the dreary sameness of existence, a measure of dramatic life may be drawn. Even the most commonplace, the deadest among the living, may play a part in a great drama."[164] In *Ulysses*, we experience once again Joyce as the "solitary artist immersing himself in and resurrecting from the ordinary, the everyday, the dramatic, the eternal, and its transmutation into poetic prose."[165]

The phases or epochs of history that Joyce and Dos Passos document are at one and the same time expansive and minute. *Ulysses* ostensibly revolves about a day in the life—16 June 1904—of an Irish Jew named Leopold Bloom, a canvasser for the *Freeman* newspaper. During the course of this day we experience the pedestrian details of a super-realistic city Bloom sees and feels around him in his epicyclic odyssey across the face and into the heart of Dublin; his encounters with a spectacular cross-section of the city's middle- to lower-class inhabitants; and, more particularly, Bloom's touching guardianship of the exiled artist returned, Stephen Dedalus. Unlike *Ulysses*, which is the penultimate chapter of Joyce's moral history of Dublin, *Manhattan Transfer* is the opening chapter of Dos Passos' natural history of urban America. Set on a spit of land thrust seaward, the synoptic novel encompasses the first twenty-five years of New York's history in the twentieth-century. As we enter the novel, New York of the gaslight era is being transformed by the Greater New York Bill (1898), immigrants are pouring in from rural districts and from Europe, and real estate developers are carving up the city and its environs. Dos Passos' New York most fully approximates Spengler's "Late City" come to fruition; the exploding silhouette of Manhattan contradicts nature and defies the land, a "city-as-world" suffering nothing beside itself.[166] As Dos Passos intends, the experience of modernity that is New York is as phantasmagoric as it is beautiful: the city overwhelms and kills minor characters culled from the heterogeneous urban lexicon, as it does in the case of Bud Korpenning and Stan Emery, sometimes paralyzes them spiritually as it does Ellen Thatcher, or drives them out, as it does the newspaper man and failed artist, Jimmy Herf.

As both Joyce and Dos Passos were aware, the vision of the myth-maker is synchronic, the artist creating archetypal characters who exist in timeless worlds and complete ever recyclable actions. By contrast, the historian's vision is diachronic, recording more than creating human existence through the (dis)continuity of temporal sequence. In *Manhattan Transfer* the human (historical) index of New York is the experience of public space— Broadway, Brooklyn Bridge, Lincoln Square, and Columbus Circle.[167] In broader terms, however, the tension this structure invariably set up between the synchronic and the diachronic poles of the novel constitutes a symbolic field of reference. Manhattan thus becomes a metaphor for an intangible "center of things," moving between what Roland Barthes terms "extreme iconographies": street and skyscraper.[168] The co-presence of these multiple temporal and iconographic levels within the space of Manhattan remains central to our understanding of the novel. From the perspective of urban history, New York occupies the site of a former agrarian economy that has been progressively annihilated by the material expansion of the city. At the same time, the proximity of the city's rural past resurfaces at key moments, for example, the finding of a ram's horns at the site of a real estate development on the outskirts of the city, to which a city dweller exclaims, "By Gad! That must have been a fine ram" (*MT* 15). Toward the center of things in Manhattan, meanwhile, between building lots, stands a derelict farmhouse: "At a corner the rickety half of a weatherboarded farmhouse was still standing. There was half a room with blueflowered paper eaten by brown stains on the walls, a smoked fireplace, a shattered builtin cupboard, and an iron bedstead bent double" (*MT* 42).

The mythic idea of Manhattan, which runs counter to the city's diachronic realities, is sustained by a longitudinal view; consequently, this reading of the metropolis situates the consciousness of the city within the context of a transhistorical continuum. Dos Passos openly groused to Jack Lawson at one point that New York seemed like a "badly drawn cartoon," a kind of "Babylon gone mad."[169] But to Germaine Lucas-Championiere, however, he revealed a more ambiguous sense of his relationship to the city when he remarked,

> New York—after all—is magnificent, a city of cavedwellers, with a frightful, brutal ugliness about it, full of thunderous voices of metal grinding on metal and of an eternal sound of wheels which turn, turn on heavy stones. People swarm meekly like ants along designated routes, crushed by the disdainful and pitiless things around them.[170]

In many ways, New York appeared for Dos Passos as it did for contemporary artists such as Georgia O' Keefe, Hugh Ferriss, Joseph Stella, and Louis Lozowick—an immense panorama full of shadows and industrial imagery, but also a vital metropolis. Inspired by the sensate historicity of this machine-age Babylon, Dos Passos ruminated further in the style of *Manhattan Transfer* that that New York reminded him of such ancient cities as

> Nineveh and Babylon, of Ur of the Chaldees, of the immense cities which loom like basilisks behind the horizon in ancient Jewish tales, where the temples rose as high as mountains and people ran trembling through dirty little alleys to the constant noise of whips with hilts of gold. O for the sound of a brazen trumpet which, like the voice of the Baptist in the desert, will sing again about the immensity of man in this nothingness of iron, steel, marble and rock. Night time especially is both marvelous and

appalling, seen from the height of a Roof Garden, where women with rau-
cous voices dance in an amber light, the bluegray bulk of the city cut up
by the enormous arabesques of electric billboards, when the streets where
automobiles scurry about like cockroaches are lost is a golden dust, and
when a pathetic little moon, pale and dazzled, looks at you across a
leaden sky.[171]

In *Manhattan Transfer*, Dos Passos juxtaposes these historic (diachronic)
and mythic (synchronic) aspects of New York as a city *in* history, setting
both on an immanent collision course. As a structuring principle, this technique creates both a terrifying and fascinating vision of beauty in which
the palindromic conception of New York, a city created according to the
dicta of a new epoch, is inexorably linked to the fate of mythical cities of
the past:

> There were Babylon and Nineveh; they were built of brick. Athens was
> gold marble columns. Rome was held up on broad arches of rubble. In
> Constantinople the minarets flame like great candles round the Golden
> Horn. [. . .] Steel, glass, tile, concrete will be the material of the skyscrap-
> ers. Crammed on the narrow island of the million-windowed buildings
> will jut glittering, pyramid on pyramid like the white cloudhead above a
> thunderstorm. (*MT* 12)

While the vertical thrust of the Manhattan skyline announced that the new
theater of modern life was the protean life of cities, Dos Passos' vision of
the city as both image and event more often than not betrays the experience of modernity as a destructive terminal force. Indeed, if the prose-poetic titles of the opening chapters—"Ferryslip," "Metropolis," and
"Dollars"—are the glittering conduits by which we begin our mental voyage to the center of things, then the closing chapters of the Third Section of
the novel— "Nickelodeon," "Revolving Doors," "Skyscraper," "Rejoicing
City That Dwelt Carelessly," and "The Burthen of Nineveh"—are the final
stages of an increasingly dark journey toward a rotten core: Manhattan as
the betrayal of John Winthrop's shining city on a hill.

Sailing into New York Harbor by steamship on the Fourth of July,
young Jimmy Herf and his cancer-ridden mother are presented with an
image of Bunyan's celestial city gone awry. In the shadow of the Statue of
Liberty (for Jimmy's mother, "Liberty enlightening the world," but for
Jimmy merely "a tall green woman in a dressing gown standing on an island holding up her hand" [*MT* 69]), we are presented with Veblenesque
image of material consumption. The river lies choked with the detritus of
material consumption: "Streak of water crusted with splinters, grocery-
boxes, orangepeel, cabbage leaves, narrowing, narrowing between the boat
and the dock." Within the city itself, the streets, "swirling with dust [. . .]
brick streets soursmelling," (*MT* 189) threaten Ellen Thatcher with the
thought of the burgeoning mass of immigrants fresh from Ellis Island,

"spreading in dark slow crouching masses like corruption oozing from broken sewers, like a mob" (*MT* 192).

Given that the events of *Manhattan Transfer* are symptomatic of the political, social, economic, and cultural history of the United States during the first quarter of the century, Dos Passos' clinical sense of satire is at its sharpest in passages that play the iconoclastic symbols of American civic identity against prose-poetic symbols of urbanism. At the same time, the title *Manhattan Transfer*, which refers to the famous interchange train station connecting New York City and Jersey City, not only serves as a point of entry into the novel and the metropolis, but is also a foreshadowing of the endless transference of meaning and energy embodied within both the text and the urban space of Manhattan. Much of that energy manifests itself in evanescent moments. In particular, the beauty of Dos Passos' Manhattan lies mainly in its lights and colors—"glowing wormtrains"(*MT* 63), the river beneath the Brooklyn Bridge glimmering like the Milky Way above, or night crushing "bright milk out of arclights" (*MT* 83). Read as part of a larger cultural tradition, Dos Passos' river, like the city itself, thus dissolves into Whitman's "Crossing Brooklyn Ferry," which also argued that there were moments in the life of New York that contained perfection and furnished their part toward eternity.

Contrary to such possibilities, Lionel Trilling identified the "characteristic element" of modernist literature as "the bitter line of hostility to civilization which runs through it,"[172] while Monroe K. Spears noted that "for the moderns [. . .] the City is seen as falling [. . .] or as fallen [. . .] and therefore moving toward the infernal city."[173] In *The Waste Land*, Eliot's allusive strategy of juxtaposing the broken and sordid culture of contemporary London with Hebraic, Hellenic, early Christian, and renaissance cities (Jerusalem, Athens, Alexandria, Vienna, and London) represents the most famous example of the modernist desire for apocalyptic renewal. At one level, the theme of social and cultural hemiplegia expressed as an entropic vision of civilization is almost immediately apparent in the "Telemachus" episode of *Ulysses*, with Stephen's loud complaint that the Irish find themselves,"living in a bogswamp, eating cheap food and the streets paved with dust, horsedung and consumptives' spits" (*U* 12). Stephen's struggle with the burden of history intimates early on an apocalyptic desire when he exclaims, "I hear the ruin of all space, shattered glass and toppling masonry, and time one livid final flame" (*U* 20). Stephen's apocalyptic thoughts, however, become more forceful much later with the symbolic collision of time and space in "Circe": "Nothung! (He lifts his ashplant high with both hands and smashes the chandelier. Time's livid flame leaps and, in the following darkness, ruin of all space, shattered glass and toppling masonry)" (*U* 475).

Yet there is much that separates Joyce's vision of Dublin from the "bitter line" of modernist art. A humane sympathy for the life of Dubliners in the midst of an endemic sense of cultural apathy, rather, is our first experience of the city in *Ulysses*. As Bloom traverses the city, beginning with "Lotus Eaters" through the final rest of "Penelope," the centripetal force of his empathetic consciousness engages with the life of the city; indeed, his odyssey evokes and contains life-sustaining memories and desires as much as it chronicles the ambivalent and complex life-world of a metropolis. Bloom begins his journey into the life of the city with the surrender to the sober life of the Dublin's streets in "Lotus Eaters." "Aeolus," on the other hand, takes us into the heart of the commercial city proper, with an anatomical view of the "HEART OF THE HIBERNIAN METROPOLIS" (*U* 96), centered, like the chapter itself, around Nelson's pillar, symbol of Great Britain's enduring presence in Ireland. This is a tentacular, quantified, and mechanistic world with machines of all kinds—tramcars, mailcars, and printing presses—clanking away. But it is also a world which Bloom nevertheless attempts to understand above the noise of the *Freeman* presses when he says, "Everything speaks in its own way" (*U* 100).

In "Proteus," Stephen attempts to comprehend his own consciousness by sensing the world around him on Sandymount Strand in aural terms. But his conceptions of "the ineluctable modality of the audible"(*U* 31), the *Nacheinander*, and "the ineluctable modality of the visible," the *Nebeneinander*, suggest the conditions of his own struggle and imprisonment. Like the fate of souls such as Pyrrhus and Caesar whose belated histories he teaches to a classroom of "mirthless" (*U* 20) students in "Nestor," Stephen realizes that his own history exists only in potential in a land that is little more than a "pawnshop" (*U* 21) for its oppressed inhabitants. In spite of these antagonisms toward Dublin, the city remains an enigma, a stream of urban life of which Stephen finally concedes, "Dublin. I have much, much to learn" (*U* 119).

By contrast, Bloom's ability to negotiate and even reconcile himself with Dublin lies in the fact that he is able to synthesize in imaginative ways the relationship between the diachronic realities of Dublin with a sense of the city's synchronous meaning. In particular, Bloom's consciousness is guided by his comically confused notion of "parallax," the position of the fixed object in space and time, and the need to understand what, if anything, constitutes the center of existence in transhistoric and transcultural ways. It is this metaphor of flux and change that Bloom returns to obsessively throughout the novel in his attempts to fix time and the object in relation to past and present conditions. For example, in the "Calypso" episode Bloom, while looking at a German advertisement offering for sale shares in citrus groves in Palestine, suddenly contemplates how the mythical cities of the past were won over to secular ends and corrupted:

A cloud began to cover the sun slowly, wholly.
Grey. Far.
No, not like that. A barren land, bare waste. Vulcanic lake, the dead sea:
no fish, weedless, sunk deep in the earth. No wind could lift those waves,
grey metal, poisonous, foggy waters. Brimstone they called it raining

down: the cities of the plain: Sodom, Gomorrah, Edom. All dead names. A dead sea in a dead land, grey and old. Old now. It bore the oldest, the first race. A bent hag crossed from Cassidy's clutching a naggin bottle by the neck. The oldest people. Wandered far away over all the earth, captivity to captivity, multiplying, dying, being born everywhere. It lay there now. Now it could bear no more. Dead: an old woman's: the grey sunken cunt of the world. (*U* 50)

In the midst of Bloom's reverie the symbolic intrusion of the old woman reinforces the degraded culture and history of these ancient sites in symbolic terms, binding their fate to that of the Jewish diaspora. But Bloom's response to the sense of desolation engendered by his daydream and the rupturing image of the old woman is twofold. First, he declares his *credo* to life with his comical dismissal of the scene: "Well, I am here now. Yes, I am here now. Morning mouth bad images. Got up wrong side of the bed" (*U* 50). He then pronounces his *nego* to death by turning quickly to warmer thoughts of domestic life with Molly, his estranged *omphalos*: "To smell the gentle smoke of tea, fume of the pan, sizzling butter. Be near her ample bedwarmed flesh. Yes, yes" (*U* 50).

Moreover, in the same way that Bloom dismisses his own mortality in "Hades" following the burial of Paddy Dignam in Glasnevin cemetery with a curt, "Back to the world again. Enough of this place" (*U* 94), Joyce's everyman repeatedly attempts to resist the destruction of potential and of possibility by the forces of time and history. But in "Wandering Rocks" the unmasking of religious control, in the form of the paternal Fr. Conmee, and political control in the form of the viceregal cavalcade, reveals that resistance is perhaps not so easy a task. Though Bloom tries to shrug off an oppressed and oppressive Dublin, the threat remains that the city may well become just another "grey sunken cunt of the world," like the old hag, like the cities of the past.

Consonant with Joyce's own conceptual approach to history, which follows the Viconian-like progression of human evolution as a series of stages characterized by birth, maturity, death, and decay, *Ulysses* presents a vision of Dublin structured around the juxtaposition of historical conceptions of cities arranged in an unhistorical miscellany. As in the case of Bloom's reverie on Dorset Street in "Calypso," the heroic cities of the past are placed alongside a secular, commercial city of the present:

> Cityful passing away, other cityful coming, passing away too: other coming on, passing on. Houses, lines of houses, streets, miles of pavements, piledup bricks, stones. Changing hands. This owner, that. Landlord never dies they say. Other steps into his shoes when he gets his notice to quit. They buy the place up with gold and still they have all the gold. Swindle in it somewhere. Piled up in cities, worn away, age after age. Pyramids in sand. Built on bread and onions. Slaves Chinese wall. Babylon. Big stones left. Round towers. Rest rubble, sprawling suburbs, jerrybuilt. (*U* 135)

However, unlike Dos Passos' concentrated ambivalence toward New York, or Eliot's pessimistic lamentation over London, there is little room in Joyce's vision for the "ruin of space, shattered glass and toppling of masonry, and time one livid flame." For while neither Dos Passos nor his artist, Jimmy Herf could establish roots amid the choking undergrowth of the city from within, Joyce, by way of exile, concludes *Ulysses* with an affirmative "Yes" to the ambiguous nature of life within the city. If New York emerges as a point of transit and port of entry into the darkened soul of America, Dublin emerges as a platform to reconciliation.

Afterword

In the course of this book, I have suggested ways in which the representative fictions of Joyce and Dos Passos constitute a poetics of transatlantic urban modernism in which the rhetoric of the metropolis is transformed into a *Weltstadt*: a topos of the imagination where the city becomes the world. As a cultural sign, the modernist city is the essential ground of modern existence, the context of modern life an urban one, and modern consciousness an urban consciousness. At the same time, in the diaphonous intersection of the politics of locality with the legacies of cultural and historical myth, the assumptions and conceptual models employed by Joyce and Dos Passos serve dissimilar ends. Whereas Joyce offers us ultimately a humanely affirmative yet skeptical vision of the subjective moral history of Ireland, Dos Passos' naturalist history of America sets itself against society, presenting a more ambivalent conception of the individual within mass society.

When in 1904 George W. Russell (A. E.) urged Joyce write an innocuous piece for *The Irish Homestead*, it was with the intention that the young writer could easily write for money by way of playing to the common understandings, social mores, and cultural expectations of a provincial nation languishing on the margins of European culture. "The Sisters," however, while earning Joyce his one pound in payment, subverted the very expectations Russell admonished his fellow Dubliner to conform to, setting in motion a bold conception of modernity predicated on a biological theory of society. But the artistic progression from *Dubliners* to *Portrait* to *Ulysses* suggests that Joyce's mapping of the urban aggregate as symptomatic of an endemic paralysis produced in time a progressive amelioration of that original vision, indeed of Joyce's reconciliation with Dublin as a city in history.

In *My Brother's Keeper*, Stanislaus Joyce defines his brother's transcendent passion for a father, city, and nation as synonymous with "the comprehending love of an artist for his subject":

The two dominant passions of my brother's life were to be love of father and of fatherland. The latter was not the love of a patriot, which is an emotion for the market-place, part hatred of some other country, part falsehood. It was the comprehending love of an artist for his subject. Both passions stemmed, I believe, from his ancient love of God, and were already at that time spreading tough roots underground in a most unpropitious climate: love of his country, or rather of his city, that was to reject him and his work; love of his father, who was like a mill-stone round his neck. The roots of feeling in some men sink all the deeper for the difficulties that surround and frustrate them; and I wonder that people do not see how much higher than the divine love, which is the preacher's theme, is that human passion which can love an unworthy object utterly without return and forgive without waiting to be supplicated.[1]

For Stanislaus, the seed of his brother's relationship with Dublin, sown fast on the hard ground of family and nation, drove its roots down into the soil of a deeper, more spiritual and ancient passion for the land and people of his birth. Moreover, the life Stanislaus eulogizes here is the very existence Joyce chose for himself from the beginning: the artist as secular Christ who comes into the world not to create the city of God but to liberate the city of Man. However, while the desire for liberation manifests itself primarily in the chronicling of urban alienation, it is precisely the paradox of the self-exiled artist's warring love-hate relationship with Dublin that remains vital to our understanding of the importance of Joyce's modernist poetics

By contrast, Dos Passos never fully reconciled himself to New York's soul-destroying texture, a city that in his mind represented American history betrayed. But the paradoxical nature of Dos Passos' own vision of the city, like that of Joyce, is intrinsic to a larger understanding of his cultural project. In *Manhattan Transfer*, Dos Passos' romantic and entropic landscape constitutes an attempt to give back to industrial society a sense of its own cultural memory. But in the course of destabilizing outmoded nineteenth-century literary conventions to make way for a new language of modernity, the American cityscape is defined for the most part by the skein of life in the form of actions and surfaces as opposed to the psychological studies Joyce presents throughout his work. However, while *Manhattan Transfer* may well appear bitter at times, Dos Passos later defended the moral tenor of his vision as a function of its larger satirical purpose: "the satirist is so full of the possibilities of human kind in general that he tends to draw a dark and garish picture when he tries to depict people as they are at any particular moment."[2]

By way of a closing comment, I would like to consider two interrelated components that play a central part in the literary construction of Joyce's Dublin and Dos Passos' New York: the role of memory and the act of remembrance. While memory can be regarded as a faculty in the service of a structuring imagination, both memory and remembrance are, finally, indentured to a selective imagination. In particular, I would like to suggest that in reading Joyce and Dos Passos remembering Dublin and New York, from within and without the city as well as across time and space, three factors affect our reception of these texts as functions of memory. In the first instance, and perhaps rather obviously, memory is highly selective. As with a photograph, the text as a literary image can tell us as much—in both positive and negative terms—about what is inside the frame as much as it fails to tell us about what is outside. At the same time, memory is recon- structive. The nature of memory is such that it is not merely a passive re- production of past actualities but a reconstructive experience. A form of mental notation, therefore, memory enables us to convince ourselves of what, finally, *must* have occurred. In memory, experience also is encoded in order that it may later be retrieved. The reconstructive nature of mem- ory also leads us to perhaps another rather obvious conclusion: the act of memory is often contaminated. Memory, surely, reinstates the immediacy of emotions and experience. More importantly, memory, as far as the re- trieval process allows, reconstructs the context of the event and/or emotion related to that event as we remember it. The text, therefore, as a function of memory and as an act of remembrance, institutes a retrieval path that enables the reader to be "present" in the textual recall of history.

Moreover, unlike the organic nature of memory, the act of remembrance is a more "holistic" experience; not only do we re-experience the traces of memory in their different forms when we remember, but we are also able to relate those parts to a larger whole in terms of how we recover, recon- struct, and re-present the past. There is, of course, always more in remem- brance than we can ever tell (the "world" outside the frame); in addition, there is always far more attached to memory than can ever be assessed at one time. In the case of Joyce's and Dos Passos' respective reconstitutions of the past, their fictional representations function as both memory and as an acts of remembrance. These can never, of course, be fully recovered. And if we add one final factor to our contemplation, that is the issue of perspective, that is the point at which and from where these writers engage in retrieving the past, then the mechanics of representation and the chroni- cling history surely become even more complex.

What then can we say about the city and memory? I would like to pro- pose that the city *is* both memory and essential ground for modern life, and that when we read urban fictions we not only recover a sense of collective urban history, but also perceive more clearly our own relationship with the cities in which we live by way of imagination. In other words, we remem- ber (or even foreshadow) our own lives in symbolic ways that enrich our lives in the present. Representations of cities are not simply portraits of the past consigned to museums of the literary imagination. When Karl Marx questioned the possibility of the city ceasing to exist, he was predicting the eventual passing away of the capitalist state as it was embodied in the op- pressive nineteenth-century industrial metropolis. And while it may appear to many in our own time that the post-industrial city has exhausted its original function as the triumph of Reason over Nature, the city as a fundamental way of experiencing life is as present to us today as its demise, ironically, was Marx's hope for a more egalitarian future.

Notes

CHAPTER ONE NOTES

[1] "Saxa loquuntur!" Literally, "Stones Speak!" So Freud exclaimed in a lecture entitled "The Aetiology of Hysteria" (1896) before a congregation of Viennese medical colleagues. See *The Standard Edition of the Complete Psychological Works of Sigmund* Freud, ed. James Strachey (London: The Institute of Psycho-Analysis, The Hogarth Press, 1953–74) 3: 189.

[2] Freud returned to Rome in 1907, 1908, 1912, and 1923.

[3] Ernest Jones, *The Life and Work of Sigmund Freud*, 3 vols. (New York: Basic Books, Inc., 1953–57) 2: 19.

[4] Freud, Letter to Martha Freud, 3 September 1901, *Letters of Sigmund Freud*, trans. Tania and James Stern. 2nd. ed. (New York: Basic Books, 1975) 25.

[5] Freud, Letter to Wilhelm Fliess, 19 September 1901, *The Complete Letters of Sigmund Freud to Wilhelm Fliess*, ed. Jeffrey Masson (Cambridge, Mass.: Harvard UP, 1985) 46.

[6] According to John Paul Russo, "if in one sense Freud's Italy was its typical image in the mind of the civilized West (to which extent alone it would merit investigation), in another, more important sense, his 'Italy' presented intriguing problems in the phenomenon of the uncanny, the return of the repressed, the pleasure principle, and the death instinct. Freud's letters on Italy, his comments on Italian art, and his analysis of his 'deeply neurotic' obsession with Rome help explain the etiology of these problems." See Russo, "Freud and Italy," *Literature and Psychology* 36. 1–2 (1990) 1–25. 1.

[7] Freud, *The Standard Edition of the Complete Psychological Works of Sigmund Freud*, trans. James Strachey. 24 vols. (New York: Norton, 1995) 3: 336.

[8] Jones, 2: 392.

[9] Freud, Letter to Martha Freud, 16 September 1912, *Letters of Sigmund Freud*, 82.

[10] Peter Gay, *Freud: A Life for Our Time* (New York: W. W. Norton, 1975) 111.

[11] As Freud biographers Ernest Jones and Ronald W. Clark point out, theories regarding Freud's relationship with Rome are, to put it mildly, diverse. They include, as Clark notes, Freud's ambition to visit one of the great European capitals; a lifelong interest in the military career of Hannibal; and, an interest in the wonders of the ancient world, especially imperial and republican Rome. Some commentators even try to apply Freud's own theories to the case by arguing that repressed wishes can be the opposite of their manifestations. In other words, that Freud's dreams about the Pope, for example, expressed an idea to go to Rome to join the Roman Catholic Church in a Faust-like pact and thus advance himself in Vienna. See Ronald W. Clark, *Freud: The Man and the Cause* (New York: Random House, 1982) 201. Jones, meanwhile, dismisses such ideas from the garden of Freud criticism. The biographer contends that such theories are as preposterous as the idea that Freud's "agile habit of darting upstairs three at a time was an expression of is secret adoration of the Trinity!" (Jones 2: 17).

[12] Jones, 2: 16.

[13] Peter Gay, *Freud: A Life for Our Time*, 132.

[14] See *The Interpretation of Dreams* (1900), especially the dream "My son, the Myops," where the city is figured as "a cloak and symbol for a number of other passionate wishes." *The Standard Edition of the Complete Psychological Works of Sigmund Freud* 4: 196–97. The city is also a recurring theme in Freud's correspondence of the late 1890s with, among others, the Berlin rhinologist Wilhelm Fliess.

[15] Sigmund Freud, *Civilization and Its Discontents*, trans. Peter Gay (New York: W. W. Norton, 1984) 16.

[16] Freud, *Civilization and Its Discontents*, 16–18.

[17] Catherine Edwards, *Writing Rome: Textual Approaches to the City* (Cambridge: Cambridge UP, 1996) 28.

[18] Mikhail M. Bakhtin, *The Dialogic Imagination*, trans. Caryl Emerson and Holquist (Austin: The U of Texas Press, 1981) 84.

[19] Russo, 20.

[20] Peter I. Barta, *Bely, Joyce, and Doblin: Peripatetics in the City Novel* (Gainesville: U Press of Florida, 1996) 15.

[21] Edward W. Soja, "History: Geography: Modernity," *Postmodern Geographies: The Reassertion of Space in Critical Social Theory* (London: Verso, 1995) 10–42.

[22] Barta, 15.

[23] Sabine Hake, "Saxa loquuntur: Freud's Archaeology of the Text," *Boundary 2* 20.1 (Spring 1993): 58.

[24] See Stephen Kern, *The Culture of Time and Space, 1880–1918* (Cambridge, MA: Harvard UP, 1983).

[25] Monroe K. Spears, *Dionysius and the City: Modernism in Twentieth Century Poetry* (Oxford: Oxford UP, 1972) 61.

[26] David Frisby quoting Georg Simmel, *Simmel and Since: Essays on Simmel's Social Theory* (New York: Routledge, 1992) 66.

²⁷ Joyce Carol Oates, "Imaginary Cities: America," *Literature and the Urban Experience: Essays on the City and Literature*, eds. Michael C. Jaye and Ann Chalmers Watts (New Brunswick, NJ: Rutgers UP, 1981) 11.

²⁸ J. M. Roberts, *The Penguin History of the World* (London: Penguin Book, 1995) 44.

²⁹ Notable contributions to contemporary discussions of the city include but are not limited to the following: *The Historian and the City*, ed., Oscar Handlin and John Burchard (Cambridge, Mass.: MIT Press, 1963) 95–114; Raymond Williams, *The Country and the City* (New York: Oxford UP, 1973; Irving Howe, "The City in Literature," *Commentary* 51.5 (May 1971): 61–68; Max Byrd, *London Transformed: Images of the City in the Eighteenth Century* (New Haven: Yale UP, 1978); Alexander Welsh, *The City of Dickens* (Oxford: Calendon Press, 1971); Donald Fanger, *Dostoevsky and Romantic Realism* (Cambridge, Mass.: Harvard UP, 1967); Richard Sennett's, *The Fall of Public Man* (New York: Knopf, 1977), *The Uses of Disorder: Personal Identity and City Life* (New York: Knopf, 1970), and *Classic Essays on the Culture of Cities*, ed., Richard Sennett (Englewood Cliffs, N.J.: Prentice-Hall, 1969); Malcolm Bradbury "The Cities of Modernism," *Modernism*, ed., Malcolm Bradbury and James McFarlane (Harmondsworth: Penguin, 1976); Monroe K. Spears, *Dionysius and the City: Modernism in Twentieth Century Poetry* (Oxford: Oxford UP, 1972); Mickael C. Jaye and Ann Chalmers Watts, eds., *Literature and the Urban Experience: Essays on the City and Literature* (New Brunswick, NJ: Rutgers UP, 1981); Peter Jukes, *A Shout in the Street: An Excursion into the Modern City* (Berkeley: U of California Press, 1990); Ilan Stavans, ed., *The Urban Muse: Stories on the American City* (New York: Delta, 1998); Joachim Schlor, *Nights in the Big City: Paris. Berlin. London: 1840–1930* , trans. Pierre Gottfried Imhoff and Dafydd Rees Roberts (London: Reaktion Books Ltd., 1998); Leonardo Benevelo, *The European City*, Trans. Carl Ipsen (Oxford: Blackwell, 1993); Elizabeth Wilson, *The Sphinx in the City: Urban Life, the Control of Disorder, and Women* (Berkeley: U of California Press, 1991); Susan Merrill Squier, ed., *Women Writers and the City: Essays in Feminist Literary Criticism* (Knoxville: The U of Tennessee Press, 1984); Marshall Berman, *All That Is Solid Melts Into Air* (New York: Simon & Schuster, 1982); Burton Pike, *The Image of the City in Modern Literature* (Princeton: Princeton UP, 1982); William Sharpe and Leonard Wallock, eds., *Visions of the Modern City: Essays in History, Art, and Literature* (Baltimore: The Johns Hopkins UP, 1987); David Harvey, *The Urban Experience* (Baltimore: The Johns Hopkins UP, 1984); Richard Lehan, *The City in Literature: An Intellectual and Cultural History* (Berkeley: U of California Press, 1998); William B. Thesing, *The London Muse: Victorian Poetic Responses to the City* (Athens: The U of Georgia Press, 1982); Donald J. Olsen, *The City as a Work of Art: London, Paris, Vienna* (New Haven: Yale UP, 1986); Edward Timms and David Kelley, eds., *Unreal City: Urban Experience in Modern European Literature and Art* (New York: St. Martin's Press, 1984); Beatriz Colomina, ed., *Sexuality and Space* (Princeton, NJ: Princeton UP, 1992); Edward Soja, *Postmodern Geographies: The Reassertion of Space in Critical Social Theory* (London: Verso, 1997); Anthony Sutcliffe, ed., *Metropolis: 1890–1940* (Chicago: The U of Chicago Press, 1984); John H. Johnson, *The Poet and the City: A Study in Urban Perspectives* (Athens: U of Georgia Press, 1984); Michael C. Jaye and Ann C. Watts, eds., *Literature and the Urban Experience* (Manchester: Manchester UP, 1981); Eos M. Gott-

diener and Alexandros P. Lagopoulos, eds., *The City and the Sign: An Introduction to Urban Semiotics* (New York: Columbia UP, 1986); Charles Williams, *The Image of the City and Other Essays* (Oxford: Oxford UP, 1958); Mary Ann Caws, ed., *City Images: Perspectives from Literature, Philosophy, and Film* (New York: Gordon and Breach, 1991); Witold Rybczynski, *City Life: Urban Expectations in a New World* (New York: Scribner, 1995); Marc Eli Blanchard, *In Search of the City: Engels, Baudelaire, Rimbaud* (New York: Anma Libri, 1985); Carl E. Schorske, *Fin-de-Siecle Vienna, Politics and Culture* (New York, 1981); Jane Jacobs, *The Death and Life of Great American Cities* (New York, 1961); Richard T. LeGates and Frederic Stout, *The City Reader* (New York: Routledge, 1996); Michael L. Ross, *Storied Cities: Literary Imaginings of Florence, Venice, and Rome* (Westport, CT: Greenwood Press, 1984); Solomon Volkov, *St. Petersburg: A Cultural History,* Trans. Antonia W. Bouis (New York: The Free Press, 1995); Debra Mancoff and N. D.J. Tela, eds., *Victorian Urban Settings: Essays on the Nineteenth-Century City and its Contexts* (New York: Garland Publishers, 1996); Hana Wirth-Nesher, *City Codes: Reading the Modern Urban Novel* (Cambridge: Cambridge UP, 1996); Gerald MacLean, Donna Landry, and Joseph P. Ward, eds., *The Country and the City Revisited: England and the Politics of Culture, 1550–1850* (New York: Cambridge UP, 1999); Setha M. Low, ed., *Theorizing the City: The New Urban Anthropology Reader* (New Brunswick, NJ: Rutgers UP, 1999); Patrizia Lombardo, ed., *Critical Quarterly: Europe: Theory of the City* 36.4 (Winter 1994); Richard Lehan, *The City in Literature: An Intellectual and Cultural History* (Berkeley: U of California Press, 1998); David A Karp, Gregory P. Stone, and William C. Yoels. *Being Urban: A Sociology of City Life.* 2nd ed. (New York: Praeger, 1991); Kenneth T. Jackson, ed., *The Encyclopedia of New York City* (New Haven: Yale UP, 1995); John Twyning, *London Dispossessed: Literature and Social Space in the Early Modern City* (New York: St. Martin's Press, 1998); Gerd Hurm, *Fragmented Urban Images: The American City in Modern Fiction from Stephen Crane to Thomas Pynchon* (Frankfurt: Peter Lang, 1999); David Frisby, *Cityscapes of Modernity: Critical Explorations* (Malden, MA: Polity Press in association with Blackwell, 2002); Hubert Damisch, *Skyline: The Narcissistic City,* trans. John Goodman (Stanford: Stanford UP, 2001); Theo Barker and Anthony Sutcliffe, eds., *Megalopolis: The Giant City in History* (New York: St. Martin's Press, 1993); Deborah Epstein Nord, *Walking the Victorian Streets: Women, Representation, and the City* (Ithaca, NY: Cornell UP, 1995); William B. Scott and Peter M. Rutkoff, *New York Modern: The Arts and the City* (Baltimore: The Johns Hopkins Press, 2002); Mark Shiel and Tony Fitzmaurice, eds., *Cinema and the City: Film and Urban Societies in a Global Context* (Oxford: Blackwell Publishers, 2001); and, Jeremy Tambling, *Lost in the American City: Dickens, James, and Kafka* (New York: Palgrave, 2001);

[30] M. Roncayolo, *La Citta, Storia e Problemi della Dimensione Urbana,* 2nd ed. (Turin, 1988) 3.

[31] Lewis Mumford, "What Is a City?" *The Lewis Mumford Reader,* ed. Donald L. Miller (New York: Pantheon Books, 1986) 104.

[32] See Jane Jacobs, *The Death and Life of Great American Cities* (New York: Vintage Books, 1961).

[33] According to Lehan, the "Idea of the West" rested on two principal articles of faith: first, "that natural rights took place over birth rights"; and second, "that man must dominate his environment, impose his will upon nature and the land,

and turn that control into wealth." *Los Angeles in Fiction*, ed. David Fine (Albuquerque: U of New Mexico Press, 1984) 29–41. 29

[34] See Carl E. Schorske, "The Idea of the City in European Thought: Voltaire to Spengler," *The Historian and the City*, ed. Oscar Handlin and John Burchard (Massachusetts: The MIT Press and Harvard UP, 1963) 96. In the preface to this collection of essays, the editors identify the marginalized place of the modern city in terms of historical scholarship. One reason for the lack of attention paid to the city, the editors contend, is that history "has followed lines of inquiry which were mostly marked out in the nineteenth century, when the development of the city seemed incidental to other, more important trends—the rise of the nation state, industrialization, and the secularization of culture. Indeed, even now it is difficult to define the subject matter of urban history, to disentangle that which is peculiar to the evolution of the city from that which is characteristic of culture as a whole"(v–vi). *The Historian and the City*, by contrast, attempts to redress this imbalance, that is "to clarify the problem of the evolution of the city and thus to establish a basis for understanding the contemporary urban world"(vii).

[35] Schorske, 109.

[36] Blanche H. Gelfant, *The American City Novel* (Norman: U of Oklahoma Press, 1954) 11.

[37] As editors Peter Preston and Paul Simpson-Housley point out in *Writing the City: Eden, Babylon and the New Jerusalem* (London and New York: Routledge, 1994), in the case of urban geography, geographers particularly have contributed classic geographical models to "predict phenomena such as growth or decline, demographic patterns, traffic flows and economic potential"(1). And while some have taken mechanistic viewpoints and used mathematical formulae to confront urban problems, scholars such as Lewis Mumford have focused on the idea of the city as a site of human habitation. For example, see *The City in History* (London: Secker & Warburg, 1961). The city in terms of historical development has been the moniker for others such as Griffith Taylor in his *Urban Geography* (London: Methuen, 1951). "Different ideological viewpoints," they continue, "have informed these descriptive-prescriptive analyses of the city; logical empiricism has dominated the debate, but Marxist-inspired work, such as that by David Harvey on the bid-rent curve, has also made its impact," for example in *Social Justice and the City* (London: Edward Arnold, 1973). See also Richard Alston, "Cities and Space," *The City in Roman and Byzantine Egypt* (London: Routledge, 2002) 4–43; Claudia Minca, *Postmodern Geography: Theory and Praxis* (Oxford: Blackwell Publishers, 2001); Tim Hall, *Urban Geography* (New York: Routledge, 2001); Edward W. Soja., *Postmodern Geographies: The Reassertion of Space in Critical Social Theory* (New York: Verso, 1989) and *Postmetropolis: Critical Studies of Cities and Regions* (Oxford: Blackwell Publishers, 2000); and, Michael J. Dear and Steven Flusty, eds., *The Spaces of Postmodernity : Readings in Human Geography* (Oxford: Blackwell Publishers, 2002).

[38] Schorske, 113.

[39] Raymond Williams, *The Country and the City* (New York: Oxford UP, 1973) 48.

[40] Williams, *The Country and the City*, 46.

[41] Williams notes that rhetorical contrasts between town and country life are in fact quite traditional, and can be traced back to Rome, the "Mother of cities": "Quintilian makes it his first example of a stock thesis, and conventional contrasts between greed and innocence, in these characteristic locations, are commonplace in later Greek and Latin Literature [Juvenal's Satires]. But it was especially in relation to Rome that that the contrast crystallised, at the point where the city could be seen as an independent organ [. . .] Rome, after all, was a special case: an imperial capital, a metropolis." *The Country and the City* 46; 48)

[42] Schorske, 7.

[43] Central to Schorske's tripartite schema of the city in European intellectual life is the Woolfian injunction that, "somewhere about 1850, there emerged in France a new mode of thought and feeling which has slowly but forcefully extended its sway over the consciousness of the West. [. . .] we know only that the pioneers of this change explicitly challenged the validity of traditional morality, social thought and art. [. . .] this great revaluation inevitably drew the idea of the city into its train" (109).

[44] See William Sharpe and Leonard Wallock, "From 'Great Town' to 'Nonplace Urban Realm': Reading the Modern City," *Visions of the Modern City: Essays in History, Art, and Literature* (Baltimore: The Johns Hopkins Press, 1987) 1–50. In the sub-section entitled "Morphology and Metaphor: Three Phases in the Life of the Modern City," Sharpe and Wallock outline three phases of nineteenth-century metropolitan development as follows: "concentrated settlement, center city with suburban ring," and "decentered urban field," which have concomitantly resulted in "a fundamental transformation of the physical and social environment, which in turn has inspired a conception of the urban no longer synonymous with locale"(11).

[45] Sharpe and Wallock, 10.

[46] See Oscar Handlin, "The Modern City as a Field of Historical Study," *The Historian and the City* 1–26. Handlin, by way of attempting to outline some of the vague concepts of the metropolis that students reach for, foreshadows some of Sharpe and Wallock's concerns when he comments, "our difficulties with nomenclature reflect the indeterminacy of these limits"(1). He argues that "the modern city is essentially different from its predecessors, and the core of the difference lies in the fact that its life is not that 'of an organism, but of an organ'. It has become 'the heart, the brain, perhaps only the digestive stem, of that great leviathan, the modern state'. Its history cannot be understood apart from that of the more comprehensive communities of which it is a part"(2–3). Note the final caveat: "we need fewer studies of the city in history than of the history of cities [. . .] how [. . .] developments unfolded, what was the causal nexus among them, we shall only learn when we make out the interplay among them by focussing upon *a* city specifically in all its uniqueness"(26).

[47] Sharpe and Wallock, 25.

[48] Sharpe and Wallock, 1.

[49] Melvin M. Webber, "The Urban Place and the Nonplace Urban Realm," *Explorations in Urban Structure*, ed. Melvin Webber et al. (Philadelphia: 1964) 79.

⁵⁰ Sharpe and Wallock argue that, beginning with the nineteenth-century, "it is possible to distinguish three major periods of metaphoric re-evaluation and changing terminology that correspond roughly to the three phases of urban growth" (11). The first outpouring coincided with the shift from a rural to an urban society in the early decades of the nineteenth century, the second straddling the cusp of the new century in which modern consciousness was transformed into an urban consciousness," and a third phase inclusive of the present day which has inspired a universal conception of the urban no longer synonymous with locale. The authors qualify their own brand of schema thus by pointing out that, although historians have usually focused on the transition from the medieval town to the early modern and modern city in Europe, and from the colonial town to the nineteenth-century and twentieth-century city in the United States, the three phases of development they outline (though not widely adopted) "have been well documented by historians and social scientists," despite of the fact that this process of development was not common in all large cities at the same time, structurally or conceptually, and that no attempt has was made on their part to differentiate typologically among the various cities extant during each developmental phase (40). In the section titled "The City and the Disciplines," Sharpe and Wallock reiterate the "three traditions of analysis" that have shaped what historians define as "the significance of the modern city" (3). In nineteenth century England (the "Age of Capital") surveys such as Freidrich Engels' *The Condition of the Working Class in England*, Henry Mayhew's *London Labor and the London Poor*, and Charles Booth's *Life and Labour of the People in London* documented "a new spatial order and a new social structure" brought about by "the concentration of a heterogeneous population and the division of labor" on an unprecedented scale. The especial significance of this primary tradition was that commentators such as Mayhew succeeded in forgerounding that, "far from being the chaotic, haphazard, and indecipherable environment perceived by many casual observers, the nineteenth-century city was an integrated, ordered, and knowable identity"(3). Following on from this first tradition was the German School—Max Weber, *The City*, Georg Simmel's "The Metropolis and Mental Life," and Oswald Spengler's *The Decline of the West*—which focused on the social, cultural, and psychological consequences of metropolitan life, and in particular the city as a key index to human association and consciousness. The third tradition found its home in the city of Chicago under the guidance of Robert Park and is commonly known as the Chicago School. In the essay "The City: Suggestions for the Study of Human Behavior in the Urban Environment," Park extended the work of Simmel by arguing for the primacy of mutually interactive physical and moral "orders" of the city—the "ecological approach"—beyond previous studies, which, to some extent, had devoted themselves to merely deciphering "congeries of individual men and social conveniences"(4).

⁵¹ Kevin Lynch, *The Image of the City* (Cambridge, Mass.: MIT Press, 1960) 3.

⁵² Lynch, 10.

⁵³ Lynch, 3.

⁵⁴ Anthony Downs, "Alternative Forms of Future Urban Growth in the United States," *Journal of the American Institute of Planners* 36 (January 1970) 9.

⁵⁵ See Ira Katznelson, *Marxism and the City* (Oxford: Clarendon Press, 1992).

[56] Jacques Derrida, "Structure, Sign and Play in the Discourse of the Human Sciences," *Modern Criticism and Theory*, ed. David Lodge (New York: Longman, 1988) 118.

[57] Richard Lehan, *The City in Literature: An Intellectual and Cultural History* (Berkeley: U of California Press, 1998) 64.

[58] C. De Seta, "Significati e simboli della rappresentazione topografica negli Atlanti dal XVI al XVII secolo," *Citta Capitali*, ed. C. De Seta (Rome: Bari, 1985) 20.

[59] Marshall Berman, *All That Is Solid Melts Into Air* (New York: Simon & Schuster, 1982) 26.

[60] Charles Baudelaire, *Selected Writings on Art and Artists*, Alex Chavret (Penguin: Harmondsworth, 1972) 106.

[61] Martin Bock, *Crossing the Shadow-Line: The Literature of Estrangement* (Columbus: Ohio State UP, 1989) 48.

[62] Charles Baudelaire, "The Painter of Modern Life," *Charles Baudelaire, The Painter of Modern Life and Other Essays*, trans. and ed. by J. Mayne (London: Penguin, 1964) 22.

[63] Baudelaire, 4.

[64] Baudelaire, 7.

[65] Baudelaire, 11.

[66] Baudelaire, 18.

[67] Baudelaire, 9–10.

[68] According to Hans-Robert Jauss, "this historical consciousness of modernité presupposes the eternal as its antithesis." David Frisby quoting Jauss, *Fragments of Modernity: Theories of Modernity in the Work of Simmel, Kracauer and Benjamin* (Cambridge, Mass.: The MIT Press, 1986) 16.

[69] Frisby quoting Dolf Oehler, *Fragments of Modernity*, 20.

[70] Marjorie Perloff, "Modernist Studies," *Redrawing the Boundaries: The Transformation of English and American Literary Studies*, ed. Stephen Greenblatt and Giles Gunn (New York: MLA of America, 1992) 155. See 175–78 for an intelligent selection of major critical works devoted to this most thorny of subjects.

[71] See Malcolm Bradbury and James McFarlane, eds., *Modernism 1890–1910* (Penguin: Harmondsworth, 1976); Anthony Sutcliffe, ed., *Metropolis, 1890–1940* (Chicago: U of Chicago Press, 1984); William Sharpe and Leonard Wallock, eds., *Visions of the Modern City: Essays in History, Art, and Literature* (Baltimore: Johns Hopkins UP, 1987); Diana Festa-McCormick, *The City as Catalyst: A Study of Ten Novels* (Rutherford: Fairleigh Dickinson UP, 1979); Monroe K. Spears, *Dionysus and the City: Modernism in Twentieth-Century Poetry* (Oxford: OUP, 1970); William B. Thesing, *The London Muse: Victorian Poetic Responses to the City* (Athens: U of Georgia Press, 1982); Burton Pike, *The Image of the City in Modern Literature*, Princeton, NJ: Princeton UP, 1981); and David Frisby, *Cityscapes of Modernity: Critical Explorations* (Cambridge; Malden, MA: Polity Press in association with Blackwell, 2001).

[72] Michael Long, "Eliot, Pound, Joyce: Unreal City?" *Unreal City: Urban Experience in Modern European Literature and Art*, eds. Edward Timms and David Kelley (New York: St. Martin's Press, 1984) 144.

[73] See Robert L. Caserio, "Various Modernisms," *The Novel in England, 1900–1950* (New York: Twayne publishers, 1999) 80–159.

[74] Raymond Williams, "The Metropolis and the Emergence of Modernism," *Unreal City*, 13–24.

[75] Timms, *Unreal City*, 2. For the Victorian background see *The Victorian City: Images and Realities*. eds. H. J. Dyos and Michael Woolff, 2 vols. (Boston: Routledge & Keegan Paul, 1973); Anthony Sutcliffe, *Towards the Planned City: Germany, Britain, the United States and France, 1780–1914* (New York: St. Martin's Press, 1981.) For equally negative responses to the American city, see Michael C. Jaye and Ann Chalmers Watts, eds. *Literature and the American Urban Experience* (Manchester: Manchester UP, 1981); and Morton and Lucia White, *The Intellectual versus the City: From Thomas Jefferson to Frank Lloyd Wright* (Cambridge: Harvard UP, 1962).

[76] Quoted in Caroline Tisdall and Angelo Bozzolla, *Futurism* (New York: Oxford UP, 1978) 43. *The First Futurist Manifesto* was followed in 1910 by Boccioni's, Carra's, and Russolo's *Manifesto of Futurist Painters* and *Technical Manifesto of Futurist Painting*.

[77] Judy Davies, "Mechanical Millennium: Sant' Elia and the Poetry of Futurism," *Unreal City*, 69. Beyond Italy, the influence of Futurism spread to Germany, the United States, Russia, and Great Britain (where it was transformed in Vorticism by Wyndham Lewis and Ezra Pound), and France.

[78] Frank Whitford, "The City in Painting," *Unreal City*, 59.

[79] Timms, *Unreal City*, 4.

[80] Ludwig Meidner, "An Introduction to Painting Big Cities," *Voices of German Expressionism*, ed. Victor H. Miesel (Englewood Cliffs, NJ: Prentice-Hall, 1970) 111.

[81] For a general survey of the interrelations between the city and cinema, see Anthony Sutcliffe, "The Metropolis in the Cinema," *Metropolis 1890–1940* 147–71; and Mark Shiel and Tony Fitzmaurice, eds., *Cinema and the City: Film and Urban Societies in a Global Context* (Oxford: Blackwell Publishers, 2001).

[82] *Metropolis*, Ufa, 1926. Directed by Fritz Lang, script by Lang and Thea von Harbou, photography by Karl Freund, Gunther Rittau, special effects by Eugen Schufftan.

[83] *Berlin, die Symphonie der Grosstadt*, Deutsche-Verenis-Film, 1927, directed by Walther Ruttmann, script by Ruttmann and Karl Freund, from an idea by Carl Mayer, photography by Reimar Kuntze, Robert Babeske, Laszlo Schaffer.

[84] Michael Minden, "The City in Early Cinema: *Metropolis, Berlin*, and *October*," *Unreal City*, 193–213.

[85] *October*, Sovkino, 1928, directed by Sergei Eisenstein and Grigori Alexandrov, photography by Edward Tisse.

[86] See Malcolm Bradbury and James McFarlane, eds., *Modernism: A Guide to European Literature 1890–1930* (Harmondsworth: Penguin Books, 1976).

[87] Bradbury, *Modernism*, 96.

[88] Bradbury, 96.

[89] Bradbury and McFarlane, *Modernism*, 11.

[90] Michel de Certeau, "Walking in the City," *The Cultural Studies Reader*, ed. Simon During (New York: Routledge, 1993) 152.

[91] Connor Cruise O'Brien, "1891–1916," *The Shaping of Modern Ireland*, ed. Connor Cruise O'Brien (London: Routledge and Kegan Paul, 1960) 13.

[92] James Joyce, *Ulysses: The Corrected Text*, edited by Hans Walter Gabler with Wolfhard Steppe and Claus Melchior (New York: Random House, Inc., 1986).

[93] Stanislaus Joyce, *My Brother's Keeper: James Joyce's Early Years* (New York: Viking, 1958) 20.

[94] Adolf Hoffmeister, "Portrait of Joyce," *Portraits of the Artist in Exile*, ed. Willard Potts (Seattle and London: U of Washington Press, 1979) 132.

[95] Hayden White, *The Tropics of Discourse: Essays in Cultural Criticism* (Baltimore: Johns Hopkins UP, 1978) 54.

[96] Frank Budgeon, *James Joyce and the Making of Ulysses*. (Bloomington: Indiana UP, 1967) 65. Concerning Joyce's boast, Thomas Flanagan's comment stands for many others: "It is one of the few claims made for that great novel that exceeds the mark, for in fact, only sections of the city are represented, and the characters are drawn from a narrow banding of the petty bourgeoisie." See 'Introduction' to *The State of Ireland*, ed. Benedict Kiely (Boston: David R. Godine, 1980) 4.

[97] See *Irish Cities*, ed. Howard B. Clarke (Dublin: Mercier Press, 1995); Andrew MacLaran, *Dublin: The Shaping of a Capital* (New York: Belhaven Press, 1984); and Desmond Clarke, *Dublin* (London: B. T. Batsford Ltd. 1977); Joesph Brady and Anngret Simms, eds. *Dublin: Through Space and Time 900–1900* (Dublin: Four Courts, 2001).

[98] Mary E. Daly, *Dublin: The Deposed Capital, A Social and Economic History, 1860–1914* (Cork: Cork UP, 1984) 2.

[99] F. S. L. Lyons, *Ireland Since the Famine* (New York: Scribner's 1971) 275.

[100] Daly, 203–26.

[101] Lyons, "James Joyce's Dublin," *Twentieth Century Studies* (November 1970): 24.

[102] Joyce, Letter to Grant Richards, 23 June 1906, *Selected Letters of James Joyce*, 90.

[103] William E. Leuchtenburg, *The Perils of Prosperity, 1914–1932* 2nd edn. (Chicago: U of Chicago Press, 1993) 225.

[104] Carol Groneman and David M. Reiners, "Immigration," *The Encyclopedia of New York City*, ed. Kenneth T. Jackson (New Haven: Yale UP, 1995) 583.

[105] David C Hammack, *Power and Society: Greater New York at the Turn of the Century* (New York: Russell Sage Foundation, 1982) 28.

[106] Gertrude Stein, *The Autobiography of Alice B. Toklas* (New York: Modern Library, 1993) 82.

107 Ann Douglas, *Terrible Honesty: Mongrel Manhattan in the 1920s* (New York: Farrar, Strauss and Giroux, 1995) 194.

108 F. Scott Fitzgerald, *The Great Gatsby* (1925; New York: Charles Scribner's Sons, 1980) 182.

109 More recent critical analyses of the American city include the following: Warner Berthoff, *The Ferment of Realism, 1884–1919* (New York: Free Press, 1965); Thomas Bender, *New York Intellect: A History of Intellectual Life in New York City, from 1750 to the Beginnings of Our Time* (Baltimore: Johns Hopkins UP, 1987); Rachel Bowlby, *Just Looking: Consumer Culture in Dreiser, Gissing, and Zola* (New York: Methuen, 1985); Alan Trachtenberg, *Incorporation of America* (New York: Hill and Wang, 1982); Eric Sunquist, *American Realism: New Essays* (Baltimore: Johns Hopkins UP, 1982); Walter Benn Michael, *Gold Standard and the Logic of Naturalism* (Berkeley: U of California Press, 1987); Richard Wightman Fox and T. J. Jackson Lear, *The Culture of Consumption: Critical Essays in American History, 1880–1980* (New York: Pantheon Books, 1983); Richard Slotkin's trilogy, *The Fatal Environment: The Myth of the Frontier in the Age of Industrialization, 1880–1980* (Norman: U of Oklahoma Press, 1989); Amy Kaplan, *The Social Construction of American Realism* (Chicago: U of Chicago Press, 1988); Miles Orvell, *The Real Thing: Imitation and Authenticity in American Culture, 1880–1940* (Chapel Hill: U of North Carolina Press, 1989); Davitt Bell, *The Problem of American Realism: Studies in the Cultural History of a Literary Idea* (Chicago: U of Chicago Press, 1993); Donald Pizer, ed., *The Cambridge Companion to American Realism and Naturalism: Howells to London* (Cambridge: Cambridge UP, 1995); David E. Shi, *Facing Facts: Realism in American Thought and Culture, 1850–1920* (Oxford: Oxford UP, 1995); Jeremy Tambling, *Lost in the American City: Dickens, James, and Kafka* (New York: Palgrave, 2001); Sven Beckert, *The Monied Metropolis: New York City and the Consolidation of the American Bourgeoisie, 1850–1896* (Cambridge: CUP, 2001); Kevin Young, *Giant Steps: The New Generation of African American Writers* (New York: Perennial, 2000); Michael Bennett and David W. Teague, eds., *The Nature of Cities: Ecocriticism and Urban Environments* (Tucson: U of Arizona Press, 1999).

110 Fitzgerald, *The Great Gatsby*, 182.

111 According to James L. Machor, "there is no denying that a belief in the superiority of either rural or urban environments has been central to America, for beneath their divergence these two ideological strains share a common assumption informing much of our history: the conviction that city and country embody diametrically opposed values." Moreover, the vital urban-pastoral dialectic within American society constitutes an important cultural component of national identity that can be traced back through the "agrarian myth" and "pastoral ideal" of the eighteenth and nineteenth centuries to John Winthrop's lay sermon aboard the ship 'Arabella,' where he defined the prospective Puritan community of New England as a "Citty upon a Hill" that would be built according to the "lawe of nature." Machor, *Pastoral Cities: Urban Ideals and the Symbolic Landscape of America* (Wisconsin: The U of Wisconsin Press, 1987) 5; 41.

112 Ralph Waldo Emerson, "The American Scholar," *Essays and Lectures*, ed. Joel Porte (New York: Library of America, 1983) 70.

[113] Eric Homberger, "Nathaniel Hawthorne and the Dream of Happiness," *Nathaniel Hawthorne: Critical Essays*, ed. Robert A. Lee (Totowa, NJ: Vision, 1982) 173.

[114] Karl Marx, *Economic and Philosophical Manuscripts of 1844*, ed. Dirk J. Struik, trans. Martin Milligan (New York: International Publishers, 1964) 96.

[115] Marx, 112.

[116] Anselm L. Strauss, "Varieties of American Urban Symbolism," *Cities in American History*, eds. Kenneth T. Jackson and Stanley K. Schultz (New York: Alfred A. Knopf, 1972) 35.

[117] Walt Whitman, *Leaves of Grass, Walt Whitman: Complete Poetry and Collected Prose*, ed. Justin Kaplan (New York: Library of America, 1982) 5.

[118] Shaun O'Connell, *Remarkable, Unspeakable New York: A Literary History* (Boston: Beacon Press, 1995) 31.

[119] Linda Miller, "The Writer in the Crowd: Poe's Urban Vision." *The American Transcendental Quarterly* 44 (Fall 1979): 326.

[120] Edgar Allan Poe, *The Unabridged Edgar Allan Poe*, ed. Tam Mossman (Philadelphia: Running Press, 1983). 1073. All subsequent references to Poe are taken from this edition.

[121] Miller, 327.

[122] Poe, 659.

[123] Amy Kaplan, "'The Knowledge of the Line'": Realism and the City in Howells' *A Hazard of New Fortune*," *PMLA* 101.1 (January 1986): 69–81. 69.

[124] Quoted in Kaplan, 69.

[125] See also Jane Addams, *Twenty Years at Hull House: With Autobiographical Notes* (New York: The Macmillan Co., 1910).

[126] Quoted in Moses Rischin, "The Lower East Side," *Cities in American History*, eds. Kenneth T. Jackson and Stanley K. Schultz (New York: Alfred A. Knopf, 1972) 190.

[127] Alan Trachtenberg, *The Incorporation of America* (New York: Hill & Wang, 1982) 102.

[128] Thorsten Veblen, *The Theory of the Leisure Class* (New York: Penguin Books, 1994) 36.

[129] Walter Benn Michaels, "Sister Carrie's Popular Economy," *Critical Inquiry* 7 (Winter 1980): 390.

[130] James Weldon Johnson, *The Autobiography of an Ex-Colored Man* (Garden City, NY: Garden City Publishing Co., 1927) 64.

[131] Lucinda H. Mackethan, "*Black Boy* and *Ex-Colored Man*: Verson and Inversion of the Slave Narrator's Quest for Voice," *CLA Journal* 32 (1988): 52.

[132] Howard Faulkner, "James Weldon Johnson's Portrait of the Artist as a Young Man," *Black American Literature Forum* 19 (1985): 50.

[133] Malcolm Bradbury, *The Modern American Novel* (New York: Viking, 1992) 80.

134 Dos Passos, "A Humble Protest," *Harvard Monthly* 62 (June 1916) 115–120.

135 John Dos Passos, "The Baker of Almorox," *Rosinante to the Road Again* (New York: George H. Doran Co., 1922) 46.

136 Dos Passos, Foreword, Blaise Cendrars, *Panama; or, The Adventures of My Seven Uncles* (New York: Harler & Brothers, 1931) vii.

137 See Jeffrey Segall, *Joyce in America: Cultural Politics and the Trials of 'Ulysses'* (Berkeley: U of California Press, 1993).

138 Dos Passos, Introduction to Blaise Cendrars, *Le Panama et Mes Sept Oncles* (1932) viii.

139 Dos Passos, "Young Spain," *Seven Arts* 2 (August 1917) 478.

140 Dos Passos, "A Humble Protest," *Harvard Monthly* 62 (June 1916) 117.

141 Joyce, Letter to C.P. Curran, Early July 1904, *Selected Letters of James Joyce*, 22.

142 Joyce, *A Portrait of the Artist as a Young Man: Text, Criticism, and Notes*, ed. Chester G. Anderson (New York: The Viking Press, 1956) 180.

143 Michael Denning, *The Cultural Front: The Laboring of American Culture in the Twentieth Century* (New York: Verso, 1996) 167.

CHAPTER TWO NOTES

1 Roland Barthes, "Semiology and Urbanism," *Via* 2 (1973): 155–158.

2 Barthes, rejecting the notion of a system of signification based on the notion of the lexicon, that is, "a list of signifieds and coincident signifiers," contends that "semiology at present never posits the existence of a final signified. This means that the signifiers always become the signifieds for other signifiers, and vice versa. In reality, any cultural (or, for that matter, psychological) complex affords us with infinite metaphorical chains, in which the signified is always deferred or becomes itself a signifier" (155).

3 Barthes, 155.

4 Barthes, 155.

5 Barthes singles out the chapter "This Will Kill That" from Victor Hugo's *The Hunchback of Notre-Dame* as an example of an author who speaks to the "significance of urban space" (158).

6 Barthes, 158.

7 Barthes, 158.

8 Joyce, Letter to C. P. Curran, Early July 1904, *Selected Letters of James Joyce*, ed. Richard Ellmann (New York: Viking Press, 1975) 22.

9 Fintan O' Toole notes that as to the larger significance of the city in Irish culture, "for the last hundred years, Irish culture and in particular Irish writing has been marked by this dominance of the rural over the urban, a dominance based on a false opposition of the country to the city which has been vital to the maintenance of a conservative political culture in the country." See "Going West: The Country

versus the City in Irish Writing," *The Crane Bag* 9 (1985): 11–16. 11. See also Norman Vance, *Irish Literature: A Social History* (Oxford: Basil Blackwell 1995).

[10] Hugh Kenner, *Dublin's Joyce* (London: Chatto and Windus, 1955) 48. Kenner, however, is by no means alone in arguing for a principle of unity at work within *Dubliners*. Brewster Ghiselin's early and influential essay, "The Unity of Joyce's *Dubliners*," *Accent*, 16 (1956): 75–88, contends that the collection is anything but loose and episodic. See also Anthony Burgess, "A Paralysed City," *Re Joyce* (New York: W.W. Norton & Company, Inc.) 35–47. For a detailed history of the writing and organization of the collection, see Florence L. Walzl, "The Life Chronology of Dubliners," *James Joyce Quarterly* 14:4 (Summer 1977): 408–415.

[11] See Joyce's letters to Grant Richards, dated 5 May 1906 and 20 May 1906, respectively, *Selected Letters of James Joyce*, 83, 88.

[12] Thomas F. Staley, "A Beginning: Signification, Story, and Discourse in Joyce's 'The Sisters,'" *The Genres of the Irish Literary Revival*, ed. Ronald Schleifer (Oklahoma: Pilgrim Books, Inc., 1980) 121.

[13] Joyce, *Dubliners: Text, Criticism, and Notes*, eds. Robert Scholes and A. Walton Litz (New York: Penguin, 1967). Subsequent references are to this edition and cited parenthetically within the text.

[14] With regard to the word "paralysis" as the first of a cluster of "signs," Colin MacCabe writes: "the reader is introduced to a set of signifiers for which there is no interpretation except strangeness and undefined evil." *James Joyce and the Revolution of the Word* (London: Harper & Row, 1975) 34.

[15] Edward Said, *Beginnings: Intention and Method* (New York: Basic Books, 1975) 24.

[16] For previous criticism of the story see Donald T. Torchiana, "The Opening of Dubliners: A Reconsideration," *Irish University Review* 1 (1971): 149–60 and Bernard Benstock, "'The Sisters' and the Critics," *James Joyce Quarterly* 4 (1966): 32–35. As Torchiana points out, the dominant readings revolve around the following: Hugh Kenner, *Dublin's Joyce* (Boston: Beacon Press, 1956): 50–53; Marvin Magalener and Richard Kain, *Joyce, the Man, the Work, the Reputation* (New York: NYU Press, 1956): 71–75; Marvin Magalener, *Time of Apprenticeship: The Fiction of Young James Joyce* (New York: New Directions, 1959): 72–86; and, William York Tindall, *A Reader's Guide to James Joyce* (1959; Syracuse: Syracuse UP, 1995). For more criticism addressing "The Sisters," see Thomas F. Staley, "A Beginning: Signification, Story, and Discourse in Joyce's 'The Sisters,'" *The Genres of the Irish Literary Revival* and Florence L. Walzl, "Joyce's 'The Sisters': A Development," *James Joyce Quarterly* 10 (1973): 375–421; David Lodge, *The Modes of Modern Writing* (London, 1977); and Fritz Senn, "'He was too Scrupulous Always": Joyce's 'The Sisters,'" *James Joyce Quarterly* 2 (1965): 66–71.

[17] Gaston Bachelard, *The Poetics of Space*, trans. Maria Jolas (New York: The Orion Press, 1964) 4–5.

[18] Bachelard, 12.

[19] See Arthur E. McGuinness, "The Ambience of Space in Joyce's *Dubliners*," *Studies in Short Fiction* 11.4 (Fall 1974): 343–51; William P. Keen, "The Rhetoric of Spatial Focus in Joyce's *Dubliners*," *Studies in Short Fiction* 16.3 (Summer 1979): 195–203; and, Hana Wirth-Nesher "Reading Joyce's City: Public Space,

Self, and Gender in *Dubliners*," *James Joyce: The Augmented Ninth*, ed. Bernard Benstock (Syracuse, NY: Syracuse UP, 1988) 282–292. See also Wirth-Nesher, *City Codes: Reading the Modern Urban Novel* (Cambridge: CUP, 1996).

[20] See James Joyce, Letter to Stanislaus Joyce, 19 July 1905, *Selected Letters of James Joyce* 69.

[21] Torchiana reads Father Flynn's character to "intimate menacingly the hegemonic forces past and present hostile to native Dubliners, and, connected to a larger web, are but tributaries to a lager and more oppressive fate that will paralyze the grown boy." "The Opening of *Dubliners*: A Reconsideration" (158).

[22] See Florence L. Walzl, "Pattern of Paralysis," *College English* 22.4 (January 1961): 221–28.

[23] Torchiana asks, "what did it mean to live in Great Britain Street behind a shop selling goods to keep water off infants? Or what pain did such a death bring denying as it did the priest's last wish to revisit the place of his birth, Irishtown, that locale south and east of Dublin where the native Irish momentarily fled after being ordered out of Dublin by the lord deputy in 1655?" "The Opening of *Dubliners*: A Reconsideration" (152).

[24] See Margot Norris, "Narration under a Blindfold: Reading Joyce's 'Clay,'" *PMLA* 102.2 (March 1987): 206–215.

[25] See Paul Delany, "Joyce's Political Development and the Aesthetic of *Dubliners*," *College English* 34.2 (November 1972): 256–68.

[26] See David Pierce and Dan Harper, *James Joyce's Ireland* (New Haven: Yale UP, 1992). In particular see chapter four, "Dubliners, Topography, and Social Class," 83–103. Pierce and Harper argue that, "we are accustomed to considering the verbal and aural qualities of Joyce's work, but his imagination was also intensely visual—never more so than in his use of maps and in his reconstruction of the streets of Dublin. Indeed, *Dubliners* is not unlike a commentary, an *ekphrasis*, on a visual representation—in this case a map of his native city. The experience of reading *Dubliners* is greatly enriched when accompanied by such a map, and for our purposes here we can make good use of Bartholemew's 1900 map of Dublin, which includes Joyce's beloved tram routes and the place-names with which he was familiar"(83).

[27] Vincent Cheng, *Joyce, Race, and Empire* (Oxford: Oxford UP, 1995) 15.

[28] See James Joyce, Letter to Nora Barnacle, 29 August 1904, *Selected Letters of James Joyce*, 25.

[29] Terry Eagleton, *Heathcliff and the Great Hunger* (London: Verso, 1995) 145.

[30] Joseph V. O'Brien, *'Dear, Dirty Dublin': A City in Distress, 1899–1916* (Berkeley: U of California Press, 1982) xii. See also Andrew MacLaran, *Dublin: The Shaping of a Capital* (New York: Belhaven Press, 1992).

[31] An example of the relative insignificance of Dublin's metropolitan presence to the urban historian can be seen in the few references made in H. J. Dyos and M. Wolff, eds. *The Victorian City* (London: Routledge & Kegan Paul, 1973).

[32] Lehan, 253.

[33] See James Joyce, Letter to Stanislaus Joyce, About 24 September 1905, *Selected Letters of James Joyce*, 78.

[34] Joyce, Letter to Grant Richards, 15 October 1905, *Selected Letters of James Joyce*, 78–79.

[35] See William A Johnsen, "Joyce's *Dubliners* and the Futility of Modernism," *James Joyce and Modern Literature*, ed. W. J. McCormack and Alistair Stead (London: Routledge & Kegan Paul) 5–21.

[36] See the special edition "Ireland & Irish Cultural Studies," *The South Atlantic Quarterly* 95.1 (Winter 1996); Seamus Deane, "Strange Country: Modernity and Nationhood in Irish Writing since 1790 (Oxford: Clarendon Press, 1997); Louis M. Cullen, *The Emergence of Modern Ireland, 1600–1900*, 2nd ed. (London: Batsford, 1972); Thomas Bartlett and Derek Haydon, eds., *Era and Golden Age: Essays in Irish History, 1690–1800* (Belfast: Ulster Historical Foundation, 1975); David J. Dickson, *New Foundations: Ireland, 1660–1800* (Dublin: Irish Academic Press, 2000); G.J. Watson, *Irish Identity and the Literary Revival: Synge, Yeats, Joyce and O'Casey* (New York: Barnes & Noble Books, 1979); Declan Kiberd, *Inventing Ireland* (1996); Terence Brown, "Yeats, Joyce and the Irish Critical Debate," *Yeats's Political Identities: Selected Essays*, ed. Jonathon Allison (Ann Arbor: The U of Michigan Press, 1996); Debra Fleming, '*A man who does not exist*': *The Irish Peasant in the Works of W. B. Yeats and J. M. Synge* (Ann Arbor: The U of Michigan Press, 1998); D. George Boyce, *Nationalism in Ireland* (New York: Routledge, 1995); Seamus Deane, "The Production of Cultural Space in Irish Writing," *Boundary* 2 21.3 (Fall 1994): 117–44; Edward Hirsch, "The Imaginary Irish Peasant," *PMLA* 106.5 (October 1991): 1116–33; *Myth and Reality in Irish Literature*, ed. Joseph Ronsley; Seamus Deane, *Celtic Revivals: Essays in Modern Irish Literature, 1880–1980* (Boston: Faber and Faber); David Lloyd, *Anomalous States: Irish Writing and the Post-Colonial Moment* (Durham: Duke UP, 1993); Ian McBride, ed., *History and Memory in Modern Ireland* (Cambridge: Cambridge UP, 2001); Colin Graham, *Deconstructing Ireland: Identity, Theory, Culture* (Edinburgh: Edinburgh UP, 2001); and, Stephen Howe, *Ireland and Empire: Colonial Legacies in Irish History and Culture* (Oxford: OUP, 2000).

[37] According to the Rev. Whitelaw's 1798 survey, the city was estimated to be fifth for magnitude in Europe with a population of approximately 170,000. Quoted in O' Brien, '*Dear, Dirty Dublin*': *A City in Distress, 1899–1916*, 46.

[38] O' Brien, '*Dear, Dirty Dublin*': *A City in Distress, 1899–1916*, 11–12.

[39] For more on the economic and social conditions of the period, see R. F. Foster, *Modern Ireland, 1600–1972* (New York: Penguin, 1988).

[40] Joyce, Letter to Grant Richards, 15 October 1905, *Selected Letters of James Joyce*, 79.

[41] As O'Brien points out, the sudden increase in population between 1901 and 1904 was due primarily to the incorporation in 1900 of the former townships of Clontarf, Clonliffe, Drumcondra, Glasnevin, and New Kilmainham. In reality, the population of the city grew by only 5 percent over the decade. '*Dear, Dirty Dublin*': *A City in Distress, 1899–1916*, 39.

[42] O'Brien also notes that at an earlier period the homes of the resident gentry extended from Dorset to Gloucester Streets between Granby Row and Mountjoy Square. Now little more than the square itself stand as testimony to the former ele-

gance of the entire district. *'Dear, Dirty Dublin': A City in Distress, 1899–1916*, 40.

[43] See Torchiana, but for more critics involved in this debate, see F. S. L. Lyons, "James Joyce's Dublin," *Twentieth Century Studies*, No. 4 (November 1970): 6–25; J. C. C. Mays, "Some Comments on the Dublin of *Ulysses*," *Ulysses Cinquante Ans Apres*," ed. Louis Bonnerot (Paris: Marcel Didier): 83–98; Terence Brown, "Dublin in Twentieth-Century Writing: Metaphor and Subject," *Irish University Review*, 8 No.1 (Spring 1978): 7–21; and Thomas Kinsella, "The Irish Writer," *Davis, Mangan, Ferguson*, ed. Roger McHugh (Dublin: Dolmen Press, 1970): 57–70.

[44] Foster, 437.

[45] O'Brien quoting H. T. O'Rourke, xviii–xix.

[46] See Joyce's letter to Grant Richards, 23 June 1906, *Selected Letters of James Joyce*, 90.

[47] See Joyce's letter to Grant Richards, 5 May 1906, *Selected Letters of James Joyce*, 81.

[48] See Julian Moynahan, "The Image of the City in Nineteenth-Century Irish Fiction," *The Irish Writer and the City*, Irish Studies 18, ed. Maurice Harmon (Gerrards Cross, Bucks: Colin Smythe, 1984) 1–17. Moynahan documents the literary presence of Dublin in Irish fiction as "the only Irish city that has a substantial presence in 19th-century Irish fiction" (1) by first identifying landmark texts such as The Reverend Stephen J. Brown's *Ireland in Fiction* (1915). See also Maurice Craig, *Dublin 1660–1860: A Social and Architectural History* (New York: Coward-McCann, 1952). Previous fictions taking the city as their focus, Moynahan argues, can be categorized into three phases of post-Union literary development. The first phase, "Early 19th Century: The Union (1800) to Catholic Emancipation (1829)" cites the influential work of Maria Edgworth, for example *The Absentee* (1812), and "Essay on Irish Bulls" (1801), Robert Charles Maturin's *Women: or, Pour et Contre* (1818), and John Banim's *The Anglo-Irish of the Nineteenth Century* (1828). The second, leaner phase, "Mid-Century: J.S. Le Fanu (1814–1873)" produced the novels *The Cock and Anchor* (1845) and *The House by the Churchyard* (1863). In the wake of the Land War, the final category is marked "The Final Phase: George Moore in the Eighties and Somerville and Ross in the Nineties," with Moore's *A Drama in Muslin* (1886) and *Parnell and His Island* (1887), Martin Ross's story "Two Sunday Afternoons," the collaborative works by Edith Somerville and Ross entitled *The Real Charlotte* (1894) and *Strayaways* (1920)

[49] Craig, 62.

[50] See *Parliamentary Papers*, 1880 (XXX), c. 2605. By 1879 not much had changed since the Dean's days. Evidence taken at the Royal Commission on Sewerage and Drainage in Dublin held in 1879 noted that the Liffey was "polluted to a fearful extent. Experiments [. . .] showed that the water was at places so filthy as to cause almost instant death to fish. [. . .] To anyone who had passed along the quays at low water, the poisonous smell of the river must have proved the absolute necessity of some remedy being quickly applied to this gross evil" (xxi–xxii).

[51] Somerville and Ross, *The Real Charlotte* (1894; London: Longmans, Green, and co., 1919) 136.

[52] See Mary and Padraic Colum, *Our Friend James Joyce* (New York: Doubleday & Company, 1958). Padraic Colum writes of turn-of-the-century Dublin: "*Dublin is a small city,* so small that one can walk from the center to the outskirts in twenty minutes. It is a city that is commercial and bureaucratic and not industrial; little business of an absorbing nature is transacted there, and the citizens are leisurely in their ways and disengaged in their minds. The size of the city and the pursuit of the inhabitants give rise to an interest in character—an interest that was present in all the coteries that Dublin of the turn of the century composed itself into" (9). See also *The Joycean Way: A Topographical Guide to 'Dubliners' & 'A Portrait of the Artist as a Young Man'* by Bruce Bidwell and Linda Heffer (Baltimore: The Johns Hopkins Press, 1982).

[53] See Florence L. Walzl, "*Dubliners*: Women in Irish Society," *Women in Joyce*, ed. Suzette Henke and Elaine Unkeless (Urbana: U of Illinois Press, 1982). See also the essays by Blanche Gelfant, Marilyn French, and Sherrill E. Grace in the section entitled "A Frame of Her Own: Joyce's Women in *Dubliners* Re-Viewed, *James Joyce: The Augmented Ninth*.

[54] David Pierce and Dan Harper, *James Joyce's Ireland* (New Haven: Yale UP, 1992) 99.

[55] According to Pierce and Harper, "through a series of homologous structures, "A Painful Case' highlights the split between the suburbs and the city centre of Dublin, between the mind and the body, between public morality and private feeling. The story focuses on lower middle-class-detachment and its intermittent desire for contact with humanity, and it brings out Mr. Duffy's *inability* to live 'as far as possible from the city of which he was a citizen'" (Pierce and Harper 100).

[56] Gelfant, 265.

[57] Bachelard, xxxi.

[58] Yi Fu Tuan, *Space and Place: The Perspective of Experience* (Minneapolis: U of Minnesota Press, 1977) 114.

[59] See Selwyn Kittredge, "The Loss of Time in 'Counterparts'," *James Joyce Quarterly* 10.3 (Spring 1973): 339–41.

[60] See Klaus Reichert, "The European Background of Joyce's Writing" in *The Cambridge Companion to James Joyce*, ed. Derek Attridge (Cambridge: CUP, 1990) 55–82.

[61] See Marvin Magalener and Richard M. Kain, *Joyce: The Man, the Work, the Reputation* (New York: NYU Press, 1956). After outlining certain "criteria of naturalism," the editors note: "the surface resemblance of the stories in *Dubliners* to some naturalist fiction has too often led to indiscriminate labeling of the book as a product of Zola's movement. [. . .] What he [Zola] designates the vital principle of naturalism, its philosophy of determinism, seems quite unimportant in Joyce's stories [. . .] from first to last, Joyce was primarily a symbolist writer" (66–67). Compare this reading with Terence Brown, "The Dublin of *Dubliners*" *James Joyce: An International Perspective: Centenary Essays in Honour of the Late Sir Desmond Cochrane*, eds. Suheil Badi Bushrui et al. (Gerrards Cross: Colin Smythe, 1982) 1–18.

[62] For major studies of naturalist fiction as a distinct literary genre, see Yves Chevrel, *Le Naturalisme* (Paris: Presses Universitaires de France: 1982) and David

Baguely, *The Entropic Vision* (Cambridge: CUP, 1990). In "The Nature of Natural-ism," *Naturalism in the European Novel: New Critical Perspectives* (New York: Berg Publishers, Inc., 1992), Baguely identifies two basic models within the French tradition. In the first instance, there is the Goncourt type, which takes up tragic scheme of the fall of a single character, is presented as a temporal process of deteri-oration, and derives its causality from particular determining factors (hereditary flaws, neurotic dispositions, adverse social conditions) rather than from the tran-scendent forces of classical tragedy (for example, Zola's *L'Assommoir*). At the same time, there is the Flaubertian type, in which the determining factor of entropy is more generalized as the insufficiency of human life itself, trapping the individual in the snare of routine existence and its debilitating compromises" (Baguely 22).

[63] Chevrel, 48. Chevrel argues for the preeminent position of Zola in the devel-opment of naturalism, while simultaneously stressing the modernity of the natural-ist period, which he dates from the preface to the Goncourt's *Germaine Lacerteux* (1864) to the premiere of Chekov's *The Cherry Orchard* (1904).

[64] Reprinted in *Le Roman experimental* (1880); see also the Preface *to Les Soirées de Médan*.

[65] See also Tullio Pagano, *Experimental Fictions: From Emile Zola's Naturalism to Giovanni Verga's Verism* (Madison: Fairleigh Dickinson UP, 1999).

[66] Edmund Gosse, "The Limits of Realism in Fiction," *Forum* 9 (June 1890): 391–400; reprinted in *Questions at Issue* (London: Heinemann, 1893): 137–54).

[67] See Clarence Decker, "Balzac's Literary Reputation in Victorian Society," *PMLA* 47 (1932): 1150–53 and "Zola's Literary Reputation in England," *PMLA* 49 (1934): 1140–53. Also, see William C. Frierson, "The English Controversy over Realism in Fiction," *PMLA* 43 (1928): 533–50. As Dekker and Frierson note, the terms realism and naturalism were used interchangeably by nineteenth-century English critics and journalists in response to the translations of novels by Balzac, Zola, and their contemporaries.

[68] Lyn Pykett, "Representing the Real: The English Debate about Naturalism, 1884–1900," *Naturalism in the European Novel*, 169.

[69] Pykett quoting Stutfield 184. As Pykett notes, the social and political causes and effects of the "New Naturalism" were also at the center of W. S. Lilly's essay on the "New Naturalism" (1885)—a criticism of Zola and Zolaism—and Arthur Waugh's "Reticence in Literature" (1894). Lilly not only recognized but also de-plored naturalism as the representative literary form of the age, arguing that the naturalists' concerns to "analyze humanity as they find it" as essentially leveling it since it "is best done in the most vulgar types (Chevrel quoting Lilly 173).

[70] Lehan, "Joyce's City," *James Joyce: The Augmented Ninth*, 248.

[71] Lehan, 249.

[72] Houston A. Baker, *Modernism and the Harlem Renaissance* (Chicago: U of Chicago Press, 1987) 6.

[73] Long, 144.

[74] Long, 146.

[75] See Anthony Ostroff, "The Moral Vision in *Dubliners*," *Western Speech* 20.4 (Fall 1956): 196–209.

[76] Chevrel, 51.

[77] See Klaus Reichert, "The European Background of Joyce's Writing." *The Cambridge Companion to James Joyce*, ed. Derek Attridge (Cambridge: CUP, 1990) 55–82. Jackson I. Cope, meanwhile, defines Joyce's intellectual debt one stage further by connecting the author's modernist revolution more particularly to two major emphases in the Victorian novelistic tradition: in the first instance, an unquestioned assumption that "the matrix of the psyche's conflicting alienation and need was the family"; while the second was the embedding of both the individual and the family in "the larger social (or anti-social) network of the city, a metaphor for the disparateness and lonely sterility of modern life." *Joyce's Cities: Archaelogies of the Soul* (Baltimore: Johns Hopkins UP, 1981) 1–28. Cope maps the ubiquitous vision of "the wasted and despairing city" (2) in English literature from the mid-nineteenth century up until Eliot's *The Waste Land*, but argues that the Dublin of "Joyce the Victorian" was influenced by the infernal Florence of Dante's *Inferno*.

[78] Baguely, "The Nature of Naturalism," 17.

[79] See David Lodge, *The Modes of Modern Writing: Metaphor, Metonymy, and the Typology of Modern Literature* (Ithaca, NY: Cornell UP,1977). Lodge points out that the title of the stories is itself a "synechdoche," and that the book "describes a representative cross-section or sample of the life of the Irish capital" (125).

[80] See Brown, "The Dublin of *Dubliners*" *James Joyce: An International Perspective* 11; and Margaret Chesnutt, "Joyce's *Dubliners*: History, Ideology, and Social Reality." *Eire* 14:2 (1979): 533–49.

[81] For an argument against Joyce's "paralysis," see Trevor L. Williams, "Resistance to Paralysis in *Dubliners*," *Modern Fiction Studies* 35.3 (Autumn 1989): 437–57

[82] Among many early considerations of the significance of Dublin for Joyce's work are Harry Levin, *James Joyce* (Norfolk, Connecticut, 1941); William York Tindall, *James Joyce: His Way of Interpreting the Modern World*. (New York: Scribner, 1950); Hugh Kenner, *Dublin's Joyce* (London: Chatto & Windus, 1955); and Anthony Burgess, *Re Joyce* (New York: W.W. Norton, 1965).

[83] Torchiana points out that there are numerous engaging testimonies regarding the importance of Dublin for Joyce's work; for example, Ellmann, Kain, Hutchins, Hart, Knuth, Atherton, and Staples. See also Torchiana, "Joyce and Dublin," *The Irish Writer and the City* 52–63 and David Pierce, *James Joyce's Ireland* (New Haven: Yale UP, 1992). For shorter studies consult F. S. L. Lyons, "James Joyce's Dublin," *Twentieth Century Studies* 4 (November 1970): 6–25; J. C. C. Mays, "Some Comments on the Dublin of Ulysses," *Ulysses Cinquante Ans Apres* Paris: Marcel Didier: 83–98; Terence Brown, "Dublin in Twentieth-Century Writing: Metaphor and Subject," *Irish University Review*. 8:1 (Spring 1978): 7–21; and Thomas Kinsella, '*The Irish Writer*,' *Davis Mangan, Ferguson?* ed. Roger McHugh (Dublin: Dolmen Press, 1970) 57–70.

[84] For more regarding Joyce's opinions on these matters, see the letters written to Stanislaus Joyce, 19 July 1905, and 6 November 1906, respectively, *Selected Letters of James Joyce*, 70, 123.

85 Richards' side of the correspondence appears in *Studies in Bibliography*, ed. Fredson Bowers (Charlottesville, VA: U of Virginia, 1963) Vol. XVI, 139–60.

86 See Joyce's letter to Grant Richards, 25 May 1906, *Selected Letters of James Joyce*, 83.

87 See Joyce's Letter to Stanislaus Joyce, 19 July 1905 *Selected Letters of James Joyce*, 70.

88 See Joyce's letter to Grant Richards, 31 May 1906, *Selected Letters of James Joyce*, 86.

89 See Joyce's letters to Grant Richards dated 23 June 1906 and 23 June 1906, *Selected Letters of James Joyce*, 89, 90.

90 See Joyce's letter to Grant Richards, 31 May 1906, *Selected Letters of James Joyce*, 86.

91 Herbert N. Schneidau, "Style and Sacrament in Modernist Writing," *The Georgia Review* 31 (1977) 429. See also Ben L. Collins, "Progression in the Work of James Joyce," *Wisconsin Studies in Literature* 2 (1965): 54–69.

92 Schneidau, 430. Jackson I. Cope argues that "to see properly the nature of Joyce's modernist revolution, one must not lose sight of Joyce the Victorian." "The Waste Land," *Joyce's Cities*, 1–28.

93 See M. G. Cooke, "From Comedy to Terror: On *Dubliners* and the Development of Tone and Structure in the Modern Short Story," *The Massachusetts Review* (Spring 1968): 331–43.

94 Joseph K. Davis, "The City as Radical Order: James Joyce's *Dubliners*," *Studies in the Literary Imagination* 3.2 (October 1970): 80. See also Hana Wirth-Nesher, who critiques Arthur E. McGuiness' essay "The Ambience of Space in Joyce's *Dubliners*," *Studies in Short Fiction* 11.4 (Fall 1974): 343–51, as well as Davis in "Reading Joyce's City: Public Space, Self, and Gender in *Dubliners*," *James Joyce: The Augmented Ninth*. In particular, Wirth-Nesher notes that, "McGuinness draws on Bachelard's conception of topophilia, felicitous space, to demonstrate that the characters of *Dubliners* are usually indifferent to any intimate spaces that could offer security or refuge, and that they are alienated from their surrounding spaces. William P. Keen maintains that the shifting spatial focus from higher (upper floors, sky, hills) to lower (ground floors, streets, depths) is related to moral attitudes. Davis discusses Joyce as parallel to Spengler, in that the Irishman's in his indictment of the city as a place of intellect, rootlessness, and sterility, and he claims that Joyce saw the city as something to be escaped. None of these readings examines the urban lexicon" (292).

CHAPTER THREE NOTES

1 Rainer Maria Rilke, Letter 5, 29 October 1903, *Letters to a Young Poet*, trans. Stephen Mitchell (New York: Modern Library, 2001) 34.

2 Mumford, Lewis. *The City in History: Its Origins, Its Transformations, and Its Prospects.* (New York: Harcourt Brace & Company, 1961) 10.

3 Mumford, *The City in History*, 7.

[4] Ellmann, *James Joyce* (1959; Oxford: OUP, 1982) 225.

[5] As Ellmann notes, "The obtrusiveness of the dead affected what he thought of Dublin, the equally Catholic city he had abandoned, a city as prehensile of its ruins, visible and invisible. His head was filled with a sense of the too successful encroachment of the dead upon the living city: there was a disrupting parallel in the way that Dublin, buried behind him, was haunting his thoughts." Ellmann *James Joyce* 244.

[6] For example, see Joyce's letter to Stanislaus, Postmark 19 August 1906, *Selected Letters of James Joyce*, 98. Like Freud, one of Joyce's first experiences of Rome was his reaction to the Tiber. In Freud's case, he claimed to have sensed the river's metonymic presence from afar. But as a postcard to Stanislaus dated 31 July 1906 reveals, the Irish writer's reaction was one of fear. *Selected Letters of James Joyce*, 90.

[7] See Joyce's letter to Stanislaus Joyce, Postmark 19 August 1906, *Selected Letters of James Joyce*, 96.

[8] See Joyce's postcard to Stanislaus Joyce, Postmark 31 July 1906 Tuesday 9:30pm, *Selected Letters of James Joyce*, 90.

[9] See Joyce's letter to Stanislaus Joyce, Postmark 3 December 1906, Sunday noon, *Selected Letters of James Joyce*, 135.

[10] See Joyce's letter to Stanislaus Joyce, 25 September 1906, *Selected Letters of James Joyce*, 108.

[11] Ellmann, *James Joyce*, 244.

[12] See Joyce's letter to Stanislaus Joyce, ?1 March 1907, *Selected Letters of James Joyce*, 109–10.

[13] Brewster Ghiselin's analysis argues convincingly for the structural unity of the text as "both a group of short stories and a novel, the separate histories of its protagonists composing one essential history, that of the soul of a people which has confused and weakened its relation to the source of spiritual life and cannot restore it." Ghiselin, "The Unities of Joyce's *Dubliners*," *Accent* 16 (1956): 75–88 and 196–213. 76. See also Edward Brandabur, "The Sisters," in Robert Scholes and A. Walton Litz, eds., *James Joyce*, Dubliners: *Text, Criticism, and Notes* (New York: Viking, 1968) 333–43.

[14] For example, see R. B. Kershner, *Joyce, Bakhtin, and Popular Culture: Chronicles of Disorder* (Chapel Hill and London: U of North Carolina Press, 1989) and Donald T. Torchiana, *Backgrounds for Joyce's "Dubliners"* (Boston: Allen, 1986). A central reason for this critical turn has much to do with the enduring power of Richard Ellmann's monumental biography *James Joyce*. See also Alan Roughley, *James Joyce and Critical Theory: An Introduction* (Ann Arbor: The U of Michigan Press, 1991).

[15] See Richard Brown, *James Joyce and Sexuality* (Cambridge: CUP, 1985); Garry Leonard, "Joyce and Lacan: 'The Woman' as a Symptom of 'Masculinity' in 'The Dead,'" *James Joyce Quarterly* 28.2 (1991): 451–72; Suzette Henke and Elaine Unkeless, eds., *Women in Joyce* (Urbana: U of Illinois Press, 1982); Bonnie Kime Scott, *Joyce and Feminism* (Bloomington: Indiana UP, 1984); and Ruth Bauerle, "Date Rape, Mate Rape: A Liturgical Interpretation of 'The Dead," *New*

Alliances in Joyce Studies, ed. Bonnie Kime Scott (Newark: U of Delaware Press, 1988) 113–125.

[16] See Colin McCabe, *James Joyce and The Revolution of the Word* (New York: Harper, 1979); and Sheldon Brivic's two studies, *Joyce Between Freud and Jung* (New York: Kennickat, 1980) and *The Veil of Signs: Joyce, Lacan, and Perception* (Urbana: U of Illinois Press, 1985). For an example of recent developments in "Dead" criticism, see Daniel R. Schwarz, ed., *James Joyce: "The Dead": Complete Authoritative Text with Biographical and Historical Contexts, Critical History, and Essays from Five Contemporary Critical Perspectives* (New York: Bedford Books of St. Martin's Press, 1994).

[17] Gerald Gould, *New Statesman* III (27 June 1914): 374–5. See also Robert H. Deming, *James Joyce: The Critical Heritage* 1902–1927 (London: Routledge & Kegan Paul, 1970). Though Gould's review focuses on "Grace" and "Araby," it nonetheless makes for an interesting early response to the text in his consideration of the originality of Joyce's approach to fiction and the success of his narrative method.

[18] John Macy, *James Joyce: The Critical Game* (Boni and Liveright, Publishers, 1922) 317–322.

[19] See Allen Tate and Caroline Gordon, *The House of Fiction* (New York: Scribner's, 1950).

[20] See C. C. Loomis, Jr., "Structure and Sympathy in Joyce's 'The Dead,'" *PMLA* 35 (1960): 149–51. Landmark interpretations from this period include Hugh Kenner, *Dublin's Joyce* (Boston: Beacon, 1956), and Northrop Frye, *Anatomy of Criticism: Four Essays* (Princeton: Princeton UP, 1957).

[21] See David Daiches, *The Novel and the Modern World* (Chicago: U of Chicago Press, 1939). Also, see the commentaries by Tate, Burke, Tindall, Walzl, Kenner, and Ellmann.

[22] See Florence L. Walzl, "Gabriel and Michael: The Conclusion of The Dead," *James Joyce Quarterly* 4:1 (Fall 1966): 17–31.

[23] Donald T. Torchiana, "Introduction: James Joyce's Method in 'Dubliners,'" *Backgrounds for Joyce's Dubliners* (London: Allen & Unwin, 1986) 1–17. For more on the "The Dead's" coda, see William York Tindall, *A Reader's Guide to James Joyce* (New York: Farrar, 1959) and Charles Peake, *James Joyce: The Citizen and the Artist* (Stanford: Stanford UP, 1977).

[24] See Ellmann, *James Joyce* 243–53. For another biographical reading of "The Dead," See Brenda Maddox, *Nora: The Real Life of Molly Bloom* (Boston: Houghton, 1981).

[25] Ellmann, *James Joyce*, 259.

[26] Allen Tate, "Three Commentaries: Poe, James, and Joyce," *Sewanee Review* 58 (1950) 409.

[27] Kenneth Burke, "The Joyce Portrait," *James Joyce, Dubliners: Text, Criticism, and Notes*, 415.

[28] Burke, *James Joyce, Dubliners: Text, Criticism, and Notes*, 415–16.

[29] Walzl, 443. Joanna Higgins' and John B. Humma's arguments are also colored along similar lines, while Tindall argues for a union of opposites in *A Reader's Guide to James Joyce*, 42–49.

[30] Walzl, 443.

[31] See John Wilson Foster's pugnacious reading of "The Dead, "Passage Through 'The Dead,'" *Criticism* 15:2 (Spring 1973): 91–108.

[32] Vincent P. Pecora, "'The Dead' and the Generosity of the Word," *PMLA* 101:2 (1986): 233–43. See also Joseph Buttigieg, "The Struggle against Meta (Phantasma)-physics: Nietzsche, Joyce, and the 'Excess of History,'" *Boundary* 2.10 (1981): 187–204.

[33] Pecora, 243.

[34] Pecora, 243.

[35] Pecora, 233.

[36] Pecora, 236.

[37] Joyce, Letter to Georg Goyert, 19 October 1927. *Selected Letters of James Joyce*, 328.

[38] Pecora, 235

[39] Pecora, 234.

[40] Pecora, 233.

[41] Pecora, 233.

[42] See Joyce's letter to Stanislaus Joyce, 25 September 1906, *Selected Letters of James Joyce*, 110.

[43] Pecora, 234.

[44] J. P. Riquelme, "Joyce's 'The Dead': The Dissolution of the Self and the Police," *Style* 25. 3 (1991): 489–505.

[45] Christopher Ames, *The Life of the Party: Festive Visions in Modern Fiction* (Athens: The U of Georgia Press, 1991) 309.

[46] Richard Lehan, *The City in Literature* (Berkeley: U of California Press, 1998) 272.

[47] Michael Wheeler, *Death and the Future Life in Victorian Literature and Theology* (Cambridge: Cambridge UP, 1990) 25. Wheeler maintains that "at the centre of these concerns [the nature of religious experience, belief and language as they relate to the processes of death and bereavement in Victorian deathbed and graveyard scenes] lies a tension between what can broadly be defined as 'horizontal' ontological and epistemological models, which tend to be anthropomorphic, historical, experiential, and gradualist in orientation, and 'vertical' models, which are often theocentric, eschatological, scriptural, and catastrophist. [. . .] The horizontal dimension of temporal process and deferral comes to the fore in the Victorian novel, and the 'sense of an ending'; in millenarian epic poems on the 'course of time'; and in doctrines of purgatory and the 'intermediate state' between death and the last judgment, whereby final dispensations are deferred" (xiii).

⁴⁸ William Wordsworth, "The Excursion" V, 554–57, *The Poetical Works of Wordsworth* (Boston: Houghton Mifflin Company, 1982) 471. Quoted by Wheeler 25.

⁴⁹ Wheeler, 27.

⁵⁰ Wordsworth's essay "Upon Epitaphs" was first published in 1810 in *The Friend* and again as an appendix to Books V–VIII of *The Excursion* in 1814. The latter two, "The Country Church-Yard," "Critical Examination of Ancient Epitaphs," and "Celebrated Epitaphs Considered," were published after Wordsworth's death in 1850.

⁵¹ Wordsworth, *The Prose Works of William Wordsworth* 3 vols. (New York: AMS Press, Inc., 1967) 2: 71.

⁵² Wordsworth, *The Prose Works*, 2: 34.

⁵³ Wordsworth, *The Prose Works*, 2: 32.

⁵⁴ See Frances Ferguson, *Wordsworth: Language as Counter-Spirit* (New Haven: Yale UP, 1977) and Alan Liu, *Wordsworth: The Sense of History* (Stanford: Stanford UP, 1989).

⁵⁵ Liu, 384.

⁵⁶ Ferguson, 155.

⁵⁷ Wordsworth, *The Poetical Works* 133. Quoted by Ferguson 155.

⁵⁸ Ferguson, 155.

⁵⁹ Liu, 381.

⁶⁰ Wordsworth, *The Prose Works*, 2: 27.

⁶¹ Wordsworth, *The Prose Works*, 2: 35.

⁶² Wordsworth, *The Prose Works*, 2: 28.

⁶³ Wordsworth, *The Prose Works*, 2: 30.

⁶⁴ Wordsworth, *The Prose Works*, 2: 28.

⁶⁵ Wordsworth, *The Prose Works*, 2: 65.

⁶⁶ Wordsworth, *The Prose Works*, 2: 65.

⁶⁷ Joyce, *The Critical Writings of James Joyce*, eds. Ellsworth Mason and Richard Ellman (New York: Viking Press, 1959) 75.

⁶⁸ Wordsworth, *The Prose Works* 2:29.

⁶⁹ Liu, 382.

⁷⁰ Dominic Manganiello, *Joyce's Politics* (London: Routledge & Kegan Paul, 1980) 25.

⁷¹ Joyce, *The Critical Writings of James Joyce*, 151.

⁷² Declan Kiberd, "The Center and the Periphery," *The South Atlantic Quarterly* 95.1 (Winter 1996): 7. See also Kiberd's "Inventing Irelands," *Yeats's Political Identities: Selected Essays*. Ed. Jonathon Allison. Ann Arbor: The U of Michigan Press, 1996. 145–64; and *Inventing Ireland* (Cambridge, MA: Harvard UP, 1996).

⁷³ Kiberd, "The Center and the Periphery," 7.

⁷⁴ Kiberd, "The Center and the Periphery," 16.

⁷⁵ Joyce, *The Critical Writings of James Joyce*, 81.

⁷⁶ Joyce, Letter to Stanislaus Joyce, 25 September 1906, *Selected Letters of James Joyce*, 109–10.

⁷⁷ Pecora, 236.

⁷⁸ Joyce, Letter to Stanislaus Joyce, 25 September 1906, *Selected Letters of James Joyce*, 110.

⁷⁹Joyce, "A Portrait of the Artist," *A Portrait of the Artist as a Young Man: Text, Criticism, and Notes*, 265–66.

⁸⁰ Pecora, 234.

⁸¹ Liu, 387.

⁸² Pecora, 234.

⁸³ Wordsworth, *The Prose Works*, 2: 36.

⁸⁴ Wordsworth, *The Prose Works*, 2: 69.

⁸⁵ Liu, 381.

⁸⁶ Wordsworth, *The Prose Works*, 2: 38.

⁸⁷ Ferguson, 31.

⁸⁸ Ferguson, 33–34.

⁸⁹ Ferguson, 31.

CHAPTER FOUR NOTES

¹ R. B. Kershner, "A Critical History of *A Portrait of the Artist as a Young Man*," *A Portrait of the Artist as a Young Man: Complete, Authoritative Text with Biographical and Historical Contexts, Critical History, and Essays from Five Contemporary Critical Perspectives*, ed. R. B Kershner (New York: Bedford Books of St. Martin's Press, 1993) 221–34. 32. For a comprehensive introduction and selective guide to Joyce and critical theory, see Alan Roughley, *James Joyce and Critical Theory* (Ann Arbor: The U of Michigan Press, 1991.

² Although rejected by the editors of the Dublin University publication *Dana*, Joyce's 1904 essay, "A Portrait of the Artist," had by 1905 been transformed into the autobiographical novel *Stephen Hero*. But by 1908 Joyce lost faith in the project. The text was reconceived to become the protracted novel *A Portrait of the Artist as a Young Man*, which Joyce completed in 1914. The novel had taken ten years: "Dublin 1904—Trieste 1914"(*P* 253). *Portrait* was serialized in *The Egoist* from 7 February 1914 to 1 September 1915. For the composition history of *Portrait* see Hans Walter Gabler, "The Seven Lost Years of *A Portrait of the Artist as a Young Man*," *Approaches to Joyce's "Portrait*," ed. Thomas F. Staley and Bernard Benstock (Pittsburgh: U of Pittsburgh Press, 1976) 25–60.

³ For a critical history of *Portrait* scholarship, see Thomas F. Staley, "Strings in the Labyrinth: Sixty Years with Joyce's *Portrait*," *Approaches to Joyce's "Portrait"* 3–24; "James Joyce," *Anglo-Irish Literature: A Review of Research*, ed. Richard J. Finneran (New York: Modern Language Association of America, 1976) 402–10; and "*A Portrait of the Artist as a Young Man*," in *An Annotated Critical Bibliogra-*

phy of James Joyce (New York: St. Martin's Press, 1989) 102–117. Also, see Mitzi M. Brunsdale, *James Joyce: A Study of the Short Fiction* (New York: Twayne Publishers, 1994) for a general overview of more recent criticism on *Portrait*. For an overview of theoretical perspectives on the novel, from Hugh Kenner through poststructuralist analyses, see David Seed, "Theoretical Perspectives," *James Joyce's "A Portrait of the Artist as a Young Man"* (New York: St. Martin's Press, 1992) 28–42; and, Thomas Rice Jackson, *James Joyce: A Guide to Research* (New York: Garland Publishing, Inc., 1982).

⁴ Arguing that *A Portrait* is "based on a literal transcript of the first twenty years of Joyce's life," Harry Levin discusses the novel in the tradition of the *kunstlerroman*, whereby a youth grows into his vocation of artistry. For more on this analysis, see Levin, *James Joyce: A Critical Introduction* (Norfolk, Connecticut: New Directions, 1941). For a summary of the range of positions assumed by Joyce scholars in their study of *Portrait*, see Chester G. Anderson, "Editor's Introduction," *A Portrait of the Artist as a Young Man: Text, Criticism, and Notes*, ed. Chester G. Anderson (New York: Viking, 1968) 446–54.

⁵ See Hugh Kenner, "The Portrait in Perspective," *Dublin's Joyce* (Boston: Beacon Press, 1956) 121. More recently, Kenner has identified the young aesthete as an extension of the paralyzed and broken figures in *Dubliners*. For example, see Kenner's "The Cubist *Portrait*," *Approaches to Joyce's "Portrait*," 177–84.

⁶ Joyce, *A Portrait of the Artist as a Young Man: Text, Criticism, and Notes*, ed. Chester G. Anderson (New York: Viking, 1968). Subsequent references are to this edition and are cited parenthetically in the text.

⁷ Kenner, *Dublin's Joyce*, 132.

⁸ For a unique commentary on Stephen's aesthetic theory in relation to the cultural and social life of the modern metropolis, see Garry Leonard, "The City, Modernism, and Aesthetic Theory," *A Portrait of the Artist as a Young Man" Novel: A Forum on Fiction* 29.1 (Fall 1995): 79–99. Isolating, among other things, issues of sexuality and commodity culture, Leonard argues that Stephen's "aesthetic contemplation must be understood within the psychological, historical, and sociological context of modernity and in relation to the metropolis" (80). In particular, Leonard notes: "The experience of modernity is fostered by the rise of the modern city, and works of modernism do not so much convey this experience as betray the strain of surviving it and detail their various strategies for doing so. Thus modernism might be regarded less as a representation of modernity and more as a symptom of it" (79).

⁹ While Simmel's direct interest in social and political affairs was minimal, he remained a prolific cultural commentator; indeed, more that two hundred of his articles appeared in a great variety of newspapers, journals, and magazines during his lifetime, and several more were published posthumously. He wrote fifteen major works in the fields of philosophy, ethics, sociology, and cultural criticism, in addition to other less significant works. Following his dissertation, he completed *On Social Differentiation* (1890), a work devoted to sociological problems. Thereafter, he published mainly in the field of ethics and the philosophy of history, returning to sociology at a later date. His two major early works include *The Problems of the Philosophy of History* and the two volumes of the *Introduction to the Science of Ethics* (1892–93). These were followed by *The Philosophy of Money* (1900), a

work that borders philosophy and sociology. Moving on to studies on religion, on Kant and Goethe, and on Nietzsche and Schopenhauer, Simmel published his major work, *Sociology: Investigations on the Forms of Sociation* in 1908. The next decade was marked by a turning away from sociological questions, but he later returned to them in 1917 with the publication of *Fundamental Questions of Sociology*. The latter part of Simmel's life up until his death in 1918 was spent working on cultural criticism, for example *Philosophische Kultur* (1911), with literary and art criticism in *Goethe* and *Rembrandt* (both published in 1916), and with the history of philosophy in *Hauptprobleme der Philosophie* (1910). His final work, *Lebensanschauung* (1918), set forth the vitalistic philosophy he had elaborated toward the end of his life. See David Frisby, *Simmel and Since: Essays on Georg Simmel's Social Theory* (New York: Routledge, 1992) 98.

[10] As Frisby points out, the more accurate translation of "Die Grossstadte und das Geistesleben" is "Metropoles and Mental Life." David Frisby, *Simmel and Since*, 96.

[11] Frisby, *Simmel and Since,* 98.

[12] Robert E. Park and E. W. Burgess, *The City* (Chicago: Chicago UP, 1967) 219.

[13] Frisby quoting H. Woodward, *Simmel and Since*, 104.

[14] For a useful consideration of Berlin as an endangered cultural sign, see Anreas Huyssen, "The Voids of Berlin," *Critical Inquiry* 24 (Autumn 1997): 57–82.

[15] The argument and elaboration of the essay's major cultural-historical idea grew out of the final section of Simmel's *The Philosophy of Money* (1900).

[16] Georg Simmel, "The Metropolis and Mental Life," *Classic Essays on the Culture of Cities*. ed. Richard Sennett (New York: Appleton-Century-Crofts, 1967) 47.

[17] The concept of circulation, as Frisby notes, was of personal importance to Simmel, in that between 1878 and 1911, Simmel moved to ten different residences within Berlin, three removals occurring within the same year. In terms of Simmel's circulation outside Berlin, he traveled abroad frequently on lecture tours to Switzerland, Italy, St. Petersburg, Vienna, Prague, Paris, Heidelburg, Frankfurt, and Munich. Frisby, *Simmel and Since*, 101–102.

[18] Frisby, *Simmel and Since*, 101.

[19] Joyce, "A Portrait of the Artist," *A Portrait of the Artist as a Young Man: Text, Criticism, and Notes*, ed. Chester G. Anderson (New York: Viking, 1968). 259.

[20] Leonard, 84.

[21] Schafer, one of Simmel's colleagues, is not only typical in his antagonism toward Simmel's lack of 'method,' but also typical of the criticisms in general leveled against sociology from within university circles in Heidelberg and Berlin. In particular, Schafer complained that, "Simmel owes his reputation to his 'sociological' activities. [. . .] In my view, however, sociology has yet to earn its position as a science. In my opinion, it is a dangerous error to wish to put 'society' in the place of the state and the church as the authoritative organ of human coexistence" David Frisby quoting Gassen, *Sociological Impressionism: A Reassessment of Georg Simmel's Social Theory*. 2nd ed. (New York: Routledge, 1981) 25.

²² Frisby, *Simmel and Since*, 5–6.

²³ See Kurt H. Wolff, *"Georg Simmel Trying Sociology* (New York: Wiley, 1974) 2–30; Frisby, *Sociological Impressionism*, 13–14.

²⁴ According to Frisby, all Simmel's concepts are relational ones, from the idea of interaction (*Wechselwirkung*) to sociation (*Vergesellschaftung*). For a more detailed analysis of Simmel's four discontinuous and informing conceptions of society (society as totality; society as sociation; society as experience and everyday knowledge; and, society as an aesthetic object), see Frisby, *Simmel and Since*, 5–19.

²⁵ Huyssen notes that, "there is perhaps no other major Western city that bears the marks of twentieth-century history as intensely and self-consciously as Berlin" (59).

²⁶ Frisby quoting Hans Simmel, *Sociological Impressionism*, 19.

²⁷ Simmel argued that metropolitan traits were the product of an urban condition social-psychological in nature; Weber, on the other hand, asserted they were the direct product of the confluence of noneconomic and economic forces called modern capitalism.

²⁸ Frisby quoting Siegfried Kracauer, *Sociological Impressionism*, 96.

²⁹ Frisby quoting Simmel, *Fragments of Modernity: Theories of Modernity in the Work of Simmel, Kracauer and Benjamin* (Cambridge, MA: The MIT Press, 1986) 96.

³⁰ As Frisby notes, at the substantive level Simmel's social theory of modernity explicitly concentrates upon the modern experience of time (as transitory), space (as fleeting), and causality (as fortuitous or arbitrary). All three arise out of a conception of modernity as the experience of the immediate present as differentiated and discontinuous. Frisby, *Fragments of Modernity*, 103.

³¹ Frisby, *Fragments of Modernity*, 104.

³² Weber's essay "The City" (written somewhere between 1911 and 1913 but not published until 1921) presents a systematic and structural investigation of the historical development and importance of the Western city as an "ideal-typical" form, with particular reference to Antiquity and the Middle Ages. Unlike Simmel, Weber assumed that modern cities were primitive institutions, and as such did not express the possibility of the city as a cultural phenomenon.

³³ Sennett, 10.

³⁴ On the question of Simmel's approach to human individuality in relation to the self, cultural objects, and social formations, see Patrick Watier, "Simmel and the Image of Individuality," *Current Sociology* 41.2 (Autumn 1993): 69–75.

³⁵ Frisby, *Simmel and Since*, 65.

³⁶ Frisby quoting Simmel, *Simmel and Since*, 150.

³⁷ Richard Lehan, *The City in Literature* (Berkeley: U of California Press, 1998) 247.

³⁸ Joyce, *Stephen Hero*, ed. John J. Slocum and Herbert Cahoon (New York: New Directions, 1963). 211.

³⁹ Leonard suggests that in the same way that Simmel's notion of urban self-protection translates itself into Stephen's "protected space of aesthetic contemplation"

(*P* 84), so "Joyce's theory of the epiphany might be seen as a similar reaction to and product of a kaleidoscopic urban environment. Indeed, like Wordsworth's "spot of time," Leonard adds, Joyce's concept of the epiphany "transforms the Wordsworthian 'moment' of oceanic connection to 'something evermore about to be' into something much more like a snapshot of a world permanently in flux" (85).

40 Frisby quoting Simmel, *Simmel and Since*, 17.

41 Frisby quoting Simmel, *Simmel and Since*, 10.

42 Simmel, *The Philosophy of Money*, trans. Tom Bottomore and David Frisby (London: Routledge & Kegan Paul, 1978) 55.

43 Frisby, *Fragments of Modernity*, 4.

44 Simmel, "The Metropolis and Mental Life," 58.

45 Simmel, "The Metropolis and Mental Life," 51.

46 Simmel, "The Metropolis and Mental Life," 52.

47 Joyce, *The Critical Writings of James Joyce*, ed. Ellsworth Mason and Richard Ellmann (New York: The Viking Press, 1959) 69.

48 See Richard F. Peterson, "Stephen and the Narrative of *A Portrait of the Artist as Young Man*," *Work in Progress: Joyce Centenary Essays*, ed. Richard F. Peterson, Alan M. Cohn, and Edmund L. Epstein (Carbondale: Southern Illinois UP, 1983) 42. Using Aristotle's principle of apprehension, Peterson examines a "separate reality," bound to Stephen's impressions, outside the young Dubliner's thoughts. Peterson goes on to add, "the errors in Stephen's thinking that disturb so many readers do not reflect the essential form of *A Portrait*. Stephen's perceptions, his discovery of his soul and his knowledge that his mission is to create the uncreated conscience of his race, form the essence of the novel" (48).

49 Simmel, "The Metropolis and Mental Life," 48.

50 Leonard terms Stephen's fixation on meeting somebody as he wanders the city's streets "Stephen's urban fantasy" (83).

51 In historical terms, William Sharpe and Leonard Wallock identify three main traditions of analysis in response to the modern city: the English school of Charles Booth and Friedrich Engels; the German school of Max Weber, Georg Simmel, and Oswald Spengler, and the Chicago of Robert Park, Ernest Burgess, and Louis Wirth. See William Sharpe and Leonard Wallock, eds. *Visions of the Modern City: Essays in History, Art, and Literature* (New York: Columbia UP, 1983) 9–10.

52 As many commentators note, the sociology of literature may be said to have begun with Madame de Stael's *De la littérature considéré dans ses rapports avec les institutions sociale*, published in Paris in 1800 (it appeared in English as *A Treatise of Ancient and Modern Literature* [1803] and *The Influence of Literature upon Society* [1812]). This landmark work was later given impetus by Hippolyte Taine, whose "triad," as Wellek and Warren identify it, of *race, milieu*, and *moment* recurs frequently in subsequent critiques, and by Karl Marx's sociology of consciousness, which profoundly affected the development of the relationship between literature and society in European and American intellectual thought. In a more recent consideration of the interdisciplinary nature of the sociology of literature, the editors of a special edition of *Critical Inquiry*, while admitting that "it [the sociology of literature] is not an established field or academic discipline, nonetheless

commit themselves to the idea of the sociology of literature as a "cluster of intellectual ventures that originate in one overriding conviction: the conviction that literature and society necessarily explain each other." See "Editors' Introduction: Mirrors, Frames, and Demons: Reflections on the Sociology of Literature" 14 [Spring 1988] 421. As Catherine Gallagher points out in her own consideration of the work of Raymond Williams, such an approach as the one taken by *Critical Inquiry* is symptomatic of the development, especially during the 1980s, of the beginnings of a progressive re-consideration of the notion of otherwise mutually exclusive realms of representation (literary versus social) "saturated with symbolic value because we do not believe there is one." Gallagher, "Raymond Williams and Cultural Studies," *Cultural Materialism: On Raymond Williams*, ed., Peter Prendergast (Minneapolis: U of Minnesota Press, 1995) 308. While the dissolution of intellectual and disciplinary boundaries is far from complete (Gallagher cites the work of Hayden White and Benedict Anderson as examples of a form of reciprocity in action), the critical and theoretical enterprises formerly referred to as the sociology of literature have mutated to become that other semantically slippery cultural practice: cultural studies. According to Gallagher, "the new reciprocity in which social and literary-critical thinkers exchange both methods and objects of inquiry seems to me to be the essence of what is now being called 'cultural studies.' 'Cultural studies' specifies neither a well-defined object nor a method of analysis, unlike 'sociological approaches to literature', which rather clumsily insisted on both." Gallagher, "Raymond Williams and Cultural Studies" 308. For an overview of commentaries from European and American perspectives, see *The Sociology of Literature*, vol. 6. ed. Peter Davison, Rolf Meyersohn, and Edward Shils (Cambridge: Chadwick-Healey Ltd., 1978); Lucien Goldmann, *Essays on Method in the Sociology of Literature*, trans. William Q. Boelhower (St. Louis, MO: Telos Press, 1980); Robert Escarpit, *The Sociology of Literature*, trans. Ernest Pick (Painesville, OH: The Lake Erie College Press, 1965); a symposium piece entitled "The Comparative Method: Sociology and the Study of Literature" by Priscilla P. Clark, Leo Lowenthal, René Wellek, Jean Alter, Louisa Jones, W. Wolfgang Holdheim and Henry H. H. Remak (editor), *Yearbook of Comparative and General Literature* 23 (1974): 5–28; Matei Calinescu and André Reszler, "Literature and the Social Sciences," *Yearbook of Comparative and General Literature* 24 (1975): 43–50; *The Sociology of Literature: Theoretical Approaches*, eds. Jane Routh and Janet Wolff (Hanley: Wood Mitchell & Co., 1977); *The Sociology of Literature: Applied Studies*, ed., Diana Laurenson (Hanley: Wood Mitchell & Co., 1978); *Critical Inquiry: The Sociology of Literature* 14.3 (Spring 1988); *The Politics of Modernism*, ed. Francis Barker et al. (U of Essex, 1979); *The Practices of Literature and Politics*, ed. Francis Barker et al. (U of Essex, 1979); David H. Miles, "Literary Sociology: Some Introductory Notes," *The German Quarterly* 68.1 (January 1975): 1–35; Priscilla B. P. Clark, "Literature and Sociology," *Interrelations of Literature*, ed. Jean-Pierre Barricelli and Joseph Gibaldi (New York: The Modern Language Association of America, 1982) 107–122; Leo Lowenthal, "On Sociology of Literature," *Critical Theory and Society: A Reader*, ed. Stephen Eric Bronner and Douglas Mackay Kellner (New York: Routledge, 1989) 40–51; Pierre Bourdieu, "The Genesis of the Concepts of Habitus and Field," *Sociocriticism* 2 (December 1985): 11–24; Peter V. Zima, "Towards Sociological Semiotics" *Sociocriticism* 2 (December 1985): 113–128. For an overview of the development of American sociology and its interrelations with literature, see Susan Mizruchi, "Fiction and the Science of Society,"

The *Columbia History of the American Novel*, ed. Emory Elliott (New York: Columbia UP, 1985) 189–215; Peter Forster and Celia Kenneford, "Sociological Theory and the Sociology of Literature," *The British Journal of Sociology* 24.3 (September 1973): 355–64; Andrew Milner, "Literature and Society: The Problem of Method" *John Milton and the English Revolution* (Totowa, NJ: Barnes & Noble Books, 1981) 1–49; Lawrence Grossberg, Cary Nelson, and Paula A. Treichler, *Cultural Studies* (New York: Routledge, 1992); and, John Storey, ed. *What is Cultural Studies: A Reader* (New York: St. Martin's Press, 1997).

[53] For an excellent analysis of the sociological novel in the American literary tradition, see Carla Cappetti, *Writing Chicago: Modernism, Ethnography, and the Novel* (New York: Columbia UP, 1997). As Capetti notes, prominent Chicago School sociologists such as Park, Redfield, Burgess, and Wirth looked upon fiction, poetry, and drama as important sociological referents, in both their respective fields of research as well as in pedagogical terms. In a lecture titled "Social Science as Humanity," Chicago sociologist Robert Redfield argued that the social sciences were explicitly concerned with human beings, and that the sources for that study were the records of human living [that] [. . .] exist in ethnography and history [. . .] in biography and in psychiatric records; and [. . .] in creative literature. He went on to add: "No one is more deeply engaged in the examination and understanding of human nature than are the dramatist and the novelist. [. . .] I doubt that the results so far achieved by the social scientists are more communicative of the truth about human nature than are the results achieved by the more personal and imaginative records of the artist. [. . .] The man [sic] of literature and art has been longest in the subject." Capetti quoting Redfield, 26–27. Moreover, as Cappetti notes, in the case of the Chicago sociologists, "combining the empirical tradition that had characterized American philosophy and social reformers' activities and writings as well as the theoretical orientation of the European sociological tradition, Chicago sociologists brought social theory physically into the city; they also brought autobiographies, life histories, case studies, and personal letters into the sociologists' monographs, and in general they brought sociology closer to literature than to hard science" (32).

[54] See Wolf Lepenies, *Between Literature and Science: The Rise of Sociology*, trans. R. J. Hollingdale (Cambridge: CUP, 1988) 12–13. For more on the interrelations of sociology and aesthetics, see Robert Nisbett, *Sociology as an Art Form* (New Brunswick, NJ: Transaction Publishers, 2002) and Richard H. Brown, *A Poetics for Sociology: Toward a Logic of Discovery for the Human Sciences* (Chicago: U of Chicago Press, 1989). For more on the relationship between literature, art, and sociology, see Morroe Berger, *Real and Imagined Worlds: The Novel and Social Science* (Cambridge. MA: Harvard UP, 1977) and Audrey Borenstein, *Redeeming the Sin: Social Science and Literature* (New York: Columbia UP, 1978). Writers working in these allied fields include Clifford Geertz, Hayden White, Vincent Crapanzano, Lawrence Stone, George E. Marcus, Dick Cushman, Paul Veyne, George E. Marcus, Michael M. J. Fischer, James Clifford, Marc Manganaro, Misia Landau, J. Edward Chamberlain Sander L. Gilman, Nancy L. Stepan, Donna Haraway, and L. J. Jordanova.

[55] In *Writing Chicago* Cappetti analyzes a range of selected theories, ethnographies, and case studies of the Chicago sociologists W. I. Thomas, Robert Park,

Ernest Burgess, Frederic Thrasher, Robert Redfield, and Louis Wirth, in conjunction with selected works by James T. Farrell, Nelson Algren, and Richard Wright.

[56] William G. Flanagan, *Contemporary Urban Sociology* (Cambridge: Cambridge UP 1993) 1. Flanagan also notes, however, that "the nominal identifying feature of urban sociology is a geographic rather than a sociological object: urban sociology is a sociology identified with place rather than with a unit of social organization" (3).

[57] Flanagan, *Contemporary Urban Sociology*, 4.

[58] James Donald, "The City, the Cinema: Modern Spaces," *Visual Culture*, ed. Chris Jencks (New York: Routledge, 1995) 81.

CHAPTER FIVE NOTES

[1] Emily Tall, "Eisenstein on Joyce: Sergei Eisenstein's Lecture on James Joyce at the State Institute of Cinematography, November 1, 1934," *James Joyce Quarterly* 24.2 (Winter 1987): 133.

[2] While the massive complex of scholarly literature on American modernism is impossible to summarize adequately here, for a unique perspective on the phenomenon from an American point of view, see the "Introduction" by Michael J. Hoffman and Patrick D. Murphy, in *Critical Essays on American Modernism*, ed., Michael J. Hoffman and Patrick D. Murphy (New York: G.K. Hill & Co., 1992) 1–15. See also Alex Davis and Lee M. Jenkins, eds. *Locations of Literary Modernism: Region and Nation in British and American Modernist Poetry* (Cambridge: CUP, 2000); and Jonathan Levin, *The Poetics of Transition: Emerson, Pragmatism, & American Literary Modernism* (Durham: Duke UP, 1999).

[3] For example, see Shari Benstock, *Women of the Left Bank* (Austin: U of Texas Press, 1986); Houston J. Baker Jr., *Modernism and the Harlem Renaissance* (Chicago: U of Chicago Press, 1987); Alice Gambrell, *Women Intellectuals, Modernism, and Difference: Transatlantic Culture, 1919–1945* (Cambridge: CUP, 1997); Thomas, Lorenzo, *Extraordinary Measures: AfroCentric Modernism and Twentieth-Century American Poetry* (Tuscaloosa: U of Alabama Press, 2000); Kimberly W. Benston, *Performing Blackness: Enactments of African-American Modernism* (London: Routledge, 2000); Robert Morse Crunden, *Body & Soul : The Making of American Modernism* (New York: Basic Books, 2000); Elizabeth Francis, *The Secret Treachery of Words: Feminism and Modernism in America* (Minneapolis: U of Minnesota Press, 2002); Jessica Berman, *Modernist Fiction, Cosmopolitanism, and the Politics of Community* (Cambridge: CUP, 2001); Martin Klepper and Joseph C. Schöpp, eds., Transatlantic Modernism (Heidelberg: C. Winter, 2001); Gregory Castle, *Modernism and the Celtic Revival* (Cambridge: CUP, 2001).

[4] Richard Poirier, "The Difficulties of Modernism and the Modernism of Difficulty," *Critical Essays on American Modernism*, ed., Michael J. Hoffman and Patrick D. Murphy (New York: G.K. Hill & Co., 1992) 106.

[5] Virginia Woolf, "Mr. Bennett and Mrs. Brown," *The Captain's Death-Bed* (New York: Harcourt Brace, 1950) 96.

[6] Henry Adams, *The Education of Henry Adams*, ed. Ernest Samuels (Boston: Houghton Mifflin Co., 1973) 382.

[7] See Paul L. Jay "American Modernism and the Uses of History: The Case of William Carlos Williams," *Critical Essays on American Modernism*. In the course of analyzing the ways in which American modernist writers not only incorporated history into their work but also invented new literary forms with which to accomplish the task, Jay comments with regard to Henry Adams: "What I want to emphasize is the *double* nature of the 'break' which Adams experiences here: both history's continuity and the traditional modes of its representation have snapped for him. Adams records in *The Education* his experience of the 'end' of history as a context for beginning it anew. Proclaiming it his 'motive' and 'duty' to help attain the end of history whose continuity has broken, he turns to the formulation of his Dynamic Theory of History because, he writes, 'the old formulas had failed, and a new one had to be made [. . .] [but] one sought no absolute truth. One sought only a spool on which to wind the thread of history without breaking it' again." Jay quoting Adams, 128.

[8] For a systematic investigation of the idea of history in English and continental modernism, see Harvey Gross, *The Contrived Corridor: History and Fatality in Modern Literature* (Ann Arbor: The U of Michigan Press, 1971).

[9] Dos Passos, "A Humble Protest," *Harvard Monthly* 62 (June 1916) 115–120.

[10] Dos Passos, "Young Spain," *Seven Arts* 2 (August 1917) 478.

[11] The debate concerning the life and language of American poetics was particularly marked in poetry. For example, see e. e. cummings, "The New Art," *The Harvard Advocate*, 24 June 1915, 154–56; Harriet Monroe, introduction, *The New Poetry: An Anthology of Twentieth-Century Verse in English*, ed. Harriet Monroe and Alice Corbin Henderson (New York: Macmillan, 1917), v–xii; Ezra Pound, "A Retrospect," *Literary Essays of Ezra Pound* (1935; Norfolk, CT: New Directions, 1954), 3–8; H.L. Mencken, "The New Poetry Movement," *Prejudices: First Series* (New York: Knopf, Inc., 1947); Louis Untermeyer, "Others," *The New Era in American Poetry* (New York: Henry Holt & Co., 1919), 309–11; Amy Lowell, "Two Generations in American Poetry," *Poetry and Poets: Essays* (Boston: Houghton Mifflin, 1930), 111–22; Hart Crane, "Modern Poetry" *The Complete Poems and Selected Letters & prose of Hart Crane*, ed. Brom Weber (New York: Liveright Publishing Corporation, 1933), 161–63.

[12] For more on this debate, see Hugh Kenner, *A Homemade World* (New York: Morrow, 1975).

[13] Marcus Klein, *Foreigners: The Making of American Literature: 1900–1940* (Chicago: U of Chicago Press, 1981) 9.

[14] Michael J. Hoffman and Patrick D. Murphy, *Critical Essays on American Modernism*, 3.

[15] T. S. Eliot, "Tradition and the Individual Talent," *Selected Prose of T. S. Eliot*, ed. Frank Kermode (New York: Harcourt Brace Jovanovich, 1975) 38.

[16] John Gould Fletcher, "It Is Time to Create Something New," *Irradiations Sand and Spray* (New York: Macmillan, 1915) xv.

[17] Ezra Pound, *The Selected Letters of Ezra Pound, 1907–1941*, ed. D.D. Paige (1950; New York: New Directions, 1971) 6.

[18] Quoted in Lisa M. Steinman, "Modernism, Modernity, and Technology: Following the Engineers," *Critical Essays on American Modernism*, 206.

[19] H. L. Mencken, "The New Poetry," *Critical Essays on American Modernism*, 41.

[20] Steinman, "Modernism, Modernity, and Technology: Following the Engineers," 206.

[21] Steinman, 199.

[22] Dos Passos, "A Humble Protest," *John Dos Passos: The Major Nonfictional Prose*, ed. Donald Pizer (Detroit: Wayne State UP, 1988) 31.

[23] Dos Passos, "A Humble Protest," 33.

[24] For example, see Dos Passos, "The Writer as Technician," *John Dos Passos: The Major Nonfictional Prose*, 169–72.

[25] Dos Passos, "Against American Literature," *The Major Nonfictional Prose*, 36.

[26] Dos Passos, "Against American Literature," 38.

[27] Dos Passos, "Against American Literature," 38.

[28] Sinclair Lewis, *John Dos Passos' 'Manhattan Transfer'* (New York: Harper & Brothers Publishers, 1926). 17. Subsequent references are to this edition and are cited parenthetically in the text.

[29] Raymond Williams, "Metropolitan Perceptions and the Emergence of Modernism," in *The Politics of Modernism*, ed. Tony Pinkey (London: Verso, 1989) 42.

[30] Richard Ellmann, *James Joyce* (1959; Oxford: OUP, 1982) 233.

[31] See Joyce's letter to Stanislaus Joyce, Postmark 3 December 1906 Sunday noon, *Selected Letters of James Joyce*, ed. Richard Ellmann (New York: The Viking Press, 1975) 135–136.

[32] See Joyce's letters to Stanislaus Joyce dated 6 November 1906 and 31 August 1906, respectively, *Selected Letters of James Joyce*, 99–100, 123.

[33] See the following essays by Dos Passos in *John Dos Passos: The Major Nonfictional Prose*: "Translator's Foreword" to *Panama; or, The Adventures of My Seven Uncles* 134–35; "Introduction" to *Three Soldiers* 146–48; "Contemporary Chronicles" 238–39; "What Makes a Novelist" 268–75; and "Portrait of a Man Reading" 293–96. For a more comprehensive analysis, see George Knox, "Dos Passos and Painting, *Dos Passos, the Critics, and the Writer's Intention*, ed. Allen Belkind (Carbondale: Southern Illinois UP, 1971) 242–64; Ben Stoltzfus, "John Dos Passos and the French," *Dos Passos, the Critics, and the Writer's Intention*, 197–218; Linda Wagner, *Dos Passos as American* (Austin: U of Texas Press, 1979); and Kathleen G. Gjerter, *Doubly Gifted: The Author as Visual Artist* (New York: Harry N. Abrams, 1986).

[34] Dos Passos, "What Makes a Novelist?" *The Major Nonfictional Prose*, 270.

[35] Dos Passos, "What Makes a Novelist?" 269.

[36] Dos Passos, "The Writer as Technician," *The Major Nonfictional Prose*, 169.

[37] Dos Passos, "Contemporary Chronicles," *The Major Nonfictional Prose*, 238–39.

[38] Dos Passos, "Contemporary Chronicles," 239.

[39] Dos Passos, "Introduction," *Three Soldiers*, *The Major Nonfictional Prose*, 147–48.

[40] Dos Passos, "Introduction," *Three Soldiers*, *The Major Nonfictional Prose*, 147.

[41] Janet Calligani Casey, *Dos Passos and the Ideology of the Feminine* (Cambridge: Cambridge UP, 1998) 2.

[42] Casey, 4. For a detailed overview of the wealth of Marxist and historicist approaches to Dos Passos, see the three most recent and comprehensive bibliographies: Jack Potter, *A Bibliography of John Dos Passos* (Chicago: Normandie House, 1950); John Rohrkemper, *John Dos Passos: A Reference Guide* (Boston: G. K. Hall, 1980); and David Sanders, *John Dos Passos: A Comprehensive Bibliography* (New York: Garland, 1987). The recent literary and cultural reconsideration of Dos Passos has been brought about by studies of proletarian literature. For example, see James F. Murphy, *The Proletarian Moment: The Controversy over Leftism in Literature* (Urbana: U of Illinois Press, 1991) and Barbara Foley, *Radical Representations: Politics and Form in U.S. Proletarian Fiction, 1929–1941* (Durham: Duke UP, 1993).

[43] For an overview of the dominant trends in recent Dos Passos scholarship, see Casey 1–17. The insistence of Dos Passos' urban vision, however, continues to elicit critical responses; for example, see Keunen Bart, "The Plurality of Chronotopes in the Modernist City Novel: the Case of *Manhattan Transfer*," *English Studies: A Journal of English Language and Literature* 82.5 (October 2001): 420–36.

[44] Michael Denning, *The Cultural Front: The Laboring of American Culture in the Twentieth Century* (New York: Verso, 1996) 132.

[45] Casey, 20.

[46] Critics like H. L. Stuart astutely linked Dos Passos with impressionist and super-naturalist writers, while Herschel Brickell tied *Manhattan Transfer* to Neo-Realism, which stressed "the ugly and sordid." But he also noted that the novel remained, ultimately, a "literary experiment." Paul Elmer Moore called the novel "an explosion in a cesspool." Still others speculated on the authors and books from which *Manhattan Transfer* might have derived, for example, Moses Harper insisted in *The New Republic* that it was "too much influenced by the French naturalists." Lloyd Morris, meanwhile, informed readers of the *New York Times Book Review* that Dos Passos' work was a "courageous but not impressive attempt to achieve an expressionistic picture of New York," and compared it to *Ulysses*. Edmund Wilson was confused by Dos Passos and his art: "I've never understood why you [Dos Passos] give so grim a picture of life as it seems in the living." For Wilson the author-in-the-flesh seemed "to enjoy life more than most people and [was] by way of being a brilliant talker," but to Wilson Dos Passos seemed always to have his characters speak in cliches, and "they always get a bad egg for breakfast." Quoted by Virginia Spencer Carr, *Dos Passos: A Life* (Garden City, New York: Doubleday & Company, Inc., 1984) 396.

[47] See Melvin Landsberg, *Dos Passos' Path to U.S.A.: A Political Biography 1912–1936* (Boulder: The Colorado Associated UP, 1972). Landsberg claims that Dos Passos was the best read of his writing generation, and connects his political

and social nonconformism to a tradition of dissenting voices, including Veblen, the International Workers of the World, and syndicalism. Dos Passos, meanwhile, among his many influences, cited Emile Verhaeren's *Les Villes Tentaculaires* and Gustave Flaubert's *Sentimental Education* as artistic influences, not to mention James Joyce's *Ulysses*.

[48] Ernest Hemingway called *Manhattan Transfer* "a spiritual Baedecker to New York. He [Dos Passos] alone of American writers has been able to show to Europeans the America they really find when they come here." After the British edition was published, D. H. Lawrence called the novel "the best modern book about New York" he had ever read. In particular, he delighted in its "endless series of glimpses of people in the vast scuffle of Manhattan Island, as they turn up again and again, in a confusion that has no obvious rhythm, but wherein at last we recognize the systole-diastole of success and failure, the end being all failure, from the point of view of life; and then another flight towards another nowhere." Lawrence, moreover, saw the book as "a very complete film [. . .] of the vast loose gang of strivers and winners and losers which seems to be very pep of New York." Quoted by Spencer Carr, *Dos Passos: A Life*, 215.

[49] See Dos Passos, "Conversation with Dos Passos," *The Major Nonfictional Prose* 233. See also *Dos Passos: A Collection of Critical Essays*, ed. Andrew Hook (Englewood Cliffs, NJ: Prentice-Hall, Inc., 1974), and Allen Belkind, *Dos Passos, the Critics, and the Writer's Intention*.

[50] See Joseph Warren Beach, *American Fiction: 1920–1949* (New York: Macmillan, 1941), and Blanche H. Gelfant, "John Dos Passos: The Synoptic Novel," *The American City Novel* (Norman: U of Oklahoma Press, 1954) 133–74.

[51] Quoted by Spencer Carr 245. Perhaps the most damaging political critique of Dos Passos' work was that penned by Mike Gold, committed Communist and agent provocateur of the intellectual Left, who complained in a review in the *New Masses* that the problem with writers like Dos Passos was that they "hug chaos to their bosoms, and all the heroes of their fiction wind up in chaos and failure." Yet this "pessimism, defeatism, and despair" was not the only possible path for writers opposed to the status quo—there was always "the world of revolutionary labor." In a review of *Manhattan Transfer*, Gold called the novel "a barbaric poem of New York" which more than anything else reflected "bewilderment." The central protagonist, Jimmy Herf, Gold commented, "is tortured by American commercialism and always seeks some escape." In Gold's view, Dos Passos did not understand how to help Herf, who at the conclusion of the novel tries to escape the chaos of Manhattan by turning his back on the city by taking to the open road away from the "center of things." Jimmy's closing response to the man who offers him a ride and asks him where he is going ("I dunno, pretty far") was an affirmation, Gold pointed out, of nothing except the negative effects of urban life. The answer to Dos Passos' problems, Gold contended, was to "read history, psychology, and economics," and to become active in the labor movement. Instead of standing aloof, Dos Passos needed to "ally himself definitely with the radical army, for in this struggle is the only true escape from middleclass bewilderment today." Gold's commentary is certainly questionable. Dos Passos, for example, was anything but aloof from the social and political issues of the day, as his involvement with the Sacco-Vanzetti trial clearly proves. At the same time, Gold astutely observed that "Dos Passos suffers with nostalgia for a clean, fair, joyous and socialized America," by which Gold

meant the egalitarian democracy of individuals that had been the ideal before the young nation one hundred years earlier. Quoted in Spencer Carr, 245.

[52] Edmund Wilson, "Dos Passos and the Social Revolution" *Dos Passos: A Collection of Critical Essays*, ed. Andrew Hook (Englewood Cliffs, N.J.: Prentice-Hall, 1974) 32–33.

[53] F. R. Leavis, "A Serious Artist," *Dos Passos: A Collection of Critical Essays*, 72; 75.

[54] Richard Chase, "The Chronicles of Dos Passos," *Dos Passos: A Collection of Critical Essays*, 176.

[55] Granville Hicks, "The Politics of Dos Passos," *Dos Passos: A Collection of Critical Essays*, 20.

[56] John Aldridge, *After the Lost Generation* (New York: McGraw-Hill, 1951) 71.

[57] Malcolm Cowley, "John Dos Passos: The Poet Against the World," *Dos Passos: A Collection of Critical Essays*, 76.

[58] Cowley, "John Dos Passos: The Poet Against the World," 84.

[59] Alfred Kazin, "Dos Passos, Society and the Individual," *Dos Passos: A Collection of Critical Essays*, 134.

[60] Lionel Trilling, "The America of John Dos Passos," *Dos Passos: A Collection of Critical Essays*, 100.

[61] Arthur Mizener, "The Gullivers of Dos Passos," *Dos Passos: A Collection of Critical Essays*, 162–63.

[62] See the essays by John Chamberlain, Horace Gregory, and Max Lerner in *Dos Passos, the Critics, and the Writer's Intention.*

[63] In addition to Joyce's influence on Dos Passos, Beach cites Dorothy Richardson, Virginia Woolf, and Carl Sandburg. But of even greater influence in Beach's estimation are Gertrude Stein and the work of French cubists and post-impressionists.

[64] Beach, *Dos Passos, the Critics, and the Writer's Intention*, 63.

[65] John D. Brantley, *The Fiction of John Dos Passos*, Studies in American Literature. Vol. 16 (The Hague: Mouton & Co., 1968) 66.

[66] Walcutt, *Dos Passos, the Critics, and the Writer's Intention*, 84. Walcutt goes on to note that although *Ulysses* is tremendously complex, its Dublin is intimately familiar, whereas Dos Passos' Manhattan is a screaming turmoil of machines and people—a clouded vortex in which the characters are arrested for poignant moments and then disappear again into the whirling background. [. . .] Joyce, who is neither cold nor sentimental in *Ulysses*, had much more to say and a much more intimate control of his material. Aimlessness, whirl, and coincidence, expressed in the form of *Manhattan Transfer*, do not add up to a novel that says much, although its frantic picture is vivid and sensational" (84–85).

[67] George J. Becker, *John Dos Passos*, Modern Literature Monographs (New York: Frederick Ungar Publishing Co., 1974) 18. Singling out Joyce's influence in particular, Becker declares: "Finally, there is the example of *Ulysses*, where the dominant narrative interest in Leopold Bloom and Stephen Dedalus is supple-

mented by a quick succession of incidental scenes giving a sense of Dublin life, most notably in the 'Wandering Rocks' episode at the center of the novel" (27).

[68] Becker, 66.

[69] "Indirect interior monologue," for example, is one device Becker identifies: thoughts conveyed in the third person rather than the first (68).

[70] E. D. Lowry argues that Dos Passos is closer to T. S. Eliot than Joyce, in that "the most obvious similarities between *The Waste Land* and *Manhattan Transfer* is their use of the structural principle of dissociation and recombination." "*Manhattan Transfer*: Dos Passos' Wasteland," *Dos Passos: A Collection of Critical Essays* 53.

[71] Marshall McLuhan, "Technique vs. Sensibility," *Dos Passos, the Critics, and the Writer's Intention*, 227.

[72] McLuhan, 230.

[73] McLuhan, 230.

[74] McLuhan, 231–32.

[75] McLuhan, 232–33.

[76] McLuhan, 233.

[77] McLuhan, 241.

[78] McLuhan, 233.

[79] Belkind, 62.

[80] James Joyce, Letter to Carlo Linati, 21 September 1920, *Selected Letters of James Joyce*, 271.

[81] James Joyce, *Selected Letters of James Joyce*, 271.

[82] A. Walton Litz, "Pound and Eliot on *Ulysses*: The Critical Tradition," *JJQ* 10.1 (Fall 1972): 6. Under Joyce's direction, Valéry Larbaud presented a talk on Joyce's *Ulysses* , in which he stressed the symbolic aspects of the novel, at the Paris séance of 7 December 1921. The talk was subsequently published in the *Nouvelle Révue Francaise* in April 1922, and in *The Criterion* in October 1922, which also contained the text of *The Waste Land* (Litz 15).

[83] For more on Pound's criticisms of Joyce from 1914 onwards, see Forrest Read, ed. *Pound/Joyce: The Letters of Ezra Pound to James Joyce*, (New York: New Directions, 1970).

[84] Litz, 16. Eliot apparently told Virginia Woolf that *Ulysses* "destroyed the whole of the 19th century. It left Joyce with nothing to write another book on. It showed up the futility of all the English styles. [. . .] There was no 'great conception': that was Joyce's intention. [. . .] Joyce did completely what he meant to do." Quoted in Louis Menand, *Discovering Modernism: T. S. Eliot and His Context* (New York: Oxford UP, 1987) 92.

[85] Arnold Goldman, *The Joyce Paradox: Form and Freedom in His Fiction* (Evanston: Northwestern UP, 1966) 42. Litz identifies Hugh Kenner and Richard Ellmann as the chief inheritors of this tradition ("Pound and Eliot on *Ulysses*: The Critical Tradition" 10).

[86] Michael Groden, afterword, *Ulysses*, James Joyce. Ed. Hans Walter Gabler (London: Bodley Head, 1993; New York: Vintage, 1996) 4.

[87] T. S. Eliot, "*Ulysses*, Order, and Myth," *Dial* 75.5 (1923): 483.

[88] See Stanley Sultan, "The Method," *Ulysses, The Waste Land, and Modernism* (Port Washington, New York: Kennikat Press, 1977) 31–52. Identifying allusion as the shared "method" that both Joyce and Eliot use, Sultan states: "The difference exemplified by *Ulysses* and *The Waste Land* lies in their extension of what earlier works had done with both the allusive relationship and the task allotted to allusion, a new modernist conception of formal and functional possibilities" (32).

[89] Litz quoting Pound, 12.

[90] See Emer Nolan, "Introduction: Modernism and Nationalism," *James Joyce and Nationalism* (New York: Routledge, 1995) 1–23.

[91] Richard Aldington, "A Sensitivist," *Manchester Guardian* (2 March 1917) 3; reprinted in *James Joyce: The Critical Heritage*, ed. Robert H. Deming, 2 vols. (London: Routledge & Kegan Paul, 1970) 92.

[92] Although disgusted by *Ulysses*, Virginia Woolf, in her essay "Modern Fiction" (1919), grudgingly acknowledged the importance of Joyce's "method."

[93] T. S. Eliot, "*Ulysses*, Order, and Myth," 483.

[94] Litz, 5. See also Robert Adams Day, "Joyce's Waste Land and Eliot's Unknown God," *Literary Monographs* 4, ed. Eric Rothstein (Madison: U of Wisconsin Press, 1971) 139–210.

[95] Litz, 14. See also Joseph Kelly, *Our Joyce: from Outcast to Icon* (Austin: U of Texas Press, 1998).

[96] Michael H. Levenson, *A Genealogy of Modernism: A Study of English Literary Doctrine 1908–1922* (Cambridge: CUP, 1984) 206.

[97] Levenson, 208.

[98] Levenson quoting Eliot, 208.

[99] See Jeffrey Segall, *Joyce in America: Cultural Politics and the Trials of Ulysses,* (Berkeley: U of California Press, 1993). Joyce was defended and castigated during the 1920s and 1930s in debates between figures such as Edmund Wilson and Paul Elmer Moore over the form and function of modernist art, but most strongly in 1934 at the First International Writers' Congress in Moscow, where Karl Radek attacked *Ulysses* for lacking a social conscience. See also Jeffrey Segall, "Between Marxism and Modernism, or How to be a Revolutionist and Still Love "*Ulysses*," *JJQ* 25.4 (Summer 1988): 421–44.

[100] Jane Heap's and Margaret Anderson's *Little Review* was sued and financially ruined for their serialization of *Ulysses* by the New York Society for the Suppression of Vice. Meanwhile, American publisher Samuel Roth took advantage of American copyright laws in order to publish pirated installments of the novel. On 6 December 1933, Joyce, represented by Random House attorney Morris Ernst put an end to Roth's actions. The trial established the moral and artistic value of *Ulysses* when Judge John M. Wolsey of the United States District Court in New York overturned the obscenity charges leveled against the novel.

[101] Segall, *Joyce in America*, 42.

[102] Segall, *Joyce in America*, 26.

[103] Because the version printed in *The Saturday Review of Literature* had been cut by one third its original length, Harper & Brothers reprinted the review in full. See Sinclair Lewis, "John Dos Passos' 'Manhattan Transfer'" (New York: Harper & Brothers Publishers, 1926). 1.

[104] Lewis, "John Dos Passos' 'Manhattan Transfer,'" 10.

[105] Lewis, "John Dos Passos' 'Manhattan Transfer,'" 3–4.

[106] John W. Aldridge, "Mr. Lewis as Essayist," *Critical Essays on Sinclair Lewis*, ed. Martin Bucco (Boston: G. K. Hall & Co., 1986) 80.

[107] Lewis, "Introduction," "John Dos Passos' 'Manhattan Transfer'," i.

[108] Quoted in Martin Bucco, "Sinclair Lewis on Authorship," *Sinclair Lewis: New Essays in Criticism*, ed. James M. Hutchison (New York: The Whitston Publishing Company, 1977) 175.

[109] Bucco, 182.

[110] Frederic I. Carpenter, "Sinclair Lewis and the Fortress of Reality," *Sinclair Lewis' Arrowsmith*, ed. Harold Bloom (New York: Chelsea House Publishers, 1988) 5. For recent interpretations of Lewis' significance, see James Lundquist, *Sinclair Lewis* (New York: Frederick Ungar, 1973); Martin Bucco, ed., *Critical Essays on Sinclair Lewis* (Boston: G. K. Hall & Co., 1986); James M. Hutchinson, ed., *Sinclair Lewis: New Essays in Criticism* (Troy, New York: The Whitson Publishing Company, 1997); Charles Johnson, Kingsblood Royal: Sinclair Lewis (New York: Modern Library (2001); and Richard Lingeman, Sinclair Lewis: Rebel from Main Street (New York: Random House, 2002).

[111] See Sinclair Lewis, "The American Scene in Fiction," *The Man From Main Street: Selected Essays and Other Writings*, eds. Harry E. Maule and Melvin Cane (New York: Random House, 1953) 142–47. Lewis typically admonished young writers to realize things generally unnoticed. For example, in the essay "Gold, Inc." he warned aspiring novelists to stay away from "bewritten Hollywood." Rather, he saw more promise in the sagas of ordinary everyday people and their travails. *Newsweek* 11 (21 February 1938): 21.

[112] Lewis, "John Dos Passos' 'Manhattan Transfer,'" 12–13.

[113] Percy H. Boynton, "Sinclair Lewis," *More Contemporary Americans* (Chicago: The U of Chicago Press) 179–98. 82.

[114] Richard Sennett, "Introduction," *Classic Essays on the Culture of Cities* (New York: Appleton-Century-Crofts, 1969) 6.

[115] Honoé de Balzac, "The Girl with the Golden Eyes," *History of the Thirteen*. Trans. Herbert J. Hunt (New York: Penguin Putnam, Inc, 1975) 309.

[116] Balzac, 324.

[117] Joyce, *The Critical Writings of James Joyce*, ed. Ellsworth Mason and Richard Ellmann (New York: Viking Press, 1959) 37. Joyce managed to maneuver the controversial essay around the college president's despite the latter's objection to the former's alleged "indifference to ethical content in drama" (37). The essay survived the university censor, and Joyce was openly criticized and applauded in equal measure.

[118] James Joyce, *Stephen Hero*, ed. Theodore Spencer (New York: New Directions, 1944) 186.

[119] Carl E. Schorske, "The Idea of the City in European Thought: Voltaire to Spengler," *The Historian and the City*. ed. Oscar Handlin and John Burchard (Harvard: The MIT Press and HUP, 1963) 110.

[120] Marshall Berman, *All That Is Solid Melts Into Air: The Experience of Modernity* (New York: Penguin Books, 1988) 36.

[121] Berman, 89.

[122] Keith Tester reads Marx's proletarian narratives as critiques of modernity that attempt to transcend the "modern hermeneutic of the world as a bounded place." *The Life and Times of Post-Modernity* (London: Routledge, 1993) 34. See also Alvin W. Gouldner, *Against Fragmentation: The Origins of Marxism and the Sociology of Intellectuals* (Oxford: OUP, 1985).

[123] With regard to commodities and their relationship with the world, Marx pronounced: "The existence of the things *qua* commodities, and the value relation between the products of labor which stamps them as commodities, is a definite social relation between men, that assumes, in their eyes, the fantastic form of a relation between things." In the fetishism of the commodity, "social productions [. . .] appear as independent beings endowed with life, and entering into relation both one another and the human race." Marx, *Capital: A Critical Analysis of Capitalist Production*, 2 vols. (London: George Allen & Unwin, 1967) 43.

[124] Karl Marx, *Economic and Philosophic Manuscripts of 1844* (Moscow: Progress Publishers, 1977) 63.

[125] For a discussion of recent developments in urban studies and urban space, see the following works by William G. Flanagan: *Contemporary Urban Sociology* (Cambridge: CUP, 1993), and Urban Sociology: Images and Structure, 3rd ed. (Boston: Allyn and Bacon, 1999).

[126] Marx, *Economic and Philosophic Manuscripts of 1844*, 84.

[127] Ferdinand Tonnies, *Community and Association (Gemeinschaft und Gesellschaft)*, trans. C.P. Loomis (London: Routledge & Kegan Paul, 1955) 37.

[128] Tonnies, 37.

[129] Tester, 70.

[130] In his later writings Nietzsche developed the idea of "the eternal recurrence of the ever-same," a contentious doctrine which carries with it two possibilities. In the first instance, Nietzsche defined the eternal return as a nihilistic phenomenon: "existence, as it is, without meaning or aim, but inevitably recurring, without a finale into nothingness." At the same time, the eternal return carried with it the possibility of affirmation in each moment of existence, an idea expressed dramatically in *Thus Spake Zarathustra* in the discussion between Zarathustra and the dwarf before the famous gateway named "Moment," the eternal point of origin and return. Quoted by David Frisby, *Fragments of Modernity: Theories of Modernity in the Work of Simmel, Kracauer and Benjamin* (Cambridge, MA: MIT Press, 1986) 34.

[131] Quoted by Frisby, *Fragments*, 30.

[132] Quoted by Frisby, *Fragments*, 30

[133] Quoted by Frisby, *Fragments*, 32.

[134] James Joyce, *Ulysses: The Corrected Text*, edited by Hans Walter Gabler with Wolfhard Steppe and Claus Melchior (New York: Random, Inc., 1986). Subsequent references are to this edition and are cited parenthetically in the text.

[135] Marx. *Basic Writings on Politics and Philosophy*, ed. L.S. Feuer (Toronto: Doubleday, 1959) 320.

[136] Quoted by Frisby, *Fragments*, 32.

[137] Quoted by Frisby, *Fragments*, 32.

[138] Richard Lehan, "Joyce's City," *James Joyce: The Augmented Ninth*, ed. Bernard Benstock (Syracuse: SUP, 1988) 247–261.

[139] Lehan 249. In Zola's *L'Asssomoir*, for example, the land question is exemplified in the following episode: "That year the whole district was being turned topsy-turvy. The Boulevard Magenta and the Boulevard Ornano were being driven through what had been the Barriere Poissonniere and made a gap through the outer boulevards. You hardly knew where you were. [. . .] It even gave rise to daily arguments between Lantier and Poisson. The former [Lantier] went on and on about the Paris demolitions, accusing the Emperor of building palaces everywhere so as to pack the workers off into the provinces, and the policeman [Poisson], white with suppressed anger, riposted that on the contrary the Emperor's first thoughts were for the workers, and that he would demolish the whole of Paris if necessary, simply to make work for them. Gervaise, too, was annoyed by these improvements, for they upset this dingy corner of Paris where she felt at home. Her annoyance came from the fact that the district was going up in the world exactly when she was going down." Emile Zola, *L'Assommoir*, trans. Leonard Tannock (Harmondsworth: Penguin Books, 1970) 367.

[140] See Raymond Williams, "Region and Class in the Novel," *Writing in Society* (London: Verso, 1983), *Marxism and Literature* (Oxford: OUP, 1977), and *The Sociology of Culture* (New York: Schocken Books, 1982).

[141] Sennett, 12.

[142] Adda B. Bozeman, "The Decline of the West? Spengler Reconsidered," *The Virginia Quarterly Review* 59.2 (Spring 1983): 181–207.

[143] Lewis Mumford, *The City in History: Its Origins, Its Transformations, and Its Prospects* (New York: Harcourt Brace & Company, 1961) 619.

[144] See Frederic Jameson, *Postmodernism, or The Cultural Logic of Late Capitalism* (Durham: Duke UP, 1991) 162.

[145] Oswald Spengler, "The Soul of the City," *Classic Essays on the Culture of Cities* (New York: Appleton-Century-Crofts, 1969) 65.

[146] Spengler, 81.

[147] Carl Pedersen, "Unreal Cities East and West: Bely's *Petersburg* and Dos Passos' *Manhattan Transfer*," *American Studies in Scandinavia* (20) 1988: 51.

[148] Spengler, 70.

[149] Dos Passos, "The Business of a Novelist," *New Republic* 78 (4 April 1934): 220.

[150] Dos Passos, *Bookman* 68 (September 1928): 26.

[151] See Townsend Luddington *John Dos Passos: A Twentieth-Century Odyssey.* (New York: E. P. Dutton, 1980). Luddington contends that Dos Passos' novel in stylistic terms is satirical, and thus goes at characters from the outside rather than treating then in depth. He points out that, "it was not that Dos Passos characterized incompletely. Rather his intention was to define by actions and surfaces, not to present psychological studies [. . .] he thought of people *en masse* or of that abstraction called society" (64).

[152] Dos Passos, interview with David Sanders, *Writers at Work: The Paris Review Interviews,* ed. George Plimpton, 4th series (New York: Viking, 1976) 68–69.

[153] Dos Passos, "What Makes a Novelist," *National Review* 20 (16 January 1968) 29–32.

[154] See Sharon Spencer, *Space, Time and Structure in the Modern Novel* (New York: NYU Press, 1971).

[155] Spencer, xx.

[156] William Brevda quoting Monroe K. Spears, "How Do I Get to Broadway? Reading Dos Passos's *Manhattan Transfer* Sign," *Texas Studies in Literature and Language* 83.1 (Spring 1996): 80.

[157] Spengler, 68.

[158] Casey, 99.

[159] Brevda, 80.

[160] With regard to the "symbolism" of Dos Passos' "center," Brevda declares: "In a ritual act whose purpose is to find the spiritual center of a locality, Dos Passos' *Manhattan Transfer* delineates the mythical geography of the new order, an order first surmised by those seers of the modern, the advertising men, who not only foresaw the new 'sacred space' at the 'center of things' but helped create it" (81).

[161] Spengler, 66.

[162] Spengler, 68.

[163] Ellmann quoting Joyce, *James Joyce,* 364.

[164] Ellmann quoting Joyce, *James Joyce,* 164.

[165] Joyce, *The Critical Writings of James Joyce,* 43.

[166] Joyce, *The Critical Writings of James Joyce,* 43.

[167] Spengler, 70.

[168] Graham Clarke, "A 'Sublime and Atrocious' Spectacle: New York and the Iconography of Manhattan Island," *The American City: Literary and Cultural Perspectives,* ed. Graham Clarke (New York: St. Martin's Press, 1988) 41.

[169] Clarke quoting Barthes, 41.

[170] Quoted by Luddington, 200.

[171] Quoted by Luddington, 200.

[172] Quoted by Luddington, 203.

[173] Lionel Trilling, *The Liberal Imagination: Essays on Literature and Society* (New York: Viking Press, 1950) 187.

[174] Monroe K. Spears, *Dionysus and the City: Modernism in Twentieth-Century Poetry* (New York: OUP, 1970) 21.

AFTERWORD NOTES

[1] Stanislaus Joyce, *My Brother's Keeper: James Joyce's Early Years*, ed. Richard Ellmann (New York: Viking Press, 1957) 238–39.

[2] Dos Passos, interview with David Sanders, *Writers at Work: The "Paris Review" Interviews*, ed. George Plimpton, 4th series (New York: Viking, 1976) 68–69.

Bibliography

Aaron, Daniel. "*U. S. A.*" *American Heritage* (July/August 1996): 63–72.

Adams, Henry. *The Education of Henry Adams*. Ed. Ernest Samuels. Boston: Houghton Mifflin Co., 1973.

Adams, Robert M. *Surface and Symbol*. New York: Oxford UP, 1962.

Addams, Jane. *Twenty Years at Hull House: With Autobiographical Notes*. New York: The Macmillan Co., 1910.

Adickes, Sandra E. *To Be Young Was Very Heaven: Women in New York Before the First World War*. New York: Palgrave, 2000.

Aldridge, John. *After the Lost Generation*. New York: McGraw-Hill, 1951.

Alkana, Joseph. "Translating the Self: Between Discord and Individualism in American Literary History." *The Social Self: Hawthorne, Howells, William James, and Nineteenth-Century Psychology*. Lexington, KY: The UP of Kentucky, 1997. 1–27.

Alston, Richard. *The City in Roman and Byzantine Egypt*. London: Routledge, 2002.

Ames, Christopher. *The Life of the Party: Festive Vision in Modern Fiction*. Athens: The U of Georgia Press, 1991.

Ammons, Elizabeth. "Expanding the Canon of American Realism." *The Cambridge Companion to American Realism and Naturalism: Howells to London*. Ed. Donald Pizer. Cambridge: Cambridge UP, 1995. 95–116.

Andrews, Malcolm. "Walt Whitman and the American City." *The American City: Literary and Cultural Perspectives*. Ed. Graham Clarke. New York: St. Martin's Press, 1988. 179–197.

Andrews, Stuart. *The Rediscovery of America: Transatlantic Crosscurrents in an Age of Revolution*. New York: St. Martin's Press, 1998.

Anesko, Michael. "Recent Critical Approaches." *The Cambridge Companion to American Realism and Naturalism: Howells to London*. Ed. Donald Pizer. Cambridge: Cambridge UP, 1995. 77–94.

Ankersmit, Frank. *Historical Representation*. Stanford: Stanford UP, 2001.

Arrington, Phillip. "The Sense of an Ending in *Manhattan Transfer*." *American Literature: A Journal of Literary History, Criticism, and Bibliography* 54.3 (October 1982): 438–43.

Attridge, Derek. Ed. *The Cambridge Companion to James Joyce*. Cambridge: Cambridge UP, 1990.

Augustine, Martin. "Joyce's Narrative Strategies in the Central Stories of *Dubliners*." *Joyce Centenary Offshoots: James Joyce, 1882–1982*. Ed. Karl-Heinz Westarp. Aarhus, Denmark: Seklos, 1983.

Bach, Rebecca Ann. *Colonial Transformations: The Cultural Production of the New Atlantic World, 1580–1640*. New York: Palgrave, 2000.

Bachelard, Gaston. *The Poetics of Space*. Trans. Maria Jolas. New York: The Orion Press, 1964.

Baguely, David. *The Entropic Vision*. Cambridge: CUP, 1990.

———. *Naturalism in the European Novel: New Critical Perspectives*. New York: Berg Publishers, Inc., 1992.

Baker, James R. and Thomes F. Staley. Eds. *James Joyce's Dubliners: A Critical Handbook*. Belmont, CA: Wadsworth Publishing Company, Inc., 1969.

Baker, Houston A. Jr. *Modernism and the Harlem Renaissance*. Chicago: U of Chicago Press, 1987.

Bakhtin, Mikhail M., *The Dialogic Imagination*. Trans. Caryl Emerson and Michael Holquist. Austin: The U of Texas Press, 1981.

Balshaw, Maria and Liam Kennedy. Eds. *Urban Space and Representation*. London: Pluto Press, 2000.

Balshaw, Maria. *Looking for Harlem: Urban Aesthetics in African American Literature*. London: Pluto Press, 2000.

Balzac, Honoré de. *History of the Thirteen*. Trans. Herbert J. Hunt. New York: Penguin Putnam, Inc, 1975.

Barker, Francis et al. Eds. *1936: The Sociology of Literature. Volume 2: Practices of Literature and Politics*. Eds.. University of Essex, 1979.

———. *The Politics of Modernism*. Colchester: U of Essex, 1979.

———. *The Practices of Literature and Politics*. Colchester: U of Essex, 1979.

Barker, Theo and Anthony Sutcliffe. Eds *Megalopolis: The Giant City in History*. New York: St. Martin's Press, 1993.

Barta, Peter I. *Bely, Joyce, and Doblin: Peripatetics in the City Novel*. Gainesville: UP of Florida, 1996.

Barthes, Roland. *Via* 2 (1973): 155–158.

Bartlett, Thomas and Derek Haydon. Eds. *Era and Golden Age: Essays in Irish History, 1690–1800*. Belfast: Ulster Historical Foundation, 1975.

Baudelaire, Charles, *Charles Baudelaire, The Painter of Modern Life and Other Essays*. Trans. J. Mayne. London: Penguin, 1964.

———. *Selected Writings on Art and Artists*. Ed. P.E. Chavret. Penguin: Harmondsworth, 1972.

Beach, Joseph Warren. *American Fiction: 1920–1949*. New York: Macmillan, 1941.

Beck, Warren. *Joyce's Dubliners: Substance, Vision, and Art*. Durham, N.C.: Duke UP, 1969.

Becker, George J. Ed. *Documents of Literary Realism*. Princeton, NJ: Princeton UP, 1963.

———. *John Dos Passos*. New York: Frederick Ungar Publishing Co., 1974.

Beckert, Sven. *The Monied Metropolis: New York City and the Consolidation of the American Bourgeoisie, 1850–1896*. Cambridge: Cambridge UP, 2001.

Beebe, Maurice. "The *Portrait* as Portrait: Joyce and Impressionism," *Irish Renaissance Annual* 1. Ed. Zack Bowen. Newark: U of Delaware Press, 1980. 13–31.

Beja, Morris. *Epiphany in the Modern Novel*. Seattle: U of Washington Press, 1971.

———. *James Joyce: Dubliners and A Portrait of the Artist as a Young Man*. London: Macmillan, 1973.

———. "One Good Look at Themselves: Epiphanies in Dubliners." *Work in Progress: Joyce Centenary Essays*. Eds. Richard F. Peterson et al. Carbondale: Southern Illinois UP, 1983. 3–14.

Belkind, Allen. Ed. *Dos Passos, the Critics, and the Writer's Intention*. Carbondale: Southern Illinois UP, 1971.

Bell, Davitt. *The Problem of American Realism: Studies in the Cultural History of a Literary Idea*. Chicago: U of Chicago Press, 1993.

Bender, Thomas. "James Fenimore Cooper and the City." *New York History* 51 (1970): 287–305.

———. *New York Intellect: A History of Intellectual Life in New York City, from 1750 to the Beginnings of Our Time*. Baltimore: Johns Hopkins UP, 1987.

———. "The Modern City as Text and Context: The Public Culture of New York." *Rivista di Studi Anglo-Americani* 6.8 (1990): 15–34.

Benevolo, Leonardo. *The European City*. Trans. Carl Ipsen. Oxford: Blackwell Press, 1993.

Benjamin, Walter. *Charles Baudelaire: A Lyric Poet in the Era of High Capitalism*. Trans. H. Zohn. London: Routledge, 1973.

Benson, Lee. *The Concept of Jacksonian Democracy: New York as a Test Case*. Princeton: Princeton UP, 1961.

Benstock, Bernard. "'The Sisters' and the Critics," *James Joyce Quarterly* 4 (1966): 32–35.

———. "A Light from Some Other World: Symbolic Structure in *A Portrait of the Artist as a Young Man*." *Approaches to Joyce's Portrait*. Eds. Thomas F. Staley and Bernard Benstock. Pittsburgh: U of Pittsburgh Press, 1976. 185–212.

———. "Joyce's Rheumatics: The Holy Ghost in *Dubliners*.'" *Southern Review* 14 (1978): 1–15.

———. *Critical Essays on James Joyce*. Boston, Mass.: G. K. Hall & Co., 1985.

Benstock, Shari. "City Spaces and Women's Places in Joyce's Dublin." *James Joyce: The Augmented Ninth. Proceedings of the Ninth International James*

Joyce Symposium, Frankfurt, 1984. Ed. Bernard Benstock. Syracuse: Syracuse UP, 1984. 293–307.

———. *Women of the Left Bank.* Austin: U of Texas Press, 1986.

Benston, Kimberly W. *Performing Blackness: Enactments of African American Modernism.* London: Routledge, 2000.

Berger, Morroe. *Real and Imagined Worlds: The Novel and Social Science.* Cambridge, MA: Harvard UP, 1977.

Berlin, die Symphonie der Grosstadt. Deutsche-Verenis-Film, 1927. Dir. Walther Ruttmann. Screenplay by Ruttmann and Karl Freund, from an idea by Carl Mayer. Photography by Reimar Kuntze, Robert Babeske, and Laszlo Schaffer.

Berman, Jessica. *Modernist Fiction, Cosmopolitanism, and the Politics of Community.* Cambridge: Cambridge UP, 2001.

Berman, Marshall. *All That Is Solid Melts into Air.* New York: Simon & Schuster, 1982.

Berthoff, Warner. *The Ferment of Realism, 1884–1919.* New York: Free Press, 1965.

Bidwell, Bruce and Linda Heffer. *The Joycean Way: A Topographical Guide to 'Dubliners' & 'A Portrait of the Artist as a Young Man.'* Baltimore: The Johns Hopkins UP, 1982.

Biersack, Aletta. "Local Knowledge, Local History: Geertz and Beyond." *The New Cultural History.* Ed. Lynn Hunt. Berkeley: U of California Press, 1989. 72–96.

Billigheimer, Rachel V. "The Living: Joyce's 'The Dead.'" *College Language Association* 31.4 (June 1988): 472–483.

Blanchard, Marc Eli. *In Search of the City: Engels, Baudelaire, Rimbaud.* Saratoga, CA: ANMA Libri, 1985.

Bloom, Harold. Ed. *James Joyce's 'A Portrait of the Artist as a Young Man.'* New York: Chelsea House Publishers, 1988.

———. *Sinclair Lewis' 'Arrowsmith.'* New York: Chelsea House Publishers, 1988.

———. Ed. *James Joyce's* Dubliners: *Modern Critical Interpretations.* New York: Chelsea House, 1989.

Blotner, Joseph. "A New Look at Dos Passos." *CEA Critic: An Official Journal of the College English Association.* 42. 4 (1980): 35–39.

Bock, Martin. *Crossing the Shadow-Line: The Literature of Estrangement.* Columbus: Ohio State U P, 1989.

Bolt, Christine. "The American City: Nightmare, Dream, or Irreducible Paradox?" *The American City: Literary and Cultural Perspectives.* Ed. Graham Clarke. New York: St. Martin's Press, 1988. 13–35.

Booth, Howard J. and Rigby Nigel. *Modernism and Empire: Writing and British Coloniality, 1890–1940.* New York: Palgrave, 2000.

Borenstein, Audrey. *Redeeming the Sin: Social Science and Literature.* New York: Columbia UP, 1978.

Bornstein, George. *Material Modernism: The Politics of the Page.* New York: Cambridge UP, 2001.

Bourdieu, Pierre. "The Genesis of the Concepts of *Habitus* and of *Field*." *Sociocriticism* 2 (1985): 11–24.

———. "Flaubert's Point of View." Trans. Priscilla Parkhurst Ferguson. *Critical Inquiry: The Sociology of Literature* 14.3 (Spring 1988): 539–62.

Bowen, Zack. "Joyce and the Epiphany Concept: A New Approach." *Journal of Modern Literature* 9.1 (1981–1982): 103–114.

Bowlby, Rachel. *Just Looking: Consumer Culture in Dreiser, Gissing, and Zola*. New York: Methuen, 1985.

Boyce, George D. *Nationalism in Ireland*. New York: Routledge, 1995.

Boyle, Robert S.J. "Ellmann's Revised Conroy." *James Joyce Quarterly* 21.3 (Spring 1984): 257–64.

Bozeman, Adda B. "The Decline of the West? Spengler Reconsidered." *The Virginia Quarterly Review* 59.2 (Spring 1983): 181–92.

Bradbury, Malcolm and James McFarlane. Eds. *Modernism 1890–1910*. Penguin: Harmondsworth, 1976.

Bradbury, Malcolm. The *Modern American Novel*. New York: Viking, 1992.

———. *Dangerous Pilgrimages: Transatlantic Mythologies and the Novel*. New York: Viking, 1996.

———. *The Modern British Novel*. London: Penguin Books, Joyce, 1993.

Brady, Joesph and Anngret Simms. Eds. *Dublin: Through Space and Time 900–1900*. Dublin: Four Courts, 2001.

Brand, Dana. *The Spectator and the City in Nineteenth-Century American Literature*. New York: Cambridge UP, 1991.

Brandabur, Edward. "The Sisters." *Dubliners Viking Critical Edition*. Ed. Robert Scholes and A. Walton Litz. New York: The Viking Press, 1969. 333–343.

Brantley, John D. *The Fiction of John Dos Passos*. The Hague: Mouton & Co., 1968.

Braun, Sidney D. Seymour Lainoff. Eds. *Transatlantic Mirrors: Essays in Franco-American Literary Relations*. Boston: Twayne Publishers, 1978.

Bremer, Sidney H. *Urban Intersections: Meetings of Life and Literature in United States Cities*. Urbana: U of Illinois Press, 1992.

Brevda, William. "How Do I Get to Broadway? Reading Dos Passos's Manhattan Transfer Sign." *Texas Studies in Literature and Language* 38.1 (Spring 1996): 79–114.

Brivic, Sheldon. *Joyce between Freud and Jung*. New York: Kennickat, 1980.

———. *The Veil of Signs: Joyce, Lacan, and Perception*. Urbana: U of Illinois Press, 1985.

Brooker, Peter. *New York Fictions: Modernity, Postmodernism, and the New Modern*. New York: Longman, 1996.

Brown, Ohmer Obed. *James Joyce's Early Fiction: The Biography of Form*. Cleveland, Ohio: Case Western Reserve UP, 1972.

Brown, Richard H. *A Poetics for Sociology: Toward a Logic of Discovery for the Human Sciences*. Chicago: U of Chicago Press, 1989.

Brown, Richard. *James Joyce and Sexuality*. Cambridge: Cambridge UP, 1985.

Brown, Terence. "Dublin in Twentieth-Century Writing: Metaphor and Subject." *Irish University Review* 8 No.1 (Spring 1978): 7–21.

———. "The Dublin of *Dubliners*," in *James Joyce: An International Perspective: Centenary Essays in Honour of the Late Sir Desmond Cochrane.* Eds. Suheil Badi Bushrui et al. Gerrards Cross: Colin Smythe, 1982. 1–18.

———. "Yeats, Joyce and the Irish Critical Debate." *Yeats's Political Identities: Selected Essays.* Ed. Jonathon Allison. Ann Arbor: The U of Michigan Press, 1996. 279–91.

Brunsdale, Mitzi M. *James Joyce: A Study of the Short Fiction.* New York: Twayne Publishers, 1994.

Bucco, Martin. Ed. *Critical Essays on Sinclair Lewis.* Boston: G. K. Hall & Co., 1986.

Buckley, Jerome Hamilton. *The Bildungsroman from Dickens to Golding.* Cambridge: Harvard UP, 1974.

Budd, Louis J. "The American Background." *The Cambridge Companion to American Realism and Naturalism: Howells to London.* Ed. Donal Pizer. Cambridge: Cambridge UP, 1995. 21–46.

Budgeon, Frank. *James Joyce and the Making of Ulysses.* Bloomington: Indiana UP, 1967.

Burgess, Anthony. *Re Joyce.* New York: W. W. Norton & Company, 1965.

Butler, Christopher. "The Concept of Modernism." *Essays for Richard Ellmann.* Kingston: McGill-Queen's UP, 1989. 49–59.

Buttigieg, Joseph A. *A Portrait of the Artist in Different Perspective.* Athens, Ohio: Ohio UP, 1987.

Cahalan, James M. *The Irish Novel: A Critical History.* Boston: Twayne Publishers, 1988.

Calinescu, Matei and André Reszler. "Literature and the Social Sciences." *Yearbook of Comparative and General Literature* 24 (1975): 43–50.

Capetti, Carla. *Writing Chicago: Modernism, Ethnography, and the Novel.* New York: Columbia UP, 1997.

Carr, Virginia Spencer. *Dos Passos: A Life.* Garden City, NY: Double Day & Company, Inc., 1984.

Carroll, Michael Thomas. *Popular Modernity in America: Experience, Technology, Mythohistory.* Albany: State U of New York Press, 2000.

Caserio, Robert L. "Various Modernisms. " *The Novel in England, 1900–1950.* New York: Twayne Publishers, 1999. 80–159.

Casey, Janet Calligani. *Dos Passos and the Ideology of the Feminine.* Cambridge: Cambridge UP, 1998.

Castle, Gregory. *Modernism and the Celtic Revival.* Cambridge: Cambridge UP, 2001.

Cavallaro, Dani. *Critical and Cultural Theory: Thematic Variations.* London: The Athlone Press, 2001.

Cheng, Vincent J. *Joyce, Race, and Empire.* Cambridge: Cambridge UP, 1995.

Chesnutt, Margaret. "Joyce's *Dubliners*: History, Ideology, and Social Reality." *Eire* 14:2 (1979): 533–49.

Chevrel, Yves. *Le Naturalisme*. Paris: Presses Universitaires de France, 1982.

———. "Toward an Aesthetic of the Naturalist Novel." *Naturalism in the European Novel: New Critical Perspectives*. Ed. David Baguely. New York: Berg Publishers, Inc., 1992. 46–65.

Chudacoff, Howard P. *The Evolution of American Urban Society*. Englewood Cliffs, NJ: Prentice-Hall, Inc., 1975.

Cixous, Helene. *The Exile of James Joyce*. Trans. Sally A. J. Purcell. New York: David Lewis, 1972.

Clark Priscilla P. et al., "The Comparative Method: Sociology and the Study of Literature." *Yearbook of Comparative and General Literature* 23 (1974): 5–28.

———. "Literature and Sociology." *Interrelations of Literature*. Eds. Jean-Pierre Barricelli and Joseph Gibaldi. New York: MLA, 1982. 107–22.

———. "The Sociology of Literature: An Historical Introduction." *Research in Sociology of Knowledge, Sciences, and Arts* 1 (1978): 237–58.

Clark, Michael. "John Dos Passos' *Manhattan Transfer*: The Woman as City." *Notes on Contemporary Literature* 12. 2 (March 1982): 5–6.

———. *Dos Passos' Early Fiction, 1912–1938*. Cranbury, NJ: Susquehanna UP, 1987.

Clark, Ronald W. *Freud: The Man and the Cause*. New York: Random House, 1982.

Clarke, Graham. Ed. *The American City: Literary and Cultural Perspectives*. New York: St. Martin's Press, 1988.

Clarke, Howard B. Ed. *Irish Cities*. Dublin: Mercier Press, 1995.

Clarke. Desmond. *Dublin*. London: B. T. Batsford Ltd., 1977.

Cohen, Barbara, Seymour Chwast and Steven Heller. Eds. *New York Observed: Artists and Writers Look at the City, 1650 to the Present*. New York: Harry N. Abrams, Inc., 1987.

Colley, Iain. *Dos Passos and the Fiction of Despair*. Totowa, N.J.: Rowman and Littlefield, 1978.

Colomina, Beatriz. Ed. *Sexuality & Space*. New York: Princeton Architectural Press, 1992.

Colum, Padraic and Mary. *Our Friend James Joyce*. Garden City, NY: Doubleday & Company, 1958.

Conder John J. "Dos Passos and Society's Self: *Manhattan Transfer*." *Naturalism in American Fiction: The Classic Phase*. Lexington, KY: The U of Kentucky Press, 1984. 118–41.

———. *Naturalism in American Fiction: The Classic Phase*. Lexington: UP of Kentucky, 1984.

Conrads, Ulrich. *Programs and Manifestoes in Twentieth-Century Architecture*. Trans. Michael Bullock. Cambridge: MIT Press, 1970.

Cooke, M.G. "From Comedy to Terror: On *Dubliners* and the Development of Tone and Structure in the Modern Short Story." *Massachusetts Review* 11:2 (Spring 1968): 331–43.

Cope, Jackson I. *Joyce's Cities: Archaeologies of the Soul.* Baltimore: Johns Hopkins UP, 1981.

Costello, Peter. *Dublin's Literary Pubs.* Montreal: McGill-Queen's University Press, 1998.

———. *The Heart Grown Brutal: The Irish Revolution in Literature, from Parnell to the Death of Yeats, 1891–1939.* London: Gill and Macmillan, 1977.

Cowan, Michael. "Walkers in the Street: American Writers and the Modern City." *Prospects: The Annual of American Cultural Studies* 6 Ed. Jack Salzman. New York: Burt Franklin and Co., Inc., 1981. 281–311.

Crane, Hart. "Modern Poetry." *The Complete Poems and Selected Letters & Prose of Hart Crane.* Ed. Brom Weber. New York: Liveright Publishing Corporation, 1933. 161–63.

Crawford, Robert. *The Savage and the City in the Work of T. S. Eliot.* New York: Oxford UP, 1987.

Cross, Richard K. *Flaubert and Joyce: The Rite of Fiction.* Princeton: Princeton UP, 1971.

Crunden, Robert Morse. *Body & Soul: The Making of American Modernism.* New York: Basic Books, 2000.

Cullen, Louis M. *The Emergence of Modern Ireland, 1600–1900.* 2nd ed. London: Batsford, 1972.

Daiches, David. "Dubliners." *The Novel and the Modern World.* Rev. ed. Chicago: U of Chicago Press, 1960. 63–82.

Daly, Mary E. *Dublin: The Deposed Capital, A Social and Economic History, 1860–1914.* Cork: Cork UP, 1984.

Damisch, Hubert. *Skyline: The Narcissistic City.* Trans. John Goodman. Stanford: Stanford UP, 2001.

Davis, Alex and Lee M. Jenkins. Eds. *Locations of Literary Modernism: Region and Nation in British and American Modernist Poetry.* Cambridge: Cambridge UP, 2000.

Davis, Joseph K. "The City as Radical Order: James Joyce's Dubliners." *Studies in the Literary Imagination* 3:2 (October 1970): 79–96.

Davison, Peter et al., Eds. *The Sociology of Literature: Literary Taste, Culture and Mass Communication* 6. Cambridge: Chadwick-Healey Ltd., 1978.

de Bolla, Peter. "Antipictorialism in the English Landscape Tradition: A Second Look at *The Country and the City.*" *Cultural Materialism: On Raymond Williams.* Ed. Christopher Prendergast. Minneapolis: U of Minnesota Press, 1995. 173–87.

Deane, Seamus. "The Literary Myths of the Revival: A Case for Their Abandonment." *Myth and Reality in Irish Literature.* Ed. Joseph Ronsley. Waterloo, Ontario: Wilfrid Lauries UP, 1977. 317–29.

———. "Joyce and Nationalism." *James Joyce: New Perspectives.* Ed. Colin MacCabe. Bloomington: Indiana UP, 1982. 168–183.

———. *A Short History of Irish Literature.* Notre Dame, Indiana: U of Notre Dame Press, 1986.

———. "The Production of Cultural Space in Irish Writing." *Boundary* 2 21.3 (Fall 1994): 117–44.

———. *Strange Country: Modernity and Nationhood in Irish Writing Since 1790.* Oxford: Clarendon Press, 1997.

Dear, Michael J. and Steven Flusty. Eds. *The Spaces of Postmodernity: Readings in Human Geography.* Oxford: Blackwell Publishers, 2002.

Deming, Robert H. *James Joyce: The Critical Heritage 1902–1927.* 2 Vols. London: Routledge & Kegan Paul, 1970.

Denning, Michael. *The Cultural Front: The Laboring of American Culture in the Twentieth Century.* New York: Verso, 1996.

Derrida, Jacques. "Structure, Sign and Play in the Discourse of the Human Sciences." *Modern Criticism and Theory.* Ed. David Lodge. New York: Longman, 1988.

Dickson, David J. *New Foundations: Ireland, 1660–1800.* 2nd. ed. Dublin: Irish Academic Press, 2000.

Diggins, John P. "Visions of Chaos and Visions of Order: Dos Passos as Historian." *American Literature: A Journal of Literary History, Criticism, and Bibliography* 46 (1974): 329–46.

Dos Passos, John. *Manhattan Transfer.* New York: Harper Brothers, 1925.

———. "Foreword." *Blaise Cendrars, Panama; or, The Adventures of My Seven Uncles.* New York: Harper & Brothers, 1933.

———. "Interview with David Sanders." *Writers at Work: The Paris Review Interviews.* Ed. George Plimpton, 4th series. New York: Viking, 1976. 68–69.

———. *The Fourteenth Chronicle: Letters and Diaries of John Dos Passos.* Ed. Townsend Luddington. Boston: Gambit, 1973.

———. *John Dos Passos: The Major Nonfictional Prose.* Ed. Donald Pizer. Detroit: Wayne State U P, 1988.

Douglas, Ann. *Terrible Honesty: Mongrel Manhattan in the 1920s.* New York: Farrar, Strauss and Giroux, 1995.

Durey, Michael. *Transatlantic Radicals and the Early American Republic.* Lawrence: UP of Kansas, 1997.

During, Simon. Ed. *The Cultural Studies Reader.* New York: Routledge, 1993.

Dyos, H. J. and M. Wolff. Eds. *The Victorian City: Images and Realities.* 2 Vols. London: Routledge & Kegan Paul, 1973.

Eagleton, Terry. "Two Approaches in the Sociology of Literature." *Critical Inquiry: The Sociology of Literature* 14.3 (Spring 1988): 469–76.

———. *Heathcliff and the Great Hunger.* London: Verso, 1995.

Eco, Umberto. "Sociology and the Novel." *Times Literary Supplement* (28 Sept. 1967): 875–76.

Edwards, Catherine. *Writing Rome: Textual Approaches to the City.* Cambridge: Cambridge UP, 1996.

Ehrlich, Heyward. Ed. *Light Rays: James Joyce and Modernism.* New York: New Horizon Press Publishers, 1989.

Ellmann, Richard *James Joyce.* 2nd ed. New York: Oxford UP, 1982.

Emerson, Ralph Waldo "The American Scholar." *Essays and Lectures.* Ed. Joel Porte. New York: Library of America, 1983.

Esbenshade, Richard S. "Remembering to Forget: Memory, History, National Identity in Postwar East-Central Europe." *Representations* 49 (Winter 1995): 72–96.

Escarpit, Robert. *Sociology of Literature.* Trans. Ernest Pick. Painesville, OH: The Lake Erie College Press, 1965.

Fairhall, James. "Joyce's Dubliners." *Explicator* 45:1 (Fall 1986): 32–34.

Faulkner, Howard. "James Weldon Johnson's Portrait of the Artist as a Young Man." *Black American Literature Forum* 19 (1985): 147–51.

Fendler, Susanne and Ruth Wittlinger. Eds. *The Idea of Europe in Literature.* New York: Palgrave, 1999.

Ferguson, Frances. *Wordsworth: Language as Counter-Spirit.* New Haven: Yale UP, 1977.

Ferguson, Priscilla Parkhurst, Philipe Desan, and Wendy Griswold. Eds. "Editors Introduction: Mirrors, Frames, and Demons: Reflections on the Sociology of Literature." *Critical Inquiry: The Sociology of Literature* 14.3 (Spring 1988): 421–430.

———. *Paris as Revolution: Writing the Nineteenth-Century City.* Berkeley: U of California Press, 1994.

Ferrall, Charles. *Modernist Writing and Reactionary Politics.* New York: Cambridge UP, 2001.

Festa, McCormick Diana. "A Pessimistic Vision of New York in Literature: *Manhattan Transfer.*" *Centerpoint: A Journal of Interdisciplinary Studies* 1. 3 (1975): 9–13.

———. *The City as Catalyst: A Study of Ten Novels.* Rutherford: Fairleigh Dickinson UP, 1979.

Fincher, Ruth and Jane M. Jacobs. Eds. *Cities of Difference.* New York: Guilford Press, 1998.

Fine, David. Ed. *Los Angeles in Fiction: A Collection of Essays: From James M. Cain to Walter Mosley.* Albuquerque: U of New Mexico Press, 1995.

Finneran Richard. J. Ed. *Anglo-Irish Literature: A Review of Research.* New York: Modern Language Association of America, 1976.

Fitzgerald, F. Scott. *The Great Gatsby.* 1925. New York: Charles Scribner's Sons, 1980.

Flanagan, William G. *Contemporary Urban Sociology.* Cambridge: Cambridge UP, 1993.

———. *Urban Sociology: Images and Structure.* 3rd ed. Boston: Allyn and Bacon, 1999.

Fleming, Deborah. *"A Man Who Does Not Exist": The Irish Peasant in the Work of W. B. Yeats and J. M. Synge.* Ann Arbor: The U of Michigan Press, 1998.

Foley, Barbara. "The Treatment of Time in *The Big Money*: An Examination of Ideology and Literary Form." *Modern Fiction Studies: John Dos Passos Special Issue* 26.3 (Autumn 1980): 447–67.

————. *Radical Representations: Politics and Form in U.S. Proletarian Fiction,* *1929–1941.* Durham: Duke UP, 1993.

Forster, Peter and Celia Kenneford. "Sociological Theory and the Sociology of Literature." *The British Journal of Sociology* 24.3 (September 1973): 355–64.

Fortuna, Diane. "The Labyrinth as Controlling Image in Joyce's *A Portrait of the Artist as a Young Man.*" *Bulletin of the New York Public Library* 76 (1972): 120–80.

Foster, Gretchen. "John Dos Passos' Use of Film Technique in *Manhattan Transfer* & *The 42nd Parallel.*" *Film Literature Quarterly* 14.3 (1986): 186–94.

Foster, John Wilson. "Passage through 'The Dead.'" *Criticism* 15 (Spring 1973): 91–108.

Foster, R. F. *Modern Ireland, 1600–1972.* New York: Penguin, 1988.

Francis, Elizabeth. *The Secret Treachery of Words: Feminism and Modernism in America.* Minneapolis: U of Minnesota Press, 2002.

Freidrich, Gerhard. "The Perspective of Joyce's *Dubliners.*" *College English* 24 (1965): 421–26.

Freud, Sigmund. *Civilization and Its Discontents.* Ed. Peter Strachey. New York: W.W. Norton, Inc., 1961.

————. *Letters of Sigmund Freud.* Trans. Tania and James Stern. 2nd ed. New York: Basic Books, 1975.

————. *Civilization and Its Discontents.* Trans. Peter Gay. New York: W. W. Norton, 1984.

————. *The Complete Letters of Sigmund Freud to Wilhelm Fliess.* Ed. Jeffrey Masson. Cambridge: Harvard UP, 1985.

————. *The Standard Edition of the Complete Psychological Works of Sigmund Freud.* 24 Vols. Ed. James Strachey. London: The Hogarth Press 1953–74.

Frierson, William C. "The English Controversy over Realism in Fiction." *PMLA* 43 (1928): 533–50.

Frisby, David. *Georg Simmel.* New York: Tavistock Publications, 1984.

————. *Fragments of Modernity: Theories of Modernity in the Work of Simmel, Kracauer and Benjamin.* Cambridge, MA: MIT Press, 1986.

————. *Simmel and Since: Essays on Simmel's Social Theory.* New York: Routledge, 1992.

————. *Sociological Impressionism: A Reassessment of Georg Simmel's Social Theory.* New York: Routledge, 1992.

————. *Cityscapes of Modernity: Critical Explorations.* Malden, MA: Polity Press in association with Blackwell, 2001.

Fuller, David. *James Joyce's Ulysses.* New York: St. Martin's Press, 1992.

Gabler, Hans Walter. "The Seven Lost Years of *A Portrait of the Artist as a Young Man,*" *Approaches to Joyce's Portrait.* Eds. Thomas F. Staley and Bernard Benstock. Pittsburgh: U of Pittsburgh Press, 1976. 25–60.

Gallagher, Catherine. "Raymond Williams and Cultural Studies," *Cultural Materialism: On Raymond Williams.* Ed. Christopher Prendergast. Minneapolis: U of Minnesota Press, 1995. 307–319.

Gambrell, Alice. *Women Intellectuals, Modernism, and Difference: Transatlantic Culture, 1919–1945.* Cambridge: Cambridge UP, 1997.

Gandal, Keith. *The Virtues of the Vicious: Jacob Riis, Stephen Crane, and the Spectacle of the Slum.* New York: Oxford University Press, 1997.

Ganim, John M. "Recent Studies on Literature, Architecture, and Urbanism." *Modern Language Quarterly* v. 56 (Sept. '95): 364–79.

Garvey, Johanna X. K. "City Limits: Reading Gender and Urban Spaces in Ulysses" *Twentieth-Century Literature* v. 41 (Spring 1995): 108–23.

Gates, Robert A. "The Dynamic City: John Dos Passos' *Manhattan Transfer.*" *The New York Vision: Interpretations of New York City in the American Novel.* Lanham, MD: University Press of America, 1987. 63–89.

———. *The New York Vision: Interpretations of New York City in the American Novel.* Lanham, MD: UP of America, 1987.

Gay, Peter. *Freud: A Life for Our Time.* New York: W. W. Norton, 1975.

Gelfant, Blanche H. *The American City Novel.* Norman: U of Oklahoma Press, 1954.

Genet, Jacqueline. Ed. *Rural Ireland, Real Ireland?* Gerrards Cross: Colin Smythe, 1996.

Ghiselin, Brewster. "The Unity of Joyce's *Dubliners.*" *Accent* 16 (1956): 75–86.

Gibson, Todd. "*Manhattan Transfer* and the International Style: The Architectural Basis of Dos Passos's Modernism." *West Virginia University Philological Papers* 41 (1995): 65–70.

Gifford, Don and Robert J. Seidman, *Joyce Annotated: Notes for Dubliners and A Portrait of the Artist As A Young Man.* 2nd ed. Berkeley: U of California Press, 1982.

Giles, James R. *The Naturalistic Inner-City Novel in America: Encounters with the Fat Man.* Benton: U of South Carolina Press, 1995.

Giles, Paul. *Transatlantic Insurrections: British Culture and the Formation of American Literature, 1730–1860.* Philadelphia: U of Pennsylvania Press, 2001.

Gillespie, Michael Patrick. Ed. *James Joyce and the Fabrication of an Irish Identity.* Amsterdam: Atlanta, GA: Rodopi, 2001.

Gjerter, Kathleen G. *Doubly Gifted: The Author as Visual Artist.* New York: Harry N. Abrams, 1986.

Goldman, Arnold. *The Joyce Paradox: Form and Freedom in His Fiction.* Evanston: Northwestern UP, 1966.

Goldmann, Lucien. *Essays on Method in the Sociology of Literature.* Trans. William Q. Boelhower. St. Louis, MO: Telos Press, 1980.

Goldsmith, Arnold L. "The Naturalistic Impression of *Manhattan Transfer.*" *The Modern American Urban Novel: Nature as "Interior Structure."* Detroit: Wayne State UP, 1991. 17–38.

Gorman, Herbert S. *James Joyce.* New York: Farrar & Rinehart, Inc., 1939.

Gould, Gerald. "Dubliners." *New Statesman* 3:64 (27 June 1914): 374–75.

Gouldner, Alvin W. *Against Fragmentation: The Origins of Marxism and the Sociology of Intellectuals.* New York: Oxford UP, 1985.

Graham, Colin. *Deconstructing Ireland: Identity, Theory, Culture*. Edinburgh: Edinburgh UP, 2001.

Grana, Cesar. *Fact and Symbol: Essays in the Sociology of Art and Literature*. New York: Oxford UP, 1971.

Green, Bryan S. *Literary Methods and Sociological Theory: Case Studies of Simmel and Weber*. Chicago: The U of Chicago Press, 1988.

Green, Martin. *Transatlantic Patterns: Cultural Comparisons of England with America*. New York: Basic Books, 1977.

Green, Paul. "The Crossing Pathways of Manhattan Transfer." *Recovering Literature: A Journal of Contextualist Criticism* 4.1 (1975): 19–42.

Gross, Harvey. *The Contrived Corridor: History and Fatality in Modern Literature*. Ann Arbor: The U of Michigan Press, 1971.

Grossberg, Lawrence, Cary Nelson, and Paula A. Treichler. Eds. *Cultural Studies*. New York: Routledge, 1992.

Habermas, Jurgen. "Georg Simmel on Philosophy and Culture: Postscript to a Collection of Essays" Trans. Mathieu Deflem, *Critical Inquiry* 22.3 (Spring 1996): 403–14.

Hall, Peter. *Cities in Civilization*. New York: Pantheon Books, 1998.

Hall, Tim. *Urban Geography*. New York: Routledge, 2001.

Halperin, John. Ed. *The Theory of the Novel: New Essays*. New York: Oxford UP, 1974.

Hamlet, Betsy L. "A Comparative Study of Two Motifs in *Howards End*, *Dubliners*, and *The Waste Land*." *Notes on Contemporary Culture*. 13:3 (May 1983): 2–4.

Hammac, David C. *Power and Society: Greater New York at the Turn of the Century*. New York: Russell Sage Foundation, 1982.

Hamon, Philippe. "The Naturalist Text and the Problem of Reference." *Naturalism in the European Novel: New Critical Perspectives*. New York: Berg Publishers, Inc., 1992. 27–45.

Handlin, Oscar and John Burchard. Eds. *The Historian and the City*. Cambridge, MA: The MIT Press and Harvard UP, 1963.

Hapgood, Lynne and Nancy L. Paxton. Eds. *Outside Modernism: In Pursuit of the English Novel, 1900–30*. New York: St. Martin's Press, 2000.

Harris, Neil. *Cultural Excursions: Marketing Appetites and Cultural Tastes in Modern America*. Chicago: The U of Chicago Press, 1987.

Hart, Clive and Leo Knuth. *A Topographical Guide to James Joyce's Ulysses*. Colchester: A Wake Newslitter Press, 1975.

Hart, Clive. Ed. *James Joyce's 'Dubliners': Critical Essays*. New York: Viking, 1969.

Harty, John. "The Doubling of Dublin's Messages in 'The Sisters.'" *NMIL* 4 (1992): 42–44.

Harvey, David. *Consciousness and the Urban Experience: Studies in the History and Theory of Capitalist Urbanization*. Baltimore: The Johns Hopkins UP, 1985.

———. *The Urban Experience*. Baltimore: The Johns Hopkins UP, 1989.

Hassan, Ihab. "Cities of Mind, Urban Words: The Dematerialization of Metropolis in Contemporary American Fiction." *Literature and the Urban Experience: Essays on the City and Literature.* Eds. Michael C. Jaye and Ann Chalmers Watts. New Brunswick: Rutgers UP, 1981. 93–121.

Hawes, Elizabeth. *New York, New York: How the Apartment House Transformed the Life of the City, 1869–1930.* New York: Alfred A. Knopf, 1993.

Hayman, David. "*A Portrait of the Artist as a Young Man* and *L'education Sentimentale*: The Structural Affinities." *Orbis Litterarum* 19 (1964): 161–75.

Henke, Suzette and Elaine Unkeless. Eds. *Women in Joyce.* Urbana: U of Illinois Press, 1982.

Higgins, Sue. "Literature and Sociology." *Southern Review: Literature and Interdisciplinary Essays* 6 (1973): 269–81.

Hirsch, Edward. "The Imaginary Irish Peasant," *PMLA* 106.5 (October 1991) 1116–1133.

Hoffman, Michael J. and Patrick D. Murphy. Eds. *Critical Essays on American Modernism.* New York: G.K. Hill & Co., 1992.

Hollis, Andy. *Beyond Boundaries: Textual Representations of European Identity.* Amsterdam: Rodopi, 2000.

Homberger, Eric. "Chicago and New York: Two Versions of American Modernism." *Modernism, 1890–1930.* Eds. Malcolm Bradbury and James McFarlane. Harmondsworth: Penguin, 1976. 151–61.

Hook, Andrew. *Dos Passos: A Collection of Critical Essays.* Englewood Cliffs, NJ: Prentice-Hall, Inc., 1974.

Horowitz, Gregg M. *Sustaining Loss: Art and Mournful Life.* Stanford: Stanford UP, 2001.

Howe, Stephen. *Ireland and Empire: Colonial Legacies in Irish History and Culture.* Oxford: Oxford UP, 2000.

Hughson, Lois. "Narration in the Making of *Manhattan Transfer.*" *Studies in the Novel* 8 (1976): 185–98.

Hughson, Lois. "Virtual History and Actual History: John Dos Passos." *Biography to History: The Historical Imagination and American Fiction, 1880–1940.* Morgantown: The UP of Virginia, 1988. 160–95.

Hurm, Gerd "The 'Architect of History': John Dos Passos's Rhetorical Construction of *U.S.A.*" *Historiographic Metafiction in Modern American and Canadian Literature.* Eds. Bernd Engler and Kurt Muller. Paderborn: Ferdinand Schoningh, 1994. 127–45.

Hutchison, James M. Ed. *Sinclair Lewis: New Essays in Criticism.* Troy, NY: The Whitson Publishing Company, 1997.

Hutchison, Ray. Ed. *New Directions in Urban Sociology.* Greenwich, CT: JAI Press, 1997.

Jackson, Kenneth T. Ed. *The Encyclopedia of New York City.* New Haven: Yale UP, 1995.

Jacobs, Jane. *The Death and Life of Great American Cities.* New York: Vintage Books, 1961.

Jacobs, Karen. *The Eye's Mind: Literary Modernism and Visual Culture.* Ithaca, NY: Cornell UP, 2001.

Jameson, Frederic. *Postmodernism, or The Cultural Logic of Late Capitalism.* Durham: Duke UP, 1991.

Jaye, Michael C. and Ann Chalmers Watts. Eds. *Literature and the Urban Experience: Essays on the City and Literature.* New Brunswick: Rutgers UP, 1981.

Jencks, Chris. Ed. *Visual Culture.* New York: Routledge, 1995.

Johnsen, William A. "Joyce's Dubliners and the Futility of Modernism." *Joyce and Modern Literature.* Eds. W.J. McCormack and Alistair Stead. Boston: Routledge & Kegan Paul, 1982: 5–21.

Johnson, James Weldon. *The Autobiography of an Ex-Colored Man.* Garden City, NY: Garden City Publishing Co., 1927.

Johnson, Charles. *Kingsblood Royal: Sinclair Lewis.* New York: Modern Library, 2001.

Johnston, John H. *The Poet and the City: A Study in Urban Perspectives.* Athens: U of Georgia Press, 1984.

Jones, Ernest. *The Life and Work of Sigmund Freud.* 3 Vols. New York: Basic Books, Inc., 1953–57.

Jones, William Powell. "'Dubliners': or the Moral History of Ireland." *James Joyce and the Common Reader.* Norman: U of Oklahoma Press, 1955: 9–23.

Joyce, James. *Stephen Hero,* ed. Theodore Spencer. New York: New Directions, 1944.

———. *The Critical Writings of James Joyce.* Eds. Ellsworth Mason and Richard Ellmann. New York: The Viking Press, 1959.

———. *Dubliners: Text, Criticism, and Notes.* Ed. Robert Scholes and A. Walton Litz. New York: Penguin Books, 1967.

———. *A Portrait of the Artist as a Young Man: Text, Criticism, and Notes,* Ed. Chester G. Anderson. New York: Viking Penguin Inc., 1968.

———. *Selected Letters of James Joyce.* Ed. Richard Ellmann. New York: The Viking Press, 1975.

———. *Ulysses: The Corrected Text.* Ed. Hans Walter Gabler with Wolfhard Steppe. New York: Random House, 1986.

———. *James Joyce's Letters to Sylvia Beach: 1921–1940* Eds. Melissa Banta and Oscar A. Silverman. Bloomington, Indiana: Indiana UP, 1987.

Joyce, Stanislaus. "James Joyce: A Memoir." *The Hudson Review.* 2:4 (Winter 1950): 485–514.

———. *My Brother's Keeper: James Joyce's Early Years.* Ed. Richard Ellmann. New York: The Viking Press, 1958.

———. *The Dublin Diary of Stanislaus Joyce.* Ed. George Harris Healy. Ithaca, NY: Cornell UP, 1962.

Juan, Rose Marie San. *Rome: A City out of Print.* Minneapolis: U of Minnesota Press, 2001.

Kaplan, Amy. "'The Knowledge of the Line'": Realism and the City in Howells's *A Hazard of New Fortune." PMLA* 101.1 (January 1986): 69–81.

————. *The Social Construction of American Realism.* Chicago: U of Chicago Press, 1988.

Karp, David A., Gregory P. Stone, and William C. Yoels. *Being Urban: A Sociology of City Life.* 2nd ed. New York: Praeger, 1991.

Katznelson, Ira. *Marxism and the City.* Oxford: Clarendon Press, 1992.

Kaufman, Will, and Heidi Slettedahl Macpherson. Eds. *Transatlantic Studies.* Lanham, MD: UP of America, 2000.

Kazin, Alfred. "New York from Melville to Mailer." *Literature and the Urban Experience: Essays on the City and Literature.* Eds. Michael C. Jaye and Ann Chalmers Watts. New Brunswick, NJ: Rutgers UP, 1981. 81–91.

Kearns, Kevin C. *Dublin Tenement Life: An Oral History.* New York: Penguin Books, 2000.

Keen, William. "The Rhetoric of Spatial Focus in Joyce's *Dubliners.*" *Studies in Short Fiction* 16.3 (Summer 1979): 195–203.

Kelleher, John V. "Irish History and Mythology in James Joyce's 'The Dead.'" *Review of Politics* 27:3 (July 1965): 414–33.

Kelley, Wyn. *Melville's City: Literary and Urban Form in Nineteenth-Century New York.* New York: Cambridge UP, 1996.

Kelly, Joseph. *Our Joyce: From Outcast to Icon.* Austin: U of Texas Press, 1998.

Kemeny, Tomasco. "The 'Unreal' Effect in Dubliners." *Myriadminded Man: Jottings on Joyce.* Eds. Rosa Maria Bosinelli et al. Bologna: Cooperativa Lib. Univ. Ed., 1986. 19–40.

Kennedy, Liam. *Race and Urban Space in Contemporary American Culture.* Edinburgh: Edinburgh UP. 2002.

Kennedy, Richard S. "John Dos Passos: New Directions in Criticism and Research." *Resources for American Literary Study* 13. 2 (Autumn 1983): 194–214.

Kenner, Hugh. *Dublin's Joyce.* Boston: Beacon, 1956.

————. "The Cubist *Portrait.*" *Approaches to Joyce's Portrait.* Eds. Thomas F. Staley and Bernard Benstock. Pittsburgh: U of Pittsburgh Press, 1976. 171–184.

————. "The Look of a Queen." *Women in Irish Legend, Life and Letters.* Ed. S. F. Gallagher. Gerrard's Cross: Colin Smythe, 1983.

Kershner, R. B. *Joyce, Bakhtin, and Popular Culture: Chronicles of Disorder.* Chapel Hill and London: U of North Carolina Press, 1989.

Keunen, Bart. "The Plurality of Chronotopes in the Modernist City Novel: the Case of *Manhattan Transfer.*" *English Studies: A Journal of English Language and Literature* 82.5 (October 2001): 420–36.

Kiberd, Declan. "Inventing Irelands." *Yeats's Political Identities: Selected Essays.* Ed. Jonathon Allison. Ann Arbor: The U of Michigan Press, 1996. 145–64.

————. "The Periphery and the Center," *South Atlantic Quarterly* 95.1 (Winter 1996): 5–22.

————. *Inventing Ireland.* Cambridge, MA: Harvard UP, 1996.

Kiely, Benedict. Ed. *The State of Ireland.* Boston: David R. Godine, 1980.

Kime Scott, Bonnie. *Joyce and Feminism*. Bloomington: Indiana UP, 1984.

King, Ross. *Emancipating Space: Geography, Architecture, and Urban Design*. New York: Guilford Press, 1996.

Kinsella, Thomas. "The Irish Writer," *Davis, Mangan, Ferguson?: Tradition and the Irish Writer*. Ed. Roger McHugh. Dublin: Dolmen 1970. 57–70.

Klein, Bernard. *Maps and the Writing of Space in Early Modern England and Ireland*. New York: Palgrave, 2001.

Klein, Marcus. *Foreigners: The Making of American Literature: 1900–1940*. Chicago: U of Chicago Press, 1981.

Klepper, Martin and Joseph C. Schöpp. Eds. *Transatlantic Modernism*. Heidelberg: C. Winter, 2001.

Knowles, Sebastian D. G. *The Dublin Helix: The Life of Language in Joyce's Ulysses*. Gainesville: U Press of Florida, 2001.

Kopper, Edward A. "Joyce's 'The Dead.'" *Explicator* 26 (February 1968): Item 46.

Kramer, Lloyd S. "Literature, Criticism, and Historical Imagination: The Literary Challenge of Hayden White and Dominick LaCapra." *The New Cultural History*. Ed. Lynn Hunt. Berkeley: U of California Press, 1989. 97–130.

Landsberg, Melvin. *Dos Passos' Path to U.S.A.: A Political Biography, 1912–1936*. Boulder: The Colorado Associated UP, 1972.

Lane, Gary. Ed. *A Word Index to James Joyce's Dubliners*. New York: Haskell House, 1972.

Lane, James B. "Manhattan Transfer as a Gateway to the 1920s." *The Centennial Review* 16 (1972): 293–311.

Langland, Elizabeth. *Society in the Novel*. Chapel Hill: The U of North Carolina Press, 1984.

Laurenson, Diana. Ed., *The Sociology of Literature: Applied Studies*. Hanley: Wood Mitchell & Co. Limited, 1978.

Lee, Robert A. Ed. *Nathaniel Hawthorne: Critical Essays*. Totowa, NJ: Vision, 1982.

Lehan, Richard. "*Sister Carrie*: The City, the Self and the Modes of Narrative Discourse." *New Essays on Sister Carrie*. Cambridge: Cambridge UP, 1991.

———. "The European Background." *The Cambridge Companion to American Realism and Naturalism: Howells to London*. Ed. Donald Pizer Cambridge: Cambridge U P, 1995. 47–76.

———. *The City in Literature: An Intellectual and Cultural History*. Berkeley: U of California Press, 1998.

Lehman, David. *The Last Avant-Garde: The Making of the New York School of Poets*. New York: Doubleday, 1998.

Leonard, Garry. "The City, Modernism, and Aesthetic Theory in *A Portrait of the Artist as a Young Man*." *Novel: A Forum on Fiction* 29.1 (Fall 1995): 79–99.

———. *Advertising and Commodity Culture in Joyce*. Gainesville: UP of Florida, 1998.

Lepenies, Wolf. *Between Literature and Science: The Rise of Sociology*. Trans.R. J. Hollingdale. Cambridge: Cambridge UP, 1988.

Leuchtenburg, William E. *The Perils of Prosperity, 1914–32.* 2nd ed. Chicago: The U of Chicago Press, 1993.

Levenson, Michael H. *A Genealogy of Modernism: A Study of English Literary Doctrine 1908–1922.* Cambridge: Cambridge UP, 1984.

Levin, Harry. *James Joyce: A Critical Introduction.* Norfolk, CT: New Directions, 1941.

———. "Revisiting Dos Passos' *U.S.A.*" *Massachusetts Review: A Quarterly of Literature, the Arts and Public Affairs* 20.3 (Autumn 1979): 401–15.

Levin, Jonathan. *The Poetics of Transition: Emerson, Pragmatism, & American Literary Modernism.* Durham: Duke UP, 1999.

Lewis, Sinclair. *John Dos Passos' 'Manhattan Transfer.'* New York: Harper & Brothers Publishers, 1926.

Li, Victor. "Policing the City: Modernism, Autonomy and Authority." *Criticism* 34.2 (Spring 1992): 261–79.

Lingeman, Richard. *Sinclair Lewis: Rebel from Main Street.* New York: Random House, 2002.

Liu, Alan. *Wordsworth: The Sense of History.* Stanford: Stanford UP, 1989.

Lloyd, David. *Anomalous States: Irish Writing and the Post-Colonial Moment.* Durham: Duke UP, 1993.

Lo, Phillip. *Writing New York: A Literary Anthology.* New York: Library of America, 1998.

Lockwood, Charles. *Manhattan Moves Uptown.* Boston: Houghton Mifflin, 1976.

Lodge, David. *The Modes of Modern Writing: Metaphor, Metonymy, and the Typology of Modern Literature.* Ithaca: Cornell UP, 1977.

Loe, Thomas. "'The Dead' as Novella." *James Joyce Quarterly* 28:2 (Winter 1991): 485–497.

Lombardo, Patrizia. Ed. *Critical Quarterly: Europe: Theory of the City* 36.4 (Winter 1994).

Long, Michael. "Eliot, Pound, Joyce: Unreal City?" *Unreal City: Urban Experience in Modern European Literature and Art.* Eds. Edward Timms and David Kelley. New York: St. Martin's Press, 1986. 144–157.

Lorenzo, Thomas. *Extraordinary Measures: Afrocentric Modernism and Twentieth-Century American Poetry.* Tuscaloosa: U of Alabama Press, 2000.

Low, Setha M. Ed. *Theorizing the City: The New Urban Anthropology Reader.* New Brunswick, NJ: Rutgers UP, 1999.

Lowell, Amy. "Two Generations in American Poetry." *Poetry and Poets: Essays.* Boston: Houghton Mifflin, 1930. 111–22.

Lowenthal, Leo. "Literature and Sociology." *Relations of Literary Study.* Ed. James Thorpe. New York: MLA, 1967. 98–110.

———. "On Sociology of Literature." *Critical Theory and Society.* Eds. Stephen Eric Bronner and Douglas MacKay Kellner. New York: Routledge, 1989. 40–51.

Lowry, E. D. "*Manhattan Transfer*: Dos Passos' Wasteland." *University Review* 30 (1963): 47–52.

———. The Lively Art of *Manhattan Transfer*." *PMLA* 84 (1969): 1628–1638.

Luddington, Townsend. *John Dos Passos: A Twentieth-Century Odyssey.* New York: E. P. Dutton, 1980.

Lukacs, Georg. "On the Nature and Form of the Essay." *Soul and Form.* Trans. A Bostock. London, 1974. 1–18.

Lundquist,James. *Sinclair Lewis.* New York: Frederick Ungar, 1973.

Lynch, Kevin. *The Image of the City.* Cambridge, MA: The MIT Press, 1960.

Lynn. Kenneth S. *Visions of America: Eleven Literary Historical Essays.* Westport, CT: Greenwood Press, 1967.

Lyons, F. S. L. "James Joyce's Dublin." *Twentieth Century Studies.* 4 (November 1970): 6–25.

———. *Ireland Since the Famine.* New York: Scribner's, 1971.

Machor, James A. "Pastoralism and the American Urban Ideal: Hawthorne, Whitman, and the Literary Pattern." *American Literature* 54.3 (October 1982): 329–43.

———. *Pastoral Cities: Urban Ideals and the Symbolic Landscape of America.* Wisconsin: The U of Wisconsin Press, 1987.

Mackethan, Lucinda H. "Black Boy and Ex-Colored Man: Version and Inversion of the Slave Narrator's Quest for Voice." *College Language Association* 32 (1988): 123–147.

MacLaran, Andrew, *Dublin: The Shaping of a Capital.* New York: Belhaven Press, 1992.

MacLean, Gerald, Donna Landry, and Joseph P. Ward. Eds. *The Country and the City Revisited: England and the Politics of Culture, 1550–1850.* New York: Cambridge UP, 1999.

Macy, John. *James Joyce: The Critical Game.* Boni and Liveright, Publishers, 1922. 317–322.

Maddox, Brenda. *Nora: The Real Life of Molly Bloom.* Boston: Houghton, 1981.

Magalener, Marvin and Richard M. Kain. *Joyce, the Man, the Work, the Reputation.* New York: NYU Press, 1956.

Magalener, Marvin. *Time of Apprenticeship: The Fiction of Young James Joyce.* New York: New Directions, 1959.

Maine, Barry. "*U. S. A.*: Dos Passos and the Rhetoric of History." *South Atlantic Review* 50. 1 (January 1985): 75–86.

Maine, Barry. Ed. *Dos Passos: The Critical Heritage.* New York: Routledge, 1988.

Mancoff, Debra N. D.J. Tela. Eds. *Victorian Urban Settings: Essays on the Nineteenth-Century City and its Contexts.* New York: Garland Publishers, 1996.

Manganiello, Dominic. *Joyce's Politics.* London: Routledge & Keegan Paul, 1980.

Mann, Susan G. *The Short Story Cycle: A Genre Companion and Reference Guide.* New York: Greenwood Press, 1995.

Marcus, Steven. "Reading the Illegible: Modern Representations of Urban Experience." *The Southern Review* 22.3 (Summer 1986): 443–64.

Marx, Karl. *Basic Writings on Politics and Philosophy.* Ed. L. S. Feuer. Toronto: Doubleday, 1959.

———. *Economic and Philosophic Manuscripts of 1844.* Ed Dirk J. Struik. Trans. Martin Milligan. New York: International Publishers, 1964.

——— *Capital: A Critical Analysis of Capitalist Production.* 2 Vols. London: George Allen & Unwin, 1967.

Marx, Leo. "The Puzzle of Anti-Urbanism in Classic American Literature." *Literature and the Urban Experience: Essays on the City and Literature.* Eds. Michael C. Jaye and Ann Chalmers Watts. New Brunswick, N.J.: Rutgers UP, 1981. 63–79.

Marz, Charles. "*U.S.A.*: Chronicle and Performance." *Modern Fiction Studies: John Dos Passos Special* 26.3 (Autumn 1980): 398–415.

Mattingly, Paul. *Suburban Landscapes: Culture and Politics in a New York Metropolitan Community.* Baltimore: The Johns Hopkins UP, 2002.

Maule, Harry E. and Melvin Cane. Eds. *The Man From Main Street: Selected Essays and Other Writings.* New York: Random House, 1953.

Mays, J. C. C. "Some Comments on the Dublin of *Ulysses,*" *Ulysses Cinquante Ans Apres*" Ed. Louis Bonnerot. Paris: Didier, 1974. 83–98.

McBride, Ian, Ed. *History and Memory in Modern Ireland.* Cambridge: Cambridge UP, 2001.

McBride, Margaret. *Ulysses and the Metamorphosis of Stephen Dedalus.* London: Associated UP, 2001.

McCabe, Colin. *James Joyce and the Revolution of the Word.* New York: Harper & Row, 1979.

McFadden, Margaret H. *Golden Cables of Sympathy: The Transatlantic Sources of Nineteenth-Century Feminism.* Lexington, KY: UP of Kentucky, 1999.

McGagern, John. "Dubliners." *Canadian Journal of Irish Studies.* 17:1 (July 1991): 31–37.

McGrath, F. C. "Laughing in His Sleeve: The Sources of Stephen's Aesthetics." *James Joyce Quarterly* 22:3 (Spring 1986): 259–275.

McGuinness, Arthur. The Ambience of Space in Joyce's *Dubliners.*" *Studies in Short Fiction* 11.4 (Fall 1974): 343–51.

McLaughlin, Joseph. *Writing the Urban Jungle: Reading Empire in London from Doyle to Eliot.* Charlottesville: UP of Virginia, 2000.

McLuhan, Marshall H. "John Dos Passos: Technique vs. Sensibility." *Dos Passos: A Collection of Critical Essays.* Ed. Andrew Hook. Englewood Cliffs, NJ: Prentice-Hall, Inc., 1974. 148–161.

McNiff, John. "James Joyce's *Dubliners*: A Study of Stagnation and Entrapment." *DLSU Dialogue.* 23:2 (1988): 29–43.

McParland, Edward. *Public Architecture in Ireland, 1680–1760.* New Haven: Yale UP, 2001.

Menand, Louis. *Discovering Modernism: T. S. Eliot and His Context.* New York: Oxford UP, 1987.

Mencken, H. L. *Prejudices: First Series.* New York: Knopf, Inc., 1947.

Metropolis. Ufa, 1926. Dir. Fritz Lang. Screenplay by Fritz Lang and Thea von Harbou. Photography by Karl Freund and Gunther Rittau. Special effects by Eugen Schufftan.

Michaels, Walter Benn. *The Gold Standard and the Logic of Naturalism: American Literature at the Turn of the Century.* Berkeley: U of California Press, 1987.

Miesel, Victor H. Ed. *Voices of German Expressionism.* Englewood Cliffs, NJ: Prentice-Hall, 1970.

Mikhail, E. H. Ed. *James Joyce: Interviews and Recollections.* New York: St. Martin's Press, 1990.

Miles, David H. "Literary Sociology: Some Introductory Notes." *The German Quarterly* 68.1 (January 1975): 1–35.

Milner, Andrew. "Literature and Society: The Problem of Method." *John Milton and the English Revolution: A Study in the Sociology of Literature.* Totowa, NJ: Barnes & Noble Books, 1981. 1–49.

Minca, Claudia. *Postmodern Geography: Theory and Praxis.* Oxford: Blackwell Publishers, 2001.

Minter, David. *A Cultural History of the American Novel: Henry James to William Faulkner.* Cambridge: Cambridge UP, 1994.

Mitchell, Breon. "A Portrait and the Bildungsroman Tradition." *Approaches to Joyce's Portrait.* Eds. Thomas F. Staley and Bernard Benstock. Pittsburgh: U of Pittsburgh Press, 1976. 61–76.

Mizruchi, Susan. "Fiction and the Science of Society." *The Columbia History of the American Novel.* Ed. Emory Elliott. New York: Columbia UP, 1994. 189–215.

Monroe, Harriet and Alice Corbin Henderson. Eds. *The New Poetry: An Anthology of Twentieth-Century Verse in English.* New York: Macmillan, 1917.

Montanelli, Indro and Mark T. Bassett. "John Dos Passos: A Portrait." *Lost Generation Journal* 8. 2 (21) Winter 1988–1989: 16–18.

Morrissey, L. J. "Inner and Outer Perceptions in Joyce's 'The Dead.'" *Short Studies in Fiction.* 25:1 (Winter 1988): 21–30.

Morrisson, Mark S. *The Public Face of Modernism: Little Magazines, Audiences, and Reception, 1905–1920.* Madison: U of Wisconsin Press, 2001.

Moynahan, Julian. "The Image of the City in Nineteenth-Century Irish Fiction." *The Irish Writer and the City.* Ed. Maurice Harmon. Gerrards Cross: Colin Smythe, 1984. 1–17.

Moynihan, William T. Ed. *Joyce's 'The Dead.'* Boston: Allyn and Bacon, 1965.

Mumford, Lewis. *The City in History: Its Origins, Its Transformations, and Its Prospects.* New York: Harcourt Brace & Company, 1961.

Murphy, James F. *The Proletarian Moment: The Controversy over Leftism in Literature.* Urbana: U of Illinois Press, 1991.

Murphy, Michael W. "Darkness in *Dubliners.*" *Modern Fiction Studies* 15 (Spring 1969): 97–104.

Naremore, James. "Consciousness and Society in *A Portrait.*" *Approaches to Joyce's Portrait.* Eds. Thomas F. Staley and Bernard Benstock. Pittsburgh: U of Pittsburgh Press, 1976. 113–134.

Niemeyer, Carl. "'Grace' and Joyce's Method of Parody." *College English* 27 (1965): 196–201.

Nisbett, Robert. *Sociology as an Art Form*. New Brunswick, NJ: Transaction Publishers, 2002.

Nolan, Emer. *James Joyce and Nationalism*. New York: Routledge, 1995.

Nord, Deborah Epstein. *Walking the Victorian Streets: Women, Representation, and the City*. Ithaca, NY: Cornell UP, 1995.

Norris, Margot. "Stifled Back Answers: The Gender Politics of Art in Joyce's 'The Dead.'" *Modern Fiction Studies* 35:3 (Autumn 1989): 479–503.

Nyman, Jopi. *Under English Eyes: Constructions of Europe in Early Twentieth-Century British Fiction*. Amsterdam: Rodopi, 2000.

O'Brien, Joseph V. *'Dear, Dirty Dublin': A City in Distress, 1899–1916*. Berkeley: U of California press, 1982.

O'Brien, Patricia. "Michel Foucault's History of Culture." *The New Cultural History*. Ed. Lynn Hunt. Berkeley: U of California Press, 1989. 25–46.

O'Connor, Frank. "Joyce and Dissociated Metaphor." *The Mirror in the Roadway: A Study of the Modern Novel*. New York: Alfred A. Knopf, 1956. 295–312.

———. "Work in Progress." *The Lonely Voice: A Study of the Short Story*. Cleveland: World, 1963. 113–27.

———. *A Short History of Irish Literature: A Backward Look*. New York: G. P. Putnam's Sons, 1967.

O'Hehir, Brendan. "Structural Symbol in Joyce's 'The Dead.'" *Twentieth Century Literature* 3 (1957): 3–13.

Oates, Joyce Carol. "Imaginary Cities: America." *Literature and the Urban Experience: Essays on the City and Literature*. Eds. Michael C. Jaye and Ann Chalmers Watts. New Brunswick, N.J.: Rutgers UP, 1981. 11–33.

O'Brien, Connor Cruise. Ed. *The Shaping of Modern Ireland*. London: Routledge and Kegan Paul, 1960.

O'Connell, Shaun. *Remarkable, Unspeakable New York: A Literary History*. Boston: Beacon Press, 1995.

October. Sovkino, 1928. Dir. Sergei Eisenstein and Grigori Alexandrov. Photography by Edward Tisse.

O'Hearn, Denis. *The Atlantic Economy: Britain, the US and Ireland*. Manchester: Manchester UP, 2001.

Olalquiaga, Celeste. *Megalopolis: Contemporary Cultural Sensibilities*. Minneapolis: U of Minnesota Press, 1992.

Orvell, Miles, *The Real Thing: Imitation and Authenticity in American Culture, 1880–1940*. Chapel Hill: U of North Carolina Press, 1989.

Ostroff, Anthony. "The Moral Vision in *Dubliners*." *Western Speech* 20.4 (Fall 1956): 196–209.

Owens, Colin. "The Mystique of the West in Joyce's 'The Dead.'" *Irish University Review* 22.1 (1992): 80–91.

Pagano, Tullio. *Experimental Fictions: From Emile Zola's Naturalism to Giovanni Verga's Verism*. Madison: Fairleigh Dickinson UP, 1999.

Park, Robert E. and E. W. Burgess. *The City*. Chicago: Chicago UP, 1967.

Parrinder, Patrick. "The Strange Necessity: James Joyce's Rejection in England (1914–30)." *James Joyce: New Perspectives.* Ed. Colin MacCabe. Bloomington: Indiana UP, 1982. 151–167.

Pease, Allison. *Modernism, Mass Culture, and the Aesthetics of Obscenity.* New York: Cambridge UP, 2000.

Pecora, Vincent P. *Self & Form in Modern Narrative.* Baltimore: The Johns Hopkins UP, 1989.

———. "'The Dead' and the Generosity of the Word," *PMLA* 109.1 (1994): 233–245.

Pedersen, Carl. "Unreal Cities East and West: Bely's *Petersurg* and Dos Passos' *Manhattan Transfer.*" *American Studies in Scandinavia* 20.2 (1988): 51–68.

Perloff, Marjorie. "Modernist Studies," *Redrawing the Boundaries: The Transformation of English and American Literary Studies.* Ed. Stephen Greenblatt and Giles Gunn. New York: MLA of America, 1992.

———. *21st-Century Modernism: The "New" Poetics.* Malden, MA: Blackwell Publishers, 2002.

Peterson, Richard F., Alan M. Cohn, and Edmund L. Epstein. Eds. *Work in Progress: Joyce Centenary Essays.* Carbondale: Southern Illinois UP, 1983.

Pierce, David and Dan Harper. *James Joyce's Ireland.* New Haven: Yale UP, 1992.

Pike, Burton. *The Image of the City in Modern Literature.* Princeton, NJ: Princeton UP, 1981.

Pinkey, Tony. Ed. *The Politics of Modernism.* London: Verso, 1989.

Pittock, Murray G.H. *Celtic Identity and the British Image.* New York: Palgrave, 2000.

Pizer, Donald and Earl N. Harbert. Eds. *American Realists and Naturalists.* Detroit: Gale, 1982.

———. *Twentieth-Century American Literary Naturalism: An Interpretation.* Carbondale: Southern Illinois UP, 1982.

———. "Frank Norris's Definition of Naturalism." *Realism and Naturalism in Nineteenth-Century American Literature.* Carbondale: Southern Illinois UP, 1984. 107–111.

———. *Dos Passos' U. S. A.* Charlottesville: UP of Virginia, 1988.

———. *Naturalism: Howells to London.* Cambridge: Cambridge UP, 1995.

———. *The Cambridge Companion to American Realism and Naturalism: Howells to London.* Cambridge: Cambridge UP, 1995.

———. "John Dos Passos: Nineteen-Nineteen." *American Expatriate Writing and the Paris Moment: Modernism and Place.* Baton Rouge: Louisiana State UP, 1996. 86–103.

———. Ed. *Documents of American Realism and Naturalism.* Carbondale: Southern Illinois UP, 1998.

Poe, Edgar Allan. *The Unabridged Edgar Allan Poe.* Ed. Tam Mossman. Philadelphia: Running.Press, 1983.

"Portrait Issue." *Jams Joyce Quarterly* 4:4 (Summer 1967): 249–356.

Potter, Jack. *A Bibliography of John Dos Passos.* Chicago: Normandie House, 1950.

Potts, Willard Ed. *Portraits of the Artist in Exile.* Seattle and London: U of Washington Press, 1979.

——. *Joyce and the two Irelands.* Austin: U of Texas Press, 2000.

Pound, Ezra. "A Retrospect." Literary Essays of Ezra Pound. 1935; Norfolk, Conn.: New Directions, 1954. 3–8.

——. *Pound/Joyce: The Letters of Ezra Pound to James Joyce, with Pound's Essays of Joyce.* Ed. Forrest Read. New York: New Directions, 1967.

——. *The Selected Letters of Ezra Pound, 1907–1941.* Ed. D. D. Paige. 1950. New York: New Directions, 1971.

——. "Dubliners and Mr. James Joyce." *Critical Essays on James Joyce.* Ed. Bernard Benstock. Boston, Massachusetts: G. K. Hall & Co. 1986. 19–21.

Prendergast, Christopher. *Paris and the Nineteenth Century.* Oxford: Blackwell, 1992.

Prendergast, Peter. Ed. *Cultural Materialism: On Raymond Williams.* Minneapolis: U of Minnesota Press, 1995.

Preston, Peter and Paul Simpson-Housley. *Writing the City: Eden, Babylon and the New Jerusalem.* New York: Routledge, 1994.

Price, Kenneth M. "Whitman, Dos Passos, and 'Our Storybook Democracy.'" *Walt Whitman: The Centennial Essays.* Ed. Ed Folsom. Iowa City: U of Iowa Press, 1994. 217–25.

Price, Martin. "The Beauty of Mortal Conditions: Joyce's *A Portrait of the Artist.*" *James Joyce's 'A Portrait of the Artist as a Young Man.'* Ed. Harold Bloom. New York: Chelsea House Publishers, 1988. 77–86.

Pykett, Lynn. "Representing the Real: The English Debate about Naturalism, 1884–1900." *Naturalism in the European Novel: New Critical Perspectives.* New York: Berg Publishers, Inc., 1992. 167–90.

Quirk, Tom and Gary Scharnhorst. Eds. *American Realism and the Canon.* Newark: U of Delaware Press, 1994.

Rabaté, Jean-Michel. *James Joyce and the Politics of Egoism.* Cambridge: Cambridge University Press, 2001.

Rachman, Stephen. "Reading Cities: Devotional Seeing in the Nineteenth Century." *American Literary History* 9.4 (Winter 1997): 653–75.

Read, Forrest. Ed. *Pound/Joyce: The Letters of Ezra Pound to James Joyce.* New York: New Directions, 1970.

Reichert, Klaus. "The European Background of Joyce's Writing." *The Cambridge Companion to James Joyce.* Ed. Derek Attridge. Cambridge: Cambridge UP, 1990. 55–82.

Reinhart, Virginia S. "John Dos Passos Bibliography: 1950–1966." *Twentieth-Century Literature: A Scholarly and Critical Journal* 13 (1967): 167–78.

Reynolds, Donald M. *The Architecture of New York City.* New York: Macmillan, 1984.

Reynolds, Mary T. "The Dantean Design of Joyce's Dubliners." *The Seventh of Joyce*. Bloomington, Indiana UP, 1982. 124–130.

Rice, Thomas Jackson. *James Joyce: A Guide to Research*. New York: Garland Publishing, Inc., 1982.

Richards, Grant. *Studies in Bibliography*. Ed. Fredson Bowers. Charlottesville, VA: Uof Virginia, 1963. 139–60.

Rilke, Rainer Maria. *Letters to a Young Poet*. Trans. Stephen Mitchell. New York: Modern Library, 2001.

Riquelme, John Paul. "Pretexts for Reading and for Writing: Title, Epigraph, and Journal in *A Portrait of the Artist as a Young Man*." *James Joyce Quarterly* 18:3 (Spring 1981): 301–21.

Ritzer, George. *Sociological Theory*. New York: Alfred A. Knopf, 1983.

Roach, Joseph R. *Cities of the Dead: Circum-Atlantic Performance*. New York: Columbia UP, 1996.

Roberts, J. M., *The Penguin History of the World*. London: Penguin Book, 1995.

Rohrkemper, John. "Criticism of John Dos Passos: A Selected Checklist." *Modern Fiction Studies: John Dos Passos Number* 26.3 (Autumn 1980): 525–38.

———. *John Dos Passos: A Reference Guide*. Boston: G. K. Hall, 1980.

Roncayolo, Marcel. *La Citta, Storia e Problemi della Dimensione Urbana*. 2nd ed. Turin: Storia, 1988.

Rose, Danis and John O'Hanlon. "The Origins of Dubliners: A Source." *Joyce Studies Annual* 4 (Summer 1993): 78–84.

Rose, Gillian. "The Dispute Over Modernism," *1936: The Sociology of Literature: Volume 1: The Politics of Modernism*. Eds. Francis Barker et al. Colchester: U of Essex, 1979. 27–36.

Rosen, Robert C. *John Dos Passos: Politics and the Writer*. Lincoln: U of Nebraska Press, 1981.

Rosenberg, Bruce A. "The Crucifixion in 'The Boarding House.'" *Studies in Short Fiction* 5 (Fall 1967): 44–53.

Ross, Kristin. *The Emergence of Social Space: Rimbaud and the Paris Commune*. Minneapolis: U of Minnesota Press, 1988.

Rossman, Charles. "Stephen Dedalus and the Spiritual-Heroic Refrigerating Apparatus: Art and Life in Joyce's *Portrait*." *Forms of Modern British Fiction*. Ed. Alan W. Friedman. Austin: U of Texas Press, 1975. 101–31.

Rotella, Carlo. *October Cities: The Redevelopment of Urban Literature*. Berkeley: U of California Press, 1998.

Roughley, Alan. *James Joyce and Critical Theory: An Introduction*. Ann Arbor: The U of Michigan Press, 1991.

Round, Phillip H. *By Nature and by Custom Cursed: Transatlantic Civil Discourse and New England Cultural Production, 1620–1660*. Hanover: UP of New England, 1999.

Routh, Jane and Janet Wolff. Eds. *The Sociology of Literature: Theoretical Approaches*. Hanley: Wood Mitchell & Co. Limited, 1977.

Ruff, Ivan. "Can There Be A Sociology of Literature?" *The British Journal of Sociology* 25.3 (September 1974): 367–72.

Ruoff, Gene W. "Social Mobility and the Artist in Manhattan Transfer and the Music of Time." *Wisconsin Studies in Contemporary Literature* 5 (1964): 64–76.

Russo, John Paul. "Freud and Italy." *Literature and Psychology* 36. 1–2 (1990): 1–25.

Ryf, Robert S. *A New Approach to Joyce: The Portrait of the Artist as a Guidebook.* Berkeley: U of California Press, 1966.

Said, Edward. *Beginnings: Intention and Method.* New York: Basic Books, 1975.

San Juan, Epifanio, Jr. *James Joyce and the Craft of Fiction: An Interpretation of 'Dubliners.'* Rutherford, NJ: Fairleigh Dickinson UP, 1972.

Sanders, David. "Manhattan Transfer and 'The Service of Things." *Themes and Directions in American Literature: Essays in Honor of Leon Howard.* Eds. Ray B. Browne and Donald Pizer. Lafayette, IN: Purdue U Studies, 1969. 171–185.

———. *John Dos Passos: A Comprehensive Bibliography.* New York: Garland Publishing, Inc., 1987.

Scandura, Jani and Michael Thurston. Eds. *Body, Memory, Capital.* New York: Columbia UP, 2002.

Scheunemann, Dietrich Ed. *European Avant-Garde: New Perspectives.* Amsterdam: Rodopi, 2000.

Schleifer, Ronald. *Modernism and Time: The Logic of Abundance in Literature, Science, and Culture, 1880–1930.* New York: Cambridge UP, 2000.

Schneidau, Herbert N. "Style and Sacrament in Modernist Writing." *The Georgia Review* 31 (1977): 427–52.

Scholes, Robert. "Some Observations on the Text of 'Dubliners': The Dead." *Studies in Bibliography.* Charlottesville: UP of Virginia XV (1962): 191–205.

———. "Joyce and the Epiphany: The Key to the Labyrinth?" *Sewanee Review* 72 (Winter 1964): 65–77.

———. "*Ulysses*: A Structuralist Perspective." *In Search of James Joyce.* Urbana: U of Illinois Press, 1978.

Schorske, Carl E. "The Idea of the City in European Thought: Voltaire to Spengler." *The Historian and the City.* Eds. Oscar Handlin and John Burchard. Cambridge, MA: The MIT Press and Harvard UP, 1963. 95–114.

Schwarz, Daniel R. Ed., *James Joyce: "The Dead": Complete Authoritative Text with Biographical and Historical Contexts, Critical History, and Essays from Five Contemporary Critical Perpsectives.* New York: Bedford Books of St. Martin's Press, 1994.

Schwarze, Tracey Teets. *Joyce and the Victorians.* Gainesville: UP of Florida, 2002.

Scott, William B. and Peter M. Rutkoff. *New York Modern: The Arts and the City.* Baltimore: The Johns Hopkins Press, 2002.

Seed, David. "Theoretical Perspectives." *James Joyce's 'A Portrait of the Artist as a Young Man.'* New York: St. Martin's Press, 1992. 28–42.

Segall, Jeffrey. *Joyce in America: Cultural Politics and the Trials of 'Ulysses.'* Berkeley: U of California Press, 1993.

Senn, Fritz. "'He was Too Scrupulous Always': Joyce's 'The Sisters.'" *James Joyce Quarterly* 2 (1965): 66–71.

Sennett, Richard. Ed. *Classic Essays on the Culture of Cities.* New York: Appleton-Century-Crofts, 1967.

Sharpe, William and Leonard Wallock. Eds. *Visions of the Modern City: Essays in History, Art, and Literature.* Baltimore: The Johns Hopkins Press, 1987.

Sherry, Vincent. *James Joyce, Ulysses.* New York: Cambridge UP, 1994.

Shi, David E. *Facing Facts: Realism in American Thought and Culture, 1850–1920.* Oxford: Oxford UP, 1995.

Shiel, Mark and Tony Fitzmaurice. Eds. *Cinema and the City: Film and Urban Societies in a Global Context.* Oxford: Blackwell Publishers, 2001.

Shields, David. "A Note on the Conclusion of Joyce's 'The Dead.'" *James Joyce Quarterly* 22:4 (Summer 1985): 427–428.

Sicari, Stephen. *Joyce's Modernist Allegory: Ulysses and the History of the Novel.* Columbia: U of South Carolina Press, 2001.

Sieglinde, Lemke. *Primitivist Modernism: Black Culture and the Origins of Transatlantic Modernism.* New York: Oxford UP, 1998.

Simmel, Georg. *The Sociology of Georg Simmel.* Trans. Kurt Wolff. New York: The Free Press, 1950.

———. "How is Society Possible?" *Essays on Sociology, Philosophy and Aesthetics by Georg Simmel et al.* Ed. K. H. Wolf. Columbus: Ohio State UP, 1959.

———. "The Metropolis and Mental Life." *Classic Essays on the Culture of Cities.* Ed. Richard Sennett. New York: Appleton-Century-Crofts, 1978. 47–60.

———. *The Philosophy of Money.* Trans. Tom Bottomore and David Frisby. London: Routledge & Kegan Paul, 1978.

———. *The Problems of the Philosophy of History: An Epistemological Essay.* Trans. Guy Oakes. New York: The Free Press, 1983.

Sisson, Annette. "Constructing the Human Consciousness in Joyce's Dubliners." *Midwest Quarterly: A Journal of Contemporary Thought.* 30:4 (Summer 1989): 492–514.

Sloan, Barbara L. "The D'Annunzian Narrator in 'A Painful Case': Silent, Exiled, and Cunning." *JJQ* 9:1 (Fall 1971): 85–92.

Slotkin, Richard. *The Fatal Environment: The Myth of the Frontier in the Age of Industrialization, 1880–1980.* 3 Vols. Norman: U of Oklahoma Press, 1989.

Smethurst, Paul. *The Postmodern Chronotope: Reading Space and Time in Contemporary Fiction.* Amsterdam: Rodopi, 2000.

Smith, Evans Lansing. *In Search of James Joyce.* Chicago: U of Illinois Press, 1992.

———. *Ricorso and Revelation: An Archetypal Poetics of Modernism.* Columbia, SC: Camden House, 1995.

Soja, Edward W. *Postmodern Geographies: The Reassertion of Space in Critical Social Theory.* London: Verso, 1995.

———. *Postmetropolis: Critical Studies of Cities and Regions.* Oxford: Blackwell Publishers, 2000.

Sommerville, Jane. "Money in *Dubliners.*'" *Studies in Short Fiction* 12.2 (Spring 1975): 109–16.

Spears, Monroe K. *Dionysius and the City: Modernism in Twentieth-Century Poetry*. New York: Oxford UP, 1972.

Spencer, Sharon. *Space, Time and Structure in the Modern Novel*. New York: NYU Press, 1971.

Spoo, Robert. *James Joyce and the Languages of History*. New York: Oxford UP, 1994.

Spykman, Nicholas J. *The Social Theory of Georg Simmel*. Aldershot: Gregg Revivals, 1992.

Squier, Susan Merrill. Ed. *Women Writers and the City: Essays in Feminist Literary Criticism*. Knoxville: U of Tennessee Press, 1984.

Staley, Thomas F. "Moral Responsibility in Joyce's 'Clay.'" *Renascence* 18:3 (Spring 1966): 215–22.

———. "James Joyce." *Anglo-Irish Literature: A Review of Research*. Ed. Richard J. Finneran. New York: Modern Language Association of America, 1976. 402–10.

———. "A Beginning: Signification, Story, and Discourse in Joyce's 'The Sisters.'" *The Genres of the Irish Literary Revival*. Ed. Ronald Schleifer. Oklahoma: Pilgrim Books, Inc., 1980. 121–138.

———. "A Portrait of the Artist as a Young Man." An Annotated Critical Bibliography of James Joyce. New York: St. Martin's Press, 1989. 102–117.

Staley, Thomas F. and Bernard Benstock. "Strings in the Labyrinth: Sixty Years with Joyce's *Portrait.*" *Approaches to Joyce's Portrait*. Eds. Thomas F. Staley and Bernard Benstock. Pittsburgh: U of Pittsburgh Press, 1976. 3–24.

Staley, Thomas F. and Bernard Benstock. Eds. *Approaches to Joyce's Portrait*. Pittsburgh: U of Pittsbburgh Press, 1976.

Stein, Gertrude. *The Autobiography of Alice B. Toklas*. New York: Modern Library, 1993.

Stern, Robert A. M. et al. Eds. *New York 1900: Metropolitan Architecture and Urbanism, 1890–1915*. New York: Rizzoli, 1983.

Stevenson, Randall. *A Reader's Guide to the Twentieth-Century Novel in Britain*. Lexington, Kentucky: The UP of Kentucky, 1993.

Still, Bayrd. *Mirror for Gotham: New York as Seen by Contemporaries from Dutch Days to the Present*. New York: New York UP, 1956.

Stoltzfus, Ben. "John Dos Passos and the French." *Comparative Literature* 15 (Spring 1963): 146–63.

Storey, John. Ed. *What is Cultural Studies?: A Reader*. New York: St. Martin's Press, 1997.

Stubbings, Diane. *Anglo-Irish Modernism and the Maternal: From Yeats to Joyce*. New York: Palgrave, 2000.

Sunquist, Eric. *American Realism: New Essays*. Baltimore: Johns Hopkins UP, 1982.

Sutcliffe, Anthony. *Towards the Planned City: Germany, Britain, the United States and France, 1780–1914.* New York: St. Martin's Press, 1981.

———. Ed. *Metropolis: 1890–1940.* Chicago: U of Chicago Press, 1984.

Tambling, Jeremy. *Lost in the American City: Dickens, James, and Kafka.* New York: Palgrave, 2001.

Tate, Allen and Caroline Gordon. *The House of Fiction.* New York: Scribner's, 1950.

Tate, Allen. "Three Commentaries: Poe, James, and Joyce." *Sewanee Review* 58 (1950): 1–15.

Taylor, Carole Anne. *The Tragedy and Comedy of Resistance: Reading Modernity through Black Women's Fiction.* Philadelphia: U of Pennsylvania Press, 2000.

Taylor, William R. *In Pursuit of Gotham: Culture and Commerce in New York.* Oxford: Oxford UP, 1992.

Templeton, Alice. "Sociology and Literature." *College Literature* 19.2 (June 1992): 19–30.

Tester, Keith. *The Life and Times of Postmodernity.* London: Routledge, 1993.

Thesing, William B. *The London Muse: Victorian Poetic Responses to the City.* Athens, GA: The U of Georgia Press, 1982.

Timms, Edward and David Kelley. Eds. *Unreal City: Urban Experience in Modern European Literature and Art.* New York: St. Martin's Press, 1984.

Tindall, William York. *James Joyce: His Way of Interpreting the World.* New York: Scribner, 1950.

———. *A Reader's Guide to James Joyce.* Syracuse: Syracuse UP, 1995.

Tisdall, Caroline and Angelo Bozzolla. *Futurism.* New York: Oxford UP, 1978.

Titche, Leon L., Jr. "Doblin and Dos Passos: Aspects of the City Novel." *Modern Fiction Studies* 17 (1973): 125–35.

Tonnies, Ferdinand. *Community and Association (Gemeinschaft und Gesellschaft)* Trans. C. P. Loomis. London: Routledge & Kegan Paul, 1955.

Torchiana, Donald T. "The Ending of 'The Dead': I Follow St. Patrick." *James Joyce Quarterly* 18:2 (Winter 1981): 123–132.

———. "Joyce and Dublin." *The Irish Writer and the City* Ed. Maurice Harmon. Irish Literary Studies 18. Gerrard's Cross, Bucks: Colin Smythe, 1984: 52–64.

———. "Introduction: James Joyce's Method in 'Dubliners.'" *Backgrounds for Joyce's Dubliners.* Boston: Allen & Unwin, 1986: 1–17.

Trachtenberg, Alan. *The Incorporation of America.* New York: Hill and Wang, 1982.

Trilling, Lionel. *The Liberal Imagination: Essays on Literature and Society.* New York: Viking Press, 1950.

———. Ed. *The Experience of Literature.* Ed. Lionel Trilling. New York: Holt, 1967.

Trotter, David. *The English Novel in History 1895–1920.* London: Routledge, 1993.

Tuan, Yi Fu. *Space and Place: The Perspective of Experience.* Minneapolis: U of Minnesota Press, 1977.

Tucker, Herbert F. "Epiphany and Browning: Character Made Manifest." *PMLA* 107.5 (October 1992): 1208–1219.

Twyning, John. *London Dispossessed: Literature and Social Space in the Early Modern City.* New York: St. Martin's Press, 1998.

Ungar, Andras. *Joyce's Ulysses as National Epic: Epic Mimesis and the Political History of the Nation State.* Gainesville: UP of Florida, 2002.

———. *University Review* 1 (1971): 149–60.

Untermeyer, Louis. "Others. " *The New Era in American Poetry.* New York: Henry Holt & Co., 1919. 309–11.

Vance, Norman. *Irish Literature: A Social History.* Oxford: Basil Blackwell, 1995.

Vanderwerken, David L. "Manhattan Transfer: Dos Passos' Babel Story." *American Literature: A Journal of Literary History, Criticism, and Bibliography* 49 (May 1977): 253–67.

Veblen, Thorsten. *The Theory of the Leisure Class.* New York: Penguin Books, 1994.

Verhoeven, W. M. and Beth Dolan Kautz. Eds. *Revolutions & Watersheds: Transatlantic Dialogues, 1775–1815.* Amsterdam: Rodopi, 1999.

Versluys, Kristiaan. "The City in Literature: A Review Article on Recent Studies." *English Studies: A Journal of English Language and Literature* 81.3 (June 2000): 229–36.

Vickery, Olga W. "The Inferno of the Moderns." *The Shaken Realist: Essays in Modern Literature in Honor of Frederick J. Hoffman.* Eds. Melvin J. Friedman, John B. Vickery and Philip R. Yannella. Baton Rouge: Louisiana State UP, 1970. 147–64.

Voelker, Joseph C. "'Chronicles of Disorder': Reading the Margins of Joyce's *Dubliners.*" *Colby Library Quarterly* 18:2 (June 1982): 126–144.

Wagner, Linda W. *Dos Passos: Artist as American.* Austin: U of Texas Press, 1979.

———. "Dos Passos: Some Directions in the Criticism." *Resources for American Literary Study* 13. 2 (Autumn 1983): 201–206.

Wall, Alan. "Modernism, Revaluation and Commitment." *1936: The Sociology of Literature: Volume 1: The Politics of Modernism,* eds. Francis Barker et al. Colchester: U of Essex, 1979. 179–89.

Walzl, Florence L. "Pattern of Paralysis in Joyce's *Dubliners*: A Study of the Original Framework." *College English* 22.4 (January 1961): 221–28.

———. "Ambiguity in the Structural Symbols of Gabriel's Vision in Joyce's 'The Dead.'" *Wisconsin Studies in English* 2. Madison: Wisconsin Teachers of English, 1965. 60–69.

———. "Gabriel and Michael: The Conclusion of 'The Dead.'" *James Joyce Quarterly* 4:1 (Fall 1966): 17–31.

———. "Joyce's 'The Sisters': A Development." *James Joyce Quarterly* 10 (1973): 375–421.

———. "The Life Chronology of *Dubliners.*'" *James Joyce Quarterly* 14:4 (Summer 1977): 408–15.

———. "*Dubliners*: Women in Irish Society." *Women in Joyce*. Eds. Suzette Henke and Elaine Unkeless. Urbana: U of Illinios Press, 1982.

———. "Dubliners." *A Companion to Joyce Studies*. Eds. Zack Bowen and James F. Carens. Westport, CT: Greenwood, 1984. 157–228.

Ward, Janet. *Weimar Surfaces: Urban Visual Culture in 1920s Germany*. Berkeley: U of California Press, 2001.

Warner, Sam Bass Jr. "If All the World Were Philadelphia: A Scaffolding for Urban History, 1774–1930." *The American Historical Review* LXXIV.1 (October 1968): 26–43.

Warren, Carrier. "'Dubliners': Joyce's Dantean Vision." *Renascence* 17:4 (Summer 1965): 211–15.

Watier, Patrick. "Simmel and the Image of Individuality." *Current Sociology* 41.2 (Autumn 1993): 69–75.

Watson, G. J. *Irish Identity and the Literary Revival: Synge, Yeats, Joyce and O'-Casey*. New York: Barnes & Noble Books, 1979.

Webber, Melvin M. Ed. *Explorations into Urban Structure*. Melvin Webber et al. Philadelphia: U of Pennsylvania Press, 1964.

Weeks, Robert P. "Fox and Hedgehog: An Essay Review." *Modern Fiction Studies: John Dos Passos Number* 26.3 (Autumn 1980): 520–23.

———. "The Novel as Poem: Whitman's Legacy to Dos Passos." *Modern Fiction Studies: John Dos Passos* 26.3 (Autumn 1980): 431–46.

Weimann, Robert. "Text, Author-Function, and Appropriation in Modern Narrative: Toward a Sociology of Representation." *Critical Inquiry: The Sociology of Literature* 14.3 (Spring 1988): 431–47.

Werner, Craig Hansen. *Dubliners: A Pluralistic World*. Boston: Twayne Publishers, 1988.

Wheeler, Michael. *Death and the Future Life in Victorian Literature and Theology*. Cambridge: Cambridge UP, 1990.

White, Hayden. *Metahistory: The Historical Imagination in Nineteenth-Century Europe*. Baltimore: The Johns Hopkins UP, 1975.

———. *Tropics of Discourse: Essays in Cultural Criticism*. Baltimore: The Johns Hopkins UP, 1978.

———. *The Content of the Form: Narrative Discourse and Historical Representation*. Baltimore: The Johns Hopkins UP, 1990.

White, Morton and Lucia. *The Intellectual Versus the City: From Thomas Jefferson to Frank Lloyd Wright*. Cambridge: Harvard UP and The MIT Press, 1962.

White, Norval. *New York: A Physical History*. New York: Atheneum, 1987.

Whitman, Walt. *Walt Whitman: Complete Poetry and Collected Prose*. Ed. Justin Kaplan. New York: Library of America, 1982.

Whitworth, Michael H. *Einstein's Wake: Relativity, Metaphor, and Modernist Literature*. New York: Oxford UP, 2001.

Whyte, William H. Jr. "Are Cities Un-American?" *The Exploding Metropolis*. New York: Doubleday & Company, Inc., 1958.

Widmer, Kingsley. "The Sociology of Literature?" *Studies in the Novel* 11.1 (Spring 1979): 99–105.

Wightman Fox, Richard and T. J. Jackson Lear. *The Culture of Consumption: Critical Essays in American History, 1880–1980*. New York: Pantheon Books, 1983.

Williams, Raymond. *The Novel from Dickens to Lawrence*. New York, Paladin, 1970.

———. *The Country and the City*. New York: Oxford UP, 1973.

———. *Marxism and Literature*. Oxford: Oxford UP, 1977.

———. *The Sociology of Culture*. New York: Schocken Books, 1982.

———. *Writing in Society*. London: Verso, 1983.

Williams, Trevor L. "Resistance to Paralysis in *Dubliners*." *Modern Fiction Studies*. 35.3 (Autumn 1989): 437–457.

Wills, Clair. "Joyce, Prostitution and the City." *South Atlantic Quarterly* 95.1 (Winter 1996): 79–96.

Wilson, Edmund. "James Joyce." *Axels' Castle: A Study in the Imaginative Literature of 1870–1930*. New York: Charles Scribner's Sons, 1948: 191–236.

Wirth-Nesher, Hana. "Reading Joyce's City: Public Space, Self, and Gender in *Dubliners*." *James Joyce: The Augmented Ninth*. Ed. Bernard Benstock. Syracuse: Syracuse UP, 1988). 282–292.

———. *City Codes: Reading the Modern Urban Novel*. Cambridge: Cambridge UP, 1996.

Wolff, Kurt H. "Georg Simmel." *Trying Sociology*. New York: Wiley, 1974. 2–30.

Wolfreys, Julian. *Writing London: The Trace of the Urban Text from Blake to Dickens*. New York: St. Martin's Press, 1998.

Woodward, Alison and Martin Kohli. Eds. *Inclusion and Exclusion in European Societies*. New York: Routledge, 2001.

Woolf, Virginia. *The Captain's Death-Bed*. New York: Harcourt Brace, 1950.

Wordsworth, *The Prose Works of William Wordsworth*. 3 Vols. New York: AMS Press, Inc., 1967.

———. *The Poetical Works of Wordsworth*. Ed. Paul D. Sheats. Boston: Houghton Mifflin Company, 1982.

Wren, John H. *John Dos Passos*. New York: Twayne, 1961.

Yi Fu, Tuan, *Space and Place: The Perspectve of Experience*. Minneapolis: The U of Minnesota Press, 1977.

Young, Kevin. Giant Steps: *The New Generation of African American Writers*. New York: Perennial, 2000.

Zima, Peter V. "Towards Sociological Semiotics." *Sociocriticism* 2 (1985): 113–28.

———. "Towards a Sociology of Fictional Texts." *New Comparisons: A Journal of Comparative and General Literary Studies* 5 (Summer 1988): 52–74.

Zola, Emile. *L'Assommoir*. Trans. Leonard Tannock. Harmondsworth: Penguin Books, 1970.

Index